Catastrophic Politics

How Extraordinary Events Redefine Perceptions of Government

Shocking moments in society create an extraordinary political environment that permits political and opinion changes that are unlikely during times of normal politics. Strong emotions felt by the public during catastrophes – even if experienced only vicariously through media coverage – are a powerful motivator of public opinion and activism. This is particularly true when emotional reactions coincide with attributing blame to governmental agencies or officials. By examining public opinion during one extraordinary event, the aftermath of Hurricane Katrina, Lonna Rae Atkeson and Cherie D. Maestas show how media information interacts with emotion in shaping a wide range of political opinions about government and political leaders. Catastrophic events bring citizens together, provide common experiences and information, and create opinions that transcend traditional political boundaries. These moments encourage citizens to reexamine their understanding of government, its leaders, and its role in a society from a less partisan perspective.

Lonna Rae Atkeson is Professor and Regents Lecturer of Political Science at the University of New Mexico. She is also Director of the Center for the Study of Voting, Elections and Democracy at the University of New Mexico.

Cherie D. Maestas is Associate Professor of Political Science and an affiliate of the Center for the Study of Democratic Performance at Florida State University.

Catastrophic Politics

How Extraordinary Events Redefine
Perceptions of Government

LONNA RAE ATKESON
University of New Mexico

CHERIE D. MAESTAS
Florida State University

CAMBRIDGE
UNIVERSITY PRESS

CAMBRIDGE UNIVERSITY PRESS
Cambridge, New York, Melbourne, Madrid, Cape Town,
Singapore, São Paulo, Delhi, Mexico City

Cambridge University Press
32 Avenue of the Americas, New York, NY 10013-2473, USA

www.cambridge.org
Information on this title: www.cambridge.org/9781107021129

First published 2012

Printed in the United States of America

A catalog record for this publication is available from the British Library.

Library of Congress Cataloging in Publication Data
Atkeson, Lonna Rae, 1965–
    Catastrophic politics : how extraordinary events redefine perceptions of
government / Lonna Rae Atkeson, Cherie D. Maestas.
        p.   cm.
    Includes bibliographical references and index.
    ISBN 978-1-107-02112-9 (hardback)
    1. Political psychology – Case studies.   2. Public opinion – United
States – Case studies.   3. Public administration – United States – Public
opinion – Case studies.   4. Political leadership – United States – Public
opinion – Case studies.   5. Disaster relief – Political aspects – United
States – Case studies.   6. Hurricane Katrina, 2005 – Political aspects.
7. Press and politics – United States – Case studies.   I. Maestas, Cherie D.,
1964– II. Title.
JA74.5.A85   2012
320.97301'9–dc23   2011045126

ISBN 978-1-107-02112-9 Hardback

For victims of catastrophes, large and small, and especially those who suffered losses from Hurricane Katrina

Contents

List of Tables		*page* x
List of Figures		xiii
Acknowledgments		xv
1	Extraordinary Events and Public Opinion	1
	Catastrophes as Regular Critical Moments in American	
	Politics	3
	The Political Importance of Collective Experiences	
	and Attributions of Blame	7
	Hurricane Katrina as a Test Case	9
	Advantages and Limits of Our Tests	14
	Overview of the Book	16
2	A Theoretical Framework for Systematically Examining	
	Extraordinary Events	22
	Normal Politics versus Extraordinary Moments	24
	Extraordinary Events as Political Context	27
	Media Coverage and the Information Environment	
	in Extraordinary Events	29
	Public Reactions: Affective Attributions of Blame	
	in Times of Crises	34
	Affective Attributions and Their Consequences for Political	
	Opinions	39
	Affective Attributions and the Anger–Punishment Link	42
	Summary and Conclusions	44

3   The Media Message Environment and the Emotional
     Context of Hurricane Katrina   46
     Media Data   46
     Public Attentiveness and Media Selection Following
         Hurricane Katrina   48
     Emotional Primes in Coverage of Hurricane Katrina   50
     Affective Engagement of the Public   54
     Media, Politics, and Blame Following Hurricane Katrina   60
     Summary and Conclusions   74

4   Affective Attributions: Assigning Blame during
     Extraordinary Times   76
     Public Agreement with Blame Frames   77
     Empirical Expectations from the Theory of Affective
         Attributions   82
     Empirical Models and Results, Attributions of Blame   84
     Race and Attributions of Blame   93
     The Emotional Fallout from Attribution of Blame   98
     Empirical Models and Results, Anger   100
     Summary and Conclusions   103

5   Federalism in a Multiple-Message Environment:
     Are the Appropriate Leaders Held Accountable?   105
     Evaluations of the Performance of Leaders during
         Hurricane Katrina   107
     Attributions and the Assignment of Political Responsibility 108
     Multiple Messages, Federalism, and Assignment
         of Responsibility   111
     Empirical Models and Results   118
     Direct Effects of Anxiety and Anger on Evaluation   129
     Conditional Effects of Anger on Evaluation   130
     Summary and Conclusions   133

6   Attributions of Blame, Political Efficacy, and Confidence
     in Government   135
     Public Confidence in Government   137
     Efficacy, Confidence, and the Case of Hurricane Katrina   139
     Empirical Results, Confidence in Government   147
     Examining Longer-Term Effects of Katrina with a Cuing
         Experiment   155
     Summary and Conclusions   158

7   Attributions, Emotions, and Policy Consequences   160
     Informational and Punitive Policy Proposals Following
         Hurricane Katrina   161

Results of Ordered-Probit Models of Agreement with Proposed Policies 170
A Closer Look at Limiting Presidential Authority and Understanding the Influence of Emotion 177
Summary and Conclusions 181

8 Extraordinary Events and Public Opinion: Some Broader Perspectives 183
A Review of Individual-Level Findings 185
Collective Trauma, Shared History, and the Political Implications of Disasters 189
Some Final Normative Thoughts 198

Appendix A. Survey Data and Methodology 201
Appendix B. Data and Methodology for Survey Experiment 202
Appendix C. Coding of News Transcripts and Video Data 204
Methodology for Video Coding of FNC and CNN Broadcasts 204
Methodology for Transcript Coding for ABC, CBS, NBC, CNN, and FNC Broadcasts 205
Appendix D. Multivariate Model Results for Chapter 4 208
Appendix E. Multivariate Model Results for Chapter 5 212
Appendix F. Multivariate Model Results for Chapter 6 214
Appendix G. Multivariate Model Results for Chapter 7 219
References 223
Index 247

Tables

1.1   Selected Major Disasters Covered by *NBC Nightly News*, 1986–2010, Ordered by Amount of Coverage   *page* 6

3.1   Emotional Engagement by Level of Attentiveness   57

3.2   Attention and Emotion, by Race (Std Errors)   59

3.3   Percentage of All News Segments Containing Implicit or Explicit Attributions of Blame, Transcript Segments   71

4.1   Distribution of Public Responses to Attributions of Blame, in Percentages   79

4.2   Distributions of Responses of Belief that State Failure Had an Effect on National Government Response Time, in Percentages   79

4.3   Agreement with Attributions by Partisanship, in Percentages   81

4.4   Ordered-Probit Models of Attributions of Blame, Select Coefficients for Focal Variables   86

4.5   Predicted Probabilities of Agreement with Societal Breakdown Frames, by Race   95

4.6   Select Ordered-Probit Coefficients from the Model of Anger   102

5.1   Evaluations of Leader Performance in the First Few Days after the Storm, in Percentages   108

5.2   Mean Evaluations of President Bush, Governor Blanco, and Mayor Nagin   114

5.3 Mean Evaluations of Bush, Blanco, and Nagin by
    Dominant Attribution Frame   117

5.4 Select Ordered-Probit Coefficients from Models of
    Evaluations of Leaders   119

5.5 Predicted Probabilities of Evaluations of Bush, Blanco,
    and Nagin, by Party and Attribution to Nature   124

5.6 Predicted Probabilities of Evaluations of Bush, Blanco,
    and Nagin, by Party and Attribution to National
    Government   125

5.7 Comparing Coefficients across Performance Models of
    Bush with and without the Angry Interaction   131

6.1 Ordered-Probit Models of External Efficacy   144

6.2 Individual-Level Confidence in Government to Handle
    Future Catastrophes, in Percentages   149

6.3 Select Ordered-Probit Coefficients from Models of
    Confidence in Government to Handle Future Crises   150

6.4 Predicted Probabilities of Feeling Less Confident, by
    Attribution Agreement and Level of Anger   152

6.5 Select Coefficients from a Negative Binomial Model of
    Lowered Confidence in Crisis Response   154

6.6 Experimental Effects of Crisis Prompts on Level of
    Confidence in Government   156

6.7 Selected Coefficients, Ordered-Probit Models of
    Confidence in Government   157

7.1 Public Opinions about Post-Katrina Policies, in
    Percentages   162

7.2 Select Coefficients from Ordered-Probit Models of
    Public Policy Preferences   171

7.3 Predicted Probability of Agreement and Disagreement
    with Policy When the Independent Variable Is at Its
    Minimum and Maximum   173

8.1 Summary of Main Hypotheses and Supportive Evidence   186

D.1 Ordered-Probit Models of Attributions of Blame   209

D.2 Ordered-Probit Model of Anger about New Orleans   211

E.1 Ordered-Probit Models of Evaluations of Leaders   212

E.2 Ordered-Probit Models of Evaluations of Leaders with
    Anger Interaction   213

F.1   Ordered-Probit Model of External Efficacy   215

F.2   Ordered-Probit Models of Confidence in National
      Government to Handle Future Catastrophes   216

F.3   Negative Binomial Model of "Less Confident" Count   217

F.4   Ordered-Probit Model of Confidence in Government to
      Assist Victims and Maintain Order   218

G.1   Ordered-Probit Models of Policy Preferences   220

G.2   Ordered-Probit Models of Policy Preferences, with
      Emotion Interactions   221

Figures

2.1 Overview of the Opinion Formation Process during
Extraordinary Events   *page* 24

2.2 Causal Linkages in Opinion Formation during
Extraordinary Events   41

3.1 Average Primetime News Viewers Based on Nielsen
Ratings for FNC, CNN, and MSNBC, Combined   47

3.2 Count of Attributions of Blame on All Networks,
Three-Day Moving Average   73

4.1 Effects of Party Identification on Agreement with
Attribution to National Government, Conditioned by
Level of Anxiety   88

4.2 Effects of Party Identification on Agreement with
Attribution to State Government, Conditioned by Level
of Anxiety   88

4.3 Effects of Party Identification on Agreement with
Criminal Behavior Attribution, Conditioned by Level of
Anxiety   90

4.4 Effects of Party Identification on Agreement with
Attribution to Nature, Conditioned by Level of Anxiety   90

4.5 Effects of Party Identification on Agreement with Non-
evacuation Attribution, Conditioned by Level of Anxiety   91

4.6 Effects of Party Identification on Agreement with
National Government Attribution, No-Anxiety and
Low-Anxiety Respondents   93

5.1 Effect of Attribution of Blame to National Government on the Probability of a "Poor" Evaluation of President Bush, Conditioned by Level of Anger   132

6.1 Predicted Probabilities of Feeling Efficacious by Levels of Blame Attribution and Anger   146

6.2 Predicted Probabilities of Confidence in Government, by Experimental Prompt   158

7.1 The Effect of Blaming National Government on Agreement with Limiting Presidential Authority, Conditioned by Level of Anger   179

7.2 The Effect of Party Identification on Agreement with Limiting Presidential Authority, Conditioned by Level of Anxiety   180

8.1 Frequency of Disaster Polling Questions, 1986–2010   196

Acknowledgments

In August 2005, we were at the American Political Science Association (APSA) annual meetings, standing in a hotel lobby, glued to televisions along with dozens of other political scientists. As we watched events unfold along the Gulf Coast, we were stunned by the destruction and desperation of the victims, and we worried for friends and colleagues who might have been affected by the storm. As human beings, we were emotionally jarred by the lack of aid and the victims' suffering. As social scientists, we couldn't help but observe the emotional reactions to this unexpected and tragic event and consider how it related to beliefs about government and its responsiveness in times of crisis.

It is fortunate that we began arm-chair theorizing about the broader public opinion ramifications of the storm, because that same weekend Cherie found herself sitting next to Brian Humes, the political science National Science Foundation (NSF) program director, who had just received word that NSF had Small Grants for Exploratory Research (SGER) funds related to Katrina. After some lively discussions about our nascent ideas pertaining to public reaction to the storm, Brian suggested we submit a proposal for review. Less than a month later, we were in the field with a survey at a time when public emotion was still intense and coverage of the blame game still high. In the early days of this project, we thought of it as a study of a particular catastrophe, but over time we realized that the story is much broader. It is a story about how humans react to unthinkable events and how such events change us as individuals and as a society.

A first book is a major academic enterprise and provides us with the opportunity to thank the plethora of people who contributed not only to this project, but also to our growth as scholars and, more generally, to the quality of our professional and personal lives. Our first debt of gratitude is to the NSF and Brian Humes for making possible the data collection that forms the core of this book. The project would have been impossible to complete without the efforts of numerous students, especially those who spent many hours reading and watching news coverage of Hurricane Katrina. They relived the horror and emotion of the catastrophe every day when they came to work. At Florida State University (FSU), these students included Thomas Croom, Caitlin Zook, and especially Lauren Bingham. At the University of New Mexico (UNM), they included Alex Adams, Lisa Bryant, Jamie Gonzales, and David Odegard. We are grateful for the many careful hours they spent coding these gut-wrenching stories. In addition to data collection, they – along with Yann Kerevel and Luciana Zilberman at UNM and Melissa Neal, Greg Ortego, Will Pollock, and Megan Wiggins at FSU – assisted with the development of the project and the analysis of the data, reviewed various versions of the manuscript, and provided valuable intellectual discussions.

A number of colleagues provided continued support, and at the same time they provided valuable criticism on how to improve our arguments and create a better book. These include R. Michael Alvarez, Kevin Arceneaux, Michael Berkman, Damarys Canache, Jamie Druckman, Brad Gomez, Wendy Hansen, Jan Leighley, Jeff Mondak, Barbara Norrander, Eric Plutzer, and Chris Reenock. There were also others who have supported us along the way whose insights and assistance may not have directly related to the book, but who have made a difference in our intellectual growth, including Jason Barabas, Sean Ehrlich, John Geer, Paul-Henri Gurian, Thad Hall, Wendy Hansen, Audrey Haynes, Rick Herrera, Pat Hurley, Jennifer Jerit, Tim Krebs, John McIver, Dale Smith, Bob Stein, Carol Weissert, and Rick Wilson. We also thank My-lien Le for assisting us with the indexing of our book as well as Andy Saff and Robert Dreesen from Cambridge University Press, who made this book a reality.

We also want to thank our mentors Walter J. Stone and Ronald Rapoport. Throughout our academic careers, they have been sources of continual support, wonderful collaborators, and, more importantly, friends. They were key players in teaching us how to think about the world of politics. The discussions we had with them over many summers and at many conferences about attitudes, cognition, and the formation of opinions in politics enriched us and gave us the foundation to write this book. Watching the care they took in writing their own book inspired us as we wrote ours.

We also want to acknowledge those personally closest to us who have made a substantial difference in our lives and have supported our growth as scholars.

Lonna's acknowledgments: I want to begin by noting the importance of the first woman political scientist in my life who inspired me to consider academics and specifically political science as a career, Barbara Sinclair. Dr. Sinclair, as I knew her then, was one of the first female professors that I met outside of the English and language departments, and her presence made me consider that I too could be a professor, a career choice that I had largely considered male. For me, descriptive representation mattered. I also want to acknowledge my mother, Bonita J. Lee, who has provided continual support throughout my life and gave me the ability to persevere. I also want to acknowledge my beautiful children: William Robert Atkeson Cary, thirteen; Jackson Ray Atkeson Cary, eleven; and Carson Bruce Atkeson Cary, seven. Every day they make my life brighter and make all that I do worthwhile. Finally, it is hard to know exactly how to detail all of the things that my twenty-seven–year relationship with my husband Robert Cary – who more recently goes by the name Bruce Cary – has contributed to my life, but I feel certain that he has been a critical figure in my journey, as well as a strong influence on the woman and scholar I am today. Moreover, he was present for the writing of this book and listened to me discuss numerous aspects of it along the way. Therefore, for all of those things that he gave me over so many years, I am truly grateful.

Cherie's acknowledgments: My husband has been an amazing source of support and sanity during the writing of this book and throughout my career. From the weekend I returned from APSA to tell him we were heading home instead of to the beach so that I could write a grant proposal, he calmly accepted this book project as an extra member of our family. My boys, Devin (twenty-six) and Eric (nineteen), were terrific sounding boards throughout the project. More important, they are a daily reminder of all that is wonderful in the world. Acknowledgments in a first book would be incomplete without mentioning those scholars and friends who set me on this path and helped me when the road was tough: my first political science professor Mel Letteer, who told an unfocused college sophomore that I should go to graduate school because I was an academic at heart; Joe Stewart, who picked up the phone when I needed advice on whether to become an economist or a political scientist and wisely guided me to the latter; and Susan Clark, who taught me not only how to think broadly, but also that one should celebrate all the big and small moments of an academic life. Finally, I want to acknowledge my mother, Billie Drake, who has passed on, and my father, Quinton Drake. I will forever be grateful for their willingness to drop whatever they were doing to read to me.

I

Extraordinary Events and Public Opinion

Extraordinary, catastrophic, and shocking moments such as the Japanese attack on Pearl Harbor, President John F. Kennedy's assassination, the Oklahoma City bombing, the terrorist attacks of 9/11, and Hurricane Katrina all have special meaning in the American psyche. They have become part of a national lexicon used by citizens, media, politicians, and policy makers to debate current events and policies. These and other crises force Americans to confront challenging questions about fundamental values in society such as the role of government in protecting its citizens, the balance between personal freedom and security, and the appropriate division of authority among different branches or levels of government. Disasters and their aftermath open up windows of opportunity for policy entrepreneurs (Kingdon 2002). They raise the salience of disaster-related issues, alter perceptions of public figures and agencies, change the distribution of power between relevant interest groups or government elites, shape political agendas, and even spawn social movements (Birkland 1997, 2006; see also Baumgartner and Jones 2009).

What makes catastrophes politically influential? We argue that it is the fact that they engage the public differently than routine political conflicts. Therefore, catastrophes create a public opinion environment that permits political changes that would be difficult or unlikely during times of normal politics. The combination of the emotional impact of an extraordinary event and the media environment that surrounds it motivates attributions of blame that suggest particular avenues for reform to avoid similarly painful crises in the future. Strong emotions felt during catastrophes – even those experienced only vicariously through media coverage – can be powerful motivators of public opinion and public activism, particularly when emotional reactions coincide with attribution of blame to governmental agencies or officials (Jennings 1999).

The purpose of this book is to develop a general framework for understanding how extraordinary events create new considerations in the minds of the public that, in turn, shape a wide range of political attitudes. Policy scholars have long recognized catastrophes as a general class of events that can reshape the lines of political debate and alter the direction of public policy (Baumgartner and Jones 2009; Birkland 1997, 2006; Wood and Doan 2003). Yet little attention has been paid to developing a general theory of how catastrophes ripple through the public psyche, shifting and reshaping political attitudes. Instead, research into public opinion following disasters tends to be event-specific. Studies of opinion following Three Mile Island (Gamson and Modigliani 1989), the *Challenger* disaster (Miller 1987), the Oklahoma City bombing (Lewis 2000), Chernobyl (Van der Brug 2001), the Persian Gulf crisis (Althaus and Kim 2006), Columbine High School (Haider-Markel and Joslyn 2001), Hurricane Katrina (Haider-Markel, Delehanty, and Bervelin 2007; Huddy and Feldman 2006), and, of course, 9/11 (Chanley 2002; Huddy et al. 2003; Huddy, Feldman, and Cassese 2007; Shambaugh et al. 2010) all explore public opinions that arise in response to a particular catastrophe. In doing so, all consider the narrow and broad significance of the catastrophe under study, but none offers an overarching theory to explain how disasters might create an environment that increases the likelihood of updating old and forming new opinions. This is an important lacuna to fill because collective tragedies have qualities that give them special status in the political landscape (Jennings 1999) and they are expected to occur regularly (Sornette 2002). The task of this book is to identify commonalities that underlie all extraordinary events, to varying degrees, to consider why they create a special individual and collective context that imparts broad political meaning.

Although our framework is intended to generalize to any disaster, we test the framework's implications by studying one highly salient, emotion-laden event: the aftermath of Hurricane Katrina. In Chapter 2, we develop an individual-level model of public opinion formation following extraordinary events that depends on external input from the media message environment. Although we provide a general theory of attitude formation that highlights the role of media messages, the specific message environment differs for each disaster. Therefore, for an in-depth and comprehensive test of our theoretical question, we rely on one case-specific analysis of media messages to generate the testable empirical hypotheses that are implied by the general theory. Hurricane Katrina is a fertile case to use for this purpose because the media environment offered a number of credible messages about political actors from different parties and different levels of government. In addition, the events surrounding Hurricane Katrina were attention grabbing and gut wrenching. The scale of the catastrophe was unprecedented and media coverage pervasive. As a result, the disaster created a sense of pain and loss in the hearts of citizens far beyond the areas directly affected by the hurricane. One indication of the disaster's impact on the public psyche was the degree to which Americans were willing to give to Katrina-related charities – an amount that exceeded donations following 9/11, the Asian tsunami crisis in 2004, and the earthquake in Pakistan in 2005 (Frank 2005). Katrina, therefore, offers an excellent testing ground to explore the paths of influence on public opinion during a catastrophic moment.

CATASTROPHES AS REGULAR CRITICAL MOMENTS IN AMERICAN POLITICS

Catastrophes leave a lasting imprint on those who experience them. They create a sense of shared history and shared meaning among diverse groups of citizens. Although any particular calamity is rare, catastrophic events happen with some degree of regularity (Sornette 2002). In fact, major catastrophes happen at least as frequently as national elections, although the timing is obviously less predictable. Like elections, such catastrophes bring public attention to political actors, institutions, and policies, and they prompt evaluations of government performance. Unlike elections, however, disasters draw scrutiny from a wide array of citizens, not just those normally interested in news and politics. In a disaster, even citizens who typically shun news, political or otherwise, tune in. Because government leaders and agencies are active players in catastrophes, disaster coverage necessarily contains a political component. As a result, catastrophes create opportunities for citizens from every segment of society to observe and evaluate government in action in a social and media context that is very different from elections or other routine political debates.

There are many different ways of defining an "extraordinary event," "catastrophe," or "disaster" (see Birkland 1997, 2006), and we adopt a broad definition here.[1] An extraordinary event, in its most basic form, is any unplanned disruption that causes loss of property and/or life. Broadly defined, this includes calamities of a personal nature, such as car accidents or residential fires, as well as epochal disasters, such as 9/11 or the Oklahoma City bombing. From a political standpoint, the set of extraordinary events that are meaningful to study consists of those that contain a collective dimension, where the intervention of one or more levels of government is both expected and necessary to resolve the problems associated with the disaster. Often this occurs because the scope or magnitude of the disaster exceeds the resources of the local emergency infrastructure, and therefore other levels of government must allocate additional resources to the task. Similarly, catastrophes may have a collective dimension because government is the only agent with sufficient authority to coordinate recovery efforts or impose regulations to prevent future similar catastrophes. Accordingly, this definition includes many different types of extraordinary events: accidental, man-made disasters that result from faulty infrastructure or decision making; major economic downturns that are national or global; terrorism; major social unrest that leads to societal ruptures; and major epidemics. Of course, it also includes natural disasters such as fire, flooding, earthquakes, tornadoes, environmental degradation, and the like.

Catastrophes vary in their breadth of relevance; some are localized, with few ramifications for the broader public, while others, regardless of their size or location, profoundly affect the nation as a whole. We are most concerned with catastrophes that are national in scope – those that capture the attention of the national press and those that require response from national leaders and agencies. They are of special

---

[1] Unless otherwise stated, we use the terms *extraordinary event*, *catastrophe*, *disaster*, *crisis*, and *calamity* interchangeably.

interest because they are most likely to generate a sense of shared experience across social strata and stimulate national-level conversations about government's role in society. However, the processes we outline in this book could be used to explain opinions following any catastrophe, whether personal, local, or national. For localized disasters, the population to which the model applies is much smaller and its effects on government policy are more limited. For national catastrophes, the model applies to a large swath of the population, thereby encouraging nationwide discussions and deliberation about policies related to the catastrophe. Of course, the larger and more shocking the catastrophe, the more likely it is that the national media will prioritize the event's coverage over all else, and the greater the chance that such an event will become a political catalyst that transforms national opinion and policy.

Table 1.1 shows a list of fifteen catastrophic events that held the lead story spot on *NBC Nightly News* for a minimum of six days during the period 1986 through 2010. Although the list is not exhaustive of all catastrophes covered in the national news, it gives a sense of the diversity and frequency of major catastrophic events that occupy the public news space. Of these, five were natural disasters, three were acts of terrorism, three were man-made catastrophes, two were unusual plane crashes, and two were mass murders.

Despite their diversity, each brought to the public news reports of government officials dealing with unexpected circumstances that highlighted both successes and failures of government. In some cases, such as the Space Shuttle *Challenger* explosion and the breach of levees in New Orleans after Hurricane Katrina, the disaster highlighted faulty government engineering and oversight. In others such as Hurricane Katrina and Hurricane Andrew, coverage highlighted weaknesses in governments' ability to respond quickly to citizens in need. Still others, such as 9/11, raised questions about national intelligence, security procedures, and disaster response. Even those catastrophes that stem from nonpolitical acts of violence, such as the Columbine High School shootings and the Virginia Tech massacre, raise the salience of political questions at the local and national levels. Questions about gun rights, student and family privacy, and school security moved to center stage in the national conversation as journalists, pundits, and public officials debated how to prevent similar tragedies in the future.

TABLE 1.1. *Selected Major Disasters Covered by* NBC Nightly News, *1986–2010, Ordered by Amount of Coverage*

Disaster	Year	Days as Lead Story during First 2 Weeks	Total Story Segments during First 2 Weeks
Exxon *Valdez* oil spill	1989	8	14
TWA crash	1996	9	16
Egypt air crash	1999	7	17
Embassy bombings	1998	6	18
Virginia Tech massacre	2006	7	18
Flooding in the Midwest	1993	9	20
Chernobyl	1986	8	24
Hurricane Andrew	1992	10	24
Challenger explosion	1986	7	26
Columbine High School shootings	1999	9	26
Indian Ocean earthquake and tsunami	2004	13	29
Haiti earthquake	2010	10	38
Oklahoma City bombing	1995	13	46
Hurricane Katrina	2005	14	54
9/11	2001	14	80[a]

Note: [a]Indexing of stories for 9/11 differs from other catastrophes. During the first three days of coverage, full broadcasts were indexed as a only a single segment each day.

Source: Search of *NBC Nightly News* broadcasts, Vanderbilt News Archives. Two coders independently counted story segments on *NBC Nightly News* in the Vanderbilt News Archives (accessed during the week of February 4, 2012). Overall, inter-coder correlations in coding both the number of lead stories and total stories were over 98 percent. Minor differences between the coders arose in coding support stories that were tangentially related to the disaster.

Catastrophes are unique because of the public's expectations for quick and effective government intervention. One fundamental principle of democratic societies is that the government has a responsibility for the safety and well-being of all its citizens. Catastrophes challenge government to uphold its end of the social contract under difficult conditions and under circumstances of intense public scrutiny. Given that citizens have expectations about how government should respond, any expectation gap will likely influence attitudes toward leaders, public policy, and government institutions (Jenkins-Smith, Silva, and Waterman 2005; Waterman, Jenkins-Smith, and Silva 1999).

Because expectations shape evaluations of government actors, especially presidents, they have additional ramifications for the ability of the president to make new policy and get things done (Genovese 2002; Kernell 1997; Lowi 1985). The public looks to elected officials for symbolic reassurance and empathy in times of crisis (Bucy 2003; Edelman1985; Merolla and Zechmeister 2009). Successes bring new political opportunities to turn political capital into public policy or career gains, whereas missteps are judged harshly by the media and political opponents. The initial response of President George W. Bush to the terrorist attacks on the World Trade Center and other U.S. targets garnered criticism from the media because he was viewed as out of touch at a time when the nation needed reassurance (Bucy 2003). Later, his response and leadership to the same catastrophe were widely praised and met with skyrocketing approval. Similarly, President Bill Clinton's reaction to the Oklahoma City bombing in 1995 was viewed as evidence of strong and empathetic leadership, and his approval ratings rose appreciably (Devroy 1995).

Of course, the president is not the only political leader to whom journalists turn for reactions in times of crisis, nor are they the only leaders to face public scrutiny. Previously unknown state or local political leaders often emerge as heroes or villains in the cast of characters during an unfolding drama. Mayor Rudolph Giuliani of New York City, for example, won high praise for his handling of the aftermath of 9/11 and rode the wave of credit to national and international fame; *Time Magazine* named him "Person of the Year" in 2001 and he handily won reelection. These anecdotes point to the importance that the press and the public attach to executive leadership during calamitous times. Assessments of crisis leadership – whether positive or negative – have significant consequences for the political capital that presidents and other leaders wield in subsequent policy debates and can help or hurt them later at the ballot box.

THE POLITICAL IMPORTANCE OF COLLECTIVE EXPERIENCES AND ATTRIBUTIONS OF BLAME

Epochal moments are politically significant because they create a shared collective experience from which society draws meaning. These events are collective by nature because people from all social and economic strata are drawn to the human relevance of the story. They are also "collective" because they prompt people to recognize the need for collective – that is, government – solutions. Epochal moments draw public attention away from parochial concerns and toward the drama of the events of the moment. The public experiences the shock of learning unexpected news as it ripples through the media and social networks. They turn to common news sources and to each other as they mentally and emotionally process the event. This creates the dynamic of a shared personal experience that transcends ordinary social or political cleavages and becomes part of the collective societal memory, and although each individual responds to the messages based on his or her personal perspectives, the novelty of the event leads many individuals to process that information with greater scrutiny and deliberation. Momentous events, such as Kennedy's assassination in 1963, 9/11, the attack on Pearl Harbor in 1941, and the *Challenger* explosion in 1986, create flashbulb memories that allow people to recall not only the circumstances in which they learned of the tragedy, but also the thoughts and emotions associated with it (Bohannan 1988; Bohannon, Gratz, and Cross 2007; Hirst et al. 2009; Kvavilashvili et al. 2009). The bundled recollection, complete with emotions, makes such an event a powerfully evocative social and political symbol. Shared tragedies, even if experienced only vicariously, become shared reminiscences that create a sense of familiarity. They help to define generational cohorts, and they provide a broader context for interpreting other social and political issues or events.

Central to this story is how the media and the public attribute blame in the aftermath of an extraordinary event. Causal stories provide a baseline from which to understand and infer responsibility, particularly political responsibility. Attributions of blame offered through the mass media provide a way to contextualize personal experiences and translate them into political problems (Mutz 1994). Attributions of blame have been studied extensively in political science because they help us to understand how and when citizens hold leaders accountable for economic, political, or social outcomes (see, for example, Arceneaux 2005; Arceneaux and Stein 2006; Atkeson and Partin 2001; Gomez and Wilson 2001, 2003, 2008; Nelson 1999), and they help us understand why citizens form preferences for some policy solutions and not others (see Iyengar 1989, 1991). We build from this broader literature, but offer new insights into why disasters and other extraordinary events hold special power in shaping political attributions. Understanding causal attributions in the wake of extreme or tragic events is especially important because the collective experience makes them long-standing political touchstones that can be drawn upon in multiple political debates (Jennings 1999). Causal attributions form an important link in a chain that runs from citizens' receipt of information (for example, from mass media, elites, friends, or personal experiences) to their issue opinions, political evaluations, and, ultimately, political choices.

Even a cursory review of policy responses following extraordinary events reveals that they can lead to significant political change, but thus far no one has carefully explored how journalistic norms and a media message environment that pins blame upon others create conditions conducive to influencing public opinions on a mass scale. Our study differs from most previous research into political attributions of blame in that it focuses on understanding the formation of opinions outside of the electoral context and beyond periods of normal politics. Blame assignment is common during catastrophes, and these attributions serve to define problems of leadership and public policy. However, people assign blame during disasters in a way that differs considerably from how they do so during ordinary times. Normal political debates and events are meant to activate predispositions; elites target their messages to energize those in their base. During extraordinary times, however, the intensity and overwhelming nature of calamity attract broad attention, allowing journalists rather than elites to take center stage in framing events. This change provides a different context for opinion formation because the media images produced by the extraordinary event cue emotions that render predispositions less important and, therefore, attitude change more likely. Therefore, by exploring emotion, public opinion, and attributions of blame following disasters, we also, by definition, examine the effects of media and elite framing on opinion.

HURRICANE KATRINA AS A TEST CASE

In the following chapters, we develop and test a general theoretical argument for how catastrophic events alter both the media message environment and individual-level processing of information generated from that environment. We combine this general theory with a detailed analysis of the media message environment that arose during and after the time that Hurricane Katrina devastated the Gulf Coast in 2005. There is no question that Hurricane Katrina falls in the category of epochal events. It was emotionally stimulating, it was personally relevant to many, and it had short- and long-term political consequences. It also continues to be a national political symbol of government failure, all of which make it an excellent test case to which to apply our theory.

To set the stage for later sections of the book, it is useful to recall the emotional and political impacts of the storm. On Monday, August 29, 2005, Hurricane Katrina hit the Gulf Coast, unleashing powerful winds gusting up to 140 miles per hour, torrential rains, and massive storm surges of over 20 feet. The devastation from the storm was shocking and America was riveted by the news coverage. Scenes of flooded towns, flattened homes, floating corpses, uncontrolled mobs, and tearful victims filled America's living rooms for weeks following the storm. Emotions ran high as journalists and citizens demanded to know why aid was so slow to arrive in New Orleans. Politicians responded with angry fingerpointing in hopes of deflecting the shrapnel of blame. Across the nation, citizens watched in stunned disbelief as an iconic American city lay exposed and bleeding from what some suggested was political neglect.

The disaster was an immediate collective crisis because the damage was so extensive that individuals on the ground could not address the myriad problems created by the storm. The levees, for example, needed to be repaired and rebuilt, as did much of the civil infrastructure along the Gulf. Thousands of victims needed shelter and relocation away from the damaged areas, and social order needed to be restored. Only government was capable of such actions. At the same time, the human tragedy and the potential broader implications of the storm made it relevant to a national audience. First, it prompted questions about the government's ability, in the face of severe tragedy, to do its job properly – something that had implications for citizens across the nation who might face future catastrophes of one kind or another. Second, the crisis had an immediate effect on gas prices and access to fuel that directly affected the personal and economic life of the nation as a whole.

As a result, Hurricane Katrina was not only a powerful natural disaster, but it was also a collective crisis and a potent political disaster that, for some, would hold devastating career consequences. Michael Brown lost his job as head of the Federal Emergency Management Agency (FEMA) while President Bush, Louisiana Governor Kathleen Blanco, and New Orleans Mayor Ray Nagin faced harsh public criticism for the roles they played in the breakdown of what should have been a coordinated government response. Each was haunted by questions about his or her performance and by the public's evaluation of his or her actions. Both the media and the Bush administration felt that Katrina was a turning point for President Bush. As Dan Bartlett, White House communications director and later counselor to the president, said, "Politically, it was the final nail in the coffin" (Murphy and Purdum 2009). For Blanco, it meant the end of her political career; she resigned rather than run for another term – a bid she would have likely lost. And for Nagin, it meant an unusually hard-fought reelection campaign and the loss of considerable local political capital and support.

After Katrina, President Bush spent the remainder of his term trying to make up for the poor governmental response that reshaped his post-9/11 image as a responsive leader. Just weeks after Hurricane Katrina, President Bush, FEMA, the Department of Homeland Security (DHS), and state and local political leaders leapt to action in response to the approach of Hurricane Rita. In 2006, FEMA, President Bush and Kansas Governor Kathleen Sebelius hastily offered assistance to victims of a string of devastating tornadoes in Greensburg, Kansas, in part "to dispel any comparisons to the [Hurricane Katrina] response" (Rutenberg 2007: 24). The 2007 firestorms in California prompted national officials to highlight the role of state officials, contrasting the laudable performance by California officials with the lamentable performance by Louisiana officials (Stolberg 2007).

Years after the storm, there is still much rebuilding to be done – structurally, emotionally, and politically. Hurricane Katrina remains in the news regularly, and has served as a frame for interpreting government performance in subsequent disasters. During 2010, Lexis-Nexis, a news indexing source, identified over three thousand news stories in

U.S. newspapers that mentioned Hurricane Katrina. A search of the
first six months of 2011 returned similar results.[2] The combined 2010
total during the first six months of just three major newspapers, the
New York Times, the *Washington Post*, and *USA Today*, was 515,
with 109 specifically mentioning Hurricane Katrina in conjunction
with the April 20 BP Gulf oil spill. In comparison, the same papers in
the first six months of 2011 offered 238 stories referencing Hurricane
Katrina. Although the story count had dropped compared to the year
before, Katrina still resonated with journalists as a political symbol
and as a benchmark for government performance, particularly for
government response to the spring tornado outbreak in the South.[3] In
part, the sustained attention stemmed from the fact that the story continued to unfold as news reports revealed a variety of ongoing problems related to Katrina, such as environmental hazards in the damaged
areas (Bellantoni 2009), toxic gases in FEMA trailers provided to victims (Robinson 2010), problems with rebuilding New Orleans (Finn
2009), problems with insurance settlements (Finn 2009), problems of
crime and corruption in the affected areas (Guarino 2009; Robertson
2009), and numerous stories of mismanagement on the part of local,
state, and federal agencies (Heath 2009; O'Harrow 2009).

However, the story of Katrina remains salient because journalists
and politicians invoke it in other contexts that are unrelated to the
storm, such as economic policy. During the fall of 2008 and the spring
of 2009, Katrina was invoked to encourage government to respond
quickly to the faltering economy. "Time is of the essence. The equiva-
lent of a hurricane has struck the US economy and we must not repeat
the mistakes of Katrina," said Representative Jim McDermott (D-WA)
when introducing a measure to extend unemployment compensation

---

[2] The source of data is a search of Lexis-Nexis News Archives, August 5, 2011. The
searches were performed in the database of major U.S. newspapers. The listing of
sources that comprise the U.S. newspapers can be found in the source lists provided by Lexis-Nexis. We searched the full database of U.S. newspapers for the term
"Hurricane Katrina" from January 1, 2010, to December 31, 2010, and again from
January 1, 2011, to December 31, 2011. Lexis-Nexis does not offer an exact count
when the number of stories exceeds three thousand. As a result, we also performed
separate searches of select newspapers – the *New York Times*, *USA Today*, and the
Washington Post – during the first six months of 2010 and 2011 (i.e., January 1,
2011, to July 1, 2011).

[3] See, for example, Sack and Williams (2011).

(Lengell 2008). After the massive stimulus package was passed, various interest groups and government watchdog groups cautioned that the government bailout funds should not be mismanaged as they were following Hurricane Katrina (Davidson 2009). Thus, the storm has moved to the status of a symbolic touchstone that is employed to frame other issues and mobilize constituencies for or against particular policies or individuals.

In each subsequent disaster, Hurricane Katrina has been used as a benchmark and symbol of government performance, especially presidential performance. For Barack Obama, Hurricane Katrina was invoked as a comparison in the U.S. government's response to the devastating earthquake in Haiti in 2010, to the BP oil spill in the Gulf in 2010, and the spring outbreak of tornadoes in 2011. The *USA Today* headline (Hall, Jervis, and Levin 2010) "Is Oil Spill Becoming Obama's Katrina?" draws potency from Katrina's symbolism and is representative of a broader range of stories where leadership in crisis is compared directly to Bush's performance during Hurricane Katrina. In this and in other disasters since Katrina, media and politicians have replayed the debates surrounding blame for the aftermath of Katrina, further reinforcing its symbolism and continued importance.

In addition to becoming a powerful political symbol, the events around and after Hurricane Katrina have prompted numerous reforms to disaster management practices, raised an ongoing debate about the proper location of FEMA in the hierarchy of the federal bureaucracy, and generated a Select Committee in the House charged with investigating the aftermath of Katrina to prevent similar response failures in the future. Thus, the crisis has had a continuous influence on both public opinion and public policy. The committee issued its final report, *A Failure of Initiative*, on February 15, 2006, a 569-page document that details errors and missteps by every level of government and its officials. The committee was charged to investigate and report, not prescribe, but the committee noted that, "Moving from our findings to legislative, organizational, and policy changes need not be a long or difficult journey" (U.S. House 2006: 359). Many of the findings from this committee have prompted reforms to existing practices or inspired new legislation. When Obama took office in 2009, he became the first president to face limits to his powers to appoint the head of FEMA. Congress, in response to Hurricane Katrina, limited presidential authority by requiring that appointees have relevant disaster management experience to be eligible for the job.

Simply stated, the political aftermath of Hurricane Katrina has reshaped the public policy and opinion landscape. Public and media attributions of blame toward government and its leaders were paramount in that process because political actors promoting policy changes drew upon the common understandings and collective image of Hurricane Katrina to tug at emotions and make persuasive arguments. Yet, the multiple-message media environment and public attentiveness to coverage make this catastrophe an ideal context for testing the arguments we develop in this book. The collection of leaders at different levels of government and from different parties can help us to untangle the relative influence of emotions and predispositions on attributions of blame and other political opinions.

ADVANTAGES AND LIMITS OF OUR TESTS

The data we use in this book are primarily drawn from two sources. The first is a national telephone survey conducted one month after the storm to investigate the opinions and perceptions of those outside the areas directly affected by the hurricane. The second is an analysis of the media coverage on each of the major news stations for the month following the disaster. We examined written transcripts of televised evening news for five networks (ABC, CBS, NBC, CNN, and FNC) and coded video footage for two, CNN and FNC. The media data provide a contextual picture of the storm and its aftermath and an accounting of the messages we examine in conjunction with our survey data of individuals. The media data permit us to generate specific, testable hypotheses implied by our general theoretical arguments. Combined, the data offer a snapshot of messages and responses to a major and unexpected national calamity. Appendix A provides methodological details about the survey component of the study, while Appendix C provides details about the media analysis.

We recognize the inherent limits in testing arguments using cross-sectional survey data – the direction of our causal arrows rests on assumption rather than a well-controlled application of treatments. However, cross-sectional survey research is complementary to experimental methods and necessary if political science is to offer valuable substantive insights about how real-world events and media messages shape public opinion. In developing our theoretical expectations about the likely public response to Hurricane Katrina, we draw heavily on the results of controlled experiments conducted in a variety of fields, including psychology, sociology, communications, and political science. Therefore, our study combines the knowledge that others have gained through experimental studies to help us form a set of theoretically grounded expectations for opinions formed during the complexity of real-world events.

Although some might argue that the absence of control and temporal sequence in cross-sectional studies makes causal inference difficult, a point we certainly acknowledge, observational studies, even with their limitations, are absolutely necessary to construct a multipronged case for the substantive importance of causal mechanisms. An examination of opinion formation during catastrophic moments would be difficult, if not impossible, to replicate in a laboratory setting. The emotion-laden information environment that occurs in the context of a real disaster is much more complex than can be reproduced in the lab. During disasters, citizens are offered many emotionally compelling cues from the media, political elites, and social networks, and these cues are embedded in a fast-paced, multiple-message, and repetitive news environment. The emotion manipulations used in lab settings simply cannot equal the organic experience of watching shocking, catastrophic events unfold as they happen.

Providing survey-based evidence from major political events is, therefore, essential to determine the political relevance of the many nuanced causal arguments that we often assume undergird political opinions. By amassing evidence from multiple sources, political scientists can offer more than just discrete theoretical advances about individual causal mechanisms. Rather, through triangulation, we can draw together the implications of multiple lab-supported causal links to say something about our expectations of how citizens grapple with politically compelling and complicated stimuli. Our study is an important step in this endeavor because our theoretical assumptions are well grounded in experimental research while identifying how the implications of these studies form a framework for interpreting and understanding real-time opinions in response to Hurricane Karina and other extraordinary events.

OVERVIEW OF THE BOOK

We develop the book in two parts, the first part comprised by Chapters 2, 3, and 4 and the second consisting of Chapters 5 through 8. In the first set of chapters, we lay out a general theory for how opinions are shaped by a combination of framed media messages and emotions triggered by extraordinary events. In these chapters, we identify common attribution patterns in the media and develop and test a theoretical model of how individuals come to agree with causal attributions in the wake of unexpected events. In the second half of the book, we examine how attributions of blame and the emotional responses during crises influence key political variables, such as evaluations of leaders, confidence in government, and preferences for policy responses.

The Emotional Underpinnings of Post-crisis Attitudes

In Chapter 2, we set the stage for understanding how post-crisis attitudes develop by outlining how extraordinary events produce a collective environment that differs appreciably from "normal politics" and consider what this means for how individuals grapple with information about shocking and unexpected events. We highlight how journalistic norms create common themes in post-catastrophe coverage. Chief among these is the norm of investigation into the causes of catastrophic outcomes, which generates a series of dominant and secondary causal attributions to which political elites and citizens respond. The public, emotionally aroused in the wake of catastrophic events, may be faced with numerous competing claims about the causes of catastrophe or may encounter a single dominant explanation. Central to understanding how crises influence a wide range of political attitudes is untangling why citizens accept or reject the causal attributions offered in the media.

We develop a theory of attribution that depends most fundamentally upon three sets of factors, one external – the media message environment – and two internal to the individual – political predispositions and emotional arousal. Each factor plays an integral, independent role in forming political attributions, but each also interacts with the others to produce important departures from the way attitudes are formed during more typical political debates. We label this theory *affective attributions* because it highlights the unique role that disaster-based anxiety plays in moderating internal and external influences on opinions.

In addition, we parse out theoretically different roles for the emotions of anxiety and anger in relationship to attributions of blame and other opinions. Only a limited body of research examines the links between emotion and the formation of attributions (but see Haider-Markel, Delehanty, and Beverlin 2007). Most focus on how attributing blame triggers the emotion of anger (Weiner 1995; Weiner, Graham, and Chandler 1982; Weiner et al. 1987).[4] However, anxiety is also relevant to our story because research on affective intelligence finds that it circumvents the normal and routine processing of information (Brader 2005; Marcus, Neuman, and MacKuen 2000; MacKuen et al. 2010; Valentino et al. 2008, 2009). Anxiety is an often critical individual emotion that is aroused during extraordinary events, and scholars have not, to our knowledge, examined the role of emotion specifically in the case of attribution of blame, nor traced its indirect effects on other opinions through attributions. Our study, then, offers a novel examination of how the emotions of anxiety and anger operate distinctly to shape opinions in the context of catastrophe.

Media Coverage, Emotional Engagement, and Causal Attributions after Hurricane Katrina

In Chapters 3 and 4, we apply our framework to understanding the media message environment, public emotional engagement, and media and public attributions of blame following Hurricane Katrina. Questions about blame and causality are fundamental to media coverage of extraordinary events, and this coverage defines the message environment in which people form their own opinions about causality. Likewise, human drama, high emotion, and arresting visuals are

---

[4] Some studies allude to the role of emotion in stimulating the attribution process by highlighting how the unexpected nature of events prompts attributions (Hewstone 1989). A broader body of work examines how attributions cause emotions such as anger or sympathy (see Forsterling 2001; Hewstone 1989; Rudolph et al. 2004; Weiner 1985, 1995; Weiner, Osborne, and Rudolph 2011), but at this time, we are aware of none that have examined how variation in emotional reactions influences the formation of attributions.

also fundamental to disaster coverage. In the first part of Chapter 3, we examine features of news coverage that triggered individual-level anxiety and assess public emotional engagement by the storm. In the second part of Chapter 3, we examine the dominant storylines of blame offered in the media following Hurricane Katrina – a "blame nature" frame that locates responsibility with the uncontrollable and overwhelming nature of the storm; a "blame government" frame that locates responsibility with government planning and execution; and two "societal breakdown" frames: one that locates responsibility with victims' refusal to evacuate, and one that locates responsibility with unruly victims. In Chapter 4, we explicitly test the implications of our theory of affective attributions. By applying our theoretical framework, we are able to identify who was more likely to accept the various attributions of blame prevalent in the media. We complete this section of the book by examining the relationship between attribution and anger – an emotion that, in conjunction with attributions, influences key political opinions that we study in later chapters.

Throughout the first half of the book, we also consider how race interacts with the unique context of Hurricane Katrina to stimulate emotions and attribution of blame. A number of studies of Hurricane Katrina have highlighted how the storm drew attention to issues of race and class in American society and, in doing so, substantially influenced opinions (Bartels 2006; Bobo 2006; and Feldman 2006a, 2006b; Potter 2007; Sweeney 2006). The power of Hurricane Katrina to shape race-related opinions is not surprising given that research on social identity and opinion demonstrates that group cohesiveness influences preferences for many different types of political opinions (Chong and Rogers 2005; Federico and Luks 2005; Gay 2004; Haider-Markel, Delehanty, and Beverlin 2007; Huddy and Feldman 2006a, 2006b; Sigelman and Welch 1993; Stets and Burke 2000). Because many of the faces of Hurricane Katrina were black, blacks felt a greater closeness or kinship with the victims, increasing their issue awareness and responsiveness to media coverage of the storm (Huddy and Feldman 2006b). We find similar results in Chapter 3 and show that race has consequences for patterns of blame attribution in Chapter 4.

We feel it important to note, however, that we see race as a case-specific part of a much larger theoretical story about how people form opinions during catastrophic events. In the case of Hurricane Katrina, the disaster coverage was steeped with racially relevant cues and therefore was important in creating a sense of social identification with victims. In disasters where race is not a primary source of identification or empathy, we would not expect race to exert any special influence on attentiveness or attributions. Thus, we consider how race influences attitudes, but under the larger rubric of how emotion, attributions, and predispositions work together.

The Effect of Causal Attributions on Political Evaluations and Policy Preferences

The political repercussions of tragedies such as Hurricane Katrina can fundamentally reshape expectations of government or lead to significant shifts in lines of authority that permanently alter the balance of power between branches and levels of government. For example, 9/11 led to the creation of a new bureaucracy, the Department of Homeland Security, and greatly expanded the power of the executive branch. Such changes were possible because of the groundswell of public support that stemmed from the disaster. Even today, Congress continues to grapple with post-Katrina recommendations that FEMA be dissolved and rebuilt, as well as proposals to increase the power of the federal government at the expense of state and local autonomy.

In this section, we examine three specific types of opinions following Hurricane Katrina: performance evaluations of political leaders, feelings of confidence in government and its responsiveness to citizens, and preferences for policy or institutional reforms. In each area, the context of Hurricane Katrina gives us opportunities to explore the effects of the attributions and emotions that we explored in the first part of the book. We also use these chapters to address other key puzzles in public opinion. For example, in Chapter 5, our examination of evaluations of leaders gives us a special opportunity to explore the effects of media framing on opinions. In disasters, new and unknown political actors came to the forefront for consideration. Political players such as Mayor Nagin and Governor Blanco were not national figures before the storm, so attitudes and evaluations of their roles in the crisis were largely determined by information obtained through the news media and not based on prior information about their ideology, policies, campaign, or style. Furthermore, because simple heuristic cues about unknown leaders were limited to partisanship, race, and gender, we can compare their relative importance to the more complex cues in the blame attributions that arose in the media. Chapter 5 also addresses larger substantive questions of when and how the public holds leaders accountable for crisis outcomes. We pay special attention to federalism, which gives both distinct and shared powers to the national and state governments, and how it affects citizens' ability to connect blame attributions properly to evaluations of leaders.

In Chapter 6, we consider how crisis events influence the public's understanding of government's place in society. We explore the long-term effects of Hurricane Katrina by examining whether the tragic events surrounding this disaster shook the confidence of Americans in government's ability to protect and aid them in future catastrophes. Our survey asked a series of questions about respondents' confidence in the ability of government to deal with other types of catastrophic events, such as terrorist attacks, health epidemics, and other natural disasters. It also asked questions about external efficacy. Responses to both series of questions were materially affected by the storm. Findings that major disasters shape these more general orientations toward government are substantively significant because of the role that efficacy and confidence play in supporting democratic legitimacy. Finally, to explore the duration of the storm's effect on confidence in government, we turn to experimental survey data collected a year after the storm. We manipulated disaster cues (9/11 or Katrina) to assess their influence on the level of confidence in the national government's ability to assist victims and maintain order following a crisis and found that catastrophes' effects persist.

In Chapter 7, we turn our attention to the question of how emotion and attributions intersect to shape preferences for policy responses following the storm. This question lies at the core of understanding why crisis events become a foundation for political change. The broad attributions of blame outlined in Chapter 3 serve as our primary explanatory factors, but we also examine how emotions heighten the connection between those attributions and the policy opinions that people hold. In addition, we revisit how anxiety helps to suspend predispositions, especially partisanship, to create greater agreement about policy goals.

We conclude the book in Chapter 8 by returning to some of the fundamental questions with which we began: What role do disasters play in structuring public understanding of the role of government in society? Do disasters create opportunities for the media to serve as watchdogs of government in ways that they might not in ordinary times? How might the characteristics of catastrophes influence the likelihood of generating preconditions for media and public oversight of government? The individual and collective understanding that emerged from the complex environment following Hurricane Katrina is an example of how disasters form the bedrock of opinion upon which future policies are built. But this one instance speaks to larger themes about public opinion formation, governance, and society. Thus, the answers to these questions are central to understanding the long-term political impact of Hurricane Katrina as well as other major natural or man-made disasters. Equally important, we consider the normative consequences of government failure on the American psyche and the potential long-term consequences of such events. Finally, we highlight how the theoretical perspectives developed and tested in this book shed new light on unresolved academic questions about the sources, quality, and duration of political attitudes.

2

A Theoretical Framework for Systematically Examining Extraordinary Events

Understanding how cataclysmic events shape political opinions requires understanding not only why such events engage public sentiment but also why they become collective crises connected to issues of governance. One key component in the process is the information environment. This includes how information is transmitted by media in times of crisis and how individuals respond to common presentations of disaster stories. Therefore, it is important for us to consider two aspects of disasters: how information about disasters is typically framed and delivered by the mass media and how individuals process this information in the context of extraordinary times. For the latter, to fully understand the relevance of catastrophes for both individual and collective opinions, we must contrast this aspect to how individuals process information during normal or routine times.

Thus far, public opinion scholars primarily have examined extraordinary events with an eye to their uniqueness rather than their regularities. This approach is not surprising given that disasters are high-salience events, albeit with different characteristics. They create identifiable collective moments that focus public attention on issues or policies that normally reside in the background (Birkland 1997, 2006). These qualities make such events excellent venues to study attitudes about particular issues or to test theories about attitudes that require identifiable variation in social context or media framing (see, for example, Haider-Markel and Joslyn 2001; Lewis 2000; Miller

1987; Van der Brug 2001). Indeed, following Hurricane Katrina, several scholars leveraged the unique social cues associated with the crisis to test how social identity theory led African Americans' attitudes to differ from non–African Americans (Haider-Markel, Delehanty, and Beverlin 2007; Huddy and Feldman 2006a, 2006b).

However, public opinion scholars thus far have not sought a more general understanding of how extraordinary events produce similar contexts for opinion formation or how they generate dynamics that spur particular types of mass attitudes, regardless of the unique features of any particular extraordinary event. In this chapter, we outline a theoretical framework that not only informs case studies of specific catastrophes, but one that also helps to identify broader implications suitable for comparative studies of catastrophes. To do so, we have drawn heavily upon insights from experimental and non-experimental work from the fields of political science, public policy, social psychology, neural and cognitive science, media studies, and communication. Experimental work provides strong grounding for the assumptions we make in our theoretical model and guides us in identifying the important implications we should observe in real-world data. Nonexperimental studies confirm experimental findings in a more realistic setting and help determine additional relevant factors to include in our analysis.

Figure 2.1 provides a simplified overview of the process that we develop more fully later in the chapter as we more carefully outline our model and its implications. The process begins with an extraordinary event that prompts citizens to tune in to learn what happened and why. This leads to attributions of blame, which then influence evaluations of leaders, government, and public policy. In this chapter, we first describe how periods of normal politics differ from periods of extraordinary politics in order to identify the key differences between the two contexts that relate to public awareness and opinion formation. Next, we examine how crises create unique news environments that assist in the development of attributions of blame that, in turn, result in new or changed opinions toward government, government leaders, and public policy. Finally, we bring together the insights from the first two sections to articulate a model of how individuals form opinions during extraordinary times and discuss its implications.

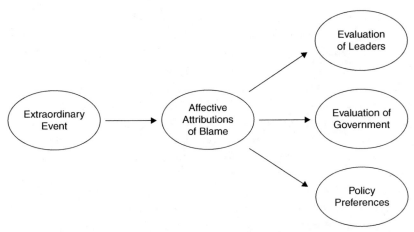

FIGURE 2.1. Overview of the Opinion Formation Process during Extraordinary Events.

NORMAL POLITICS VERSUS EXTRAORDINARY MOMENTS

Politics for most people is a remote activity that happens in musty chambers, hallways, and offices in distant capital cities. Although some individuals are attentive, many make little or no effort to follow politics or seek information about the day-to-day political debates that emerge from the normal business of budgeting, lawmaking, or electioneering. Politics is relatively predictable, with certain topics such as education, taxes, health care, and social security making the perennial list of concerns. Conflicts or controversies over these predictable topics follow well-trodden lines of debate. Even debates about policies that are quite relevant to individuals may not compel substantial attention. The policy-making process is slow and rather dull for most laypeople busy with their own lives (Downs 1957). More than half a century of research attests to the lack of attentiveness and political knowledge of citizens (see, for example, Converse 1964; Delli Carpini and Keeter 1996). Americans, on average, know very little about leading political figures, government institutions, or policy details. Instead, they rely on simple cues and heuristics, and as a result, periods of normal politics are defined by habituation, normalcy, and familiar content.

Political news during periods of normal politics is filtered and framed by political elites and transmitted via the news media to the public. Media norms and constraints bias coverage toward "indexing" or echoing elite debates rather than encouraging independent critical analysis (Bennett, Lawrence, and Livingston 2007; Entman 2003; Schiffer 2009). Political debates typically stem from long-standing ideological or partisan conflicts. Issues rise and fall on the public agenda with no clear linear story connecting political choices to substantive outcomes. These debates lack a natural beginning and a clear progression of events to help the public sort out claims about cause and effect. Instead, the American political world provides an ongoing partisan explanation of events and policies in a multimessage environment in which elites attempt to manipulate and spin information to satisfy their own personal or partisan goals.

Despite the cacophony (or perhaps because of it), most people develop strategies to help them respond to normal politics with minimal cognitive effort and maximum psychological comfort. Citizens use the perceptual lenses of partisanship or ideology along with their individual values to filter the messages that inform their political opinions. When faced with the common platter of competing elite messages, they are able to identify their group interests easily and they gravitate toward arguments that uphold their core attitudes and beliefs while filtering those that do not (DiMaggio 1997; Gaines et al. 2007; Kunda 1987, 1990; McAllister, Mitchell, and Beach 1979; Tetlock 1983; Zaller 1992).

In social psychological terms, we call the phenomenon that encourages particular strategies for thinking "motivated reasoning" (see DiMaggio 1997; Kunda 1987, 1990; Lodge and Taber 2005). The most common form of motivated reasoning is directional, in which individuals seek and process information in ways that support their already-formed opinions and attitudes (DiMaggio 1997; Gaines et al. 2007; McAllister, Mitchell, and Beach 1979; Tetlock 1983). They may selectively encode and recall only a subset of material or they may discount information incongruent with preexisting beliefs (Kunda 1990; Zaller 1992). In an effort to minimize cognitive costs, directionally motivated reasoners may also rely on heuristics, or decision-making shortcuts, to determine their preferences quickly and easily. The use of heuristics reduces the cognitive costs associated with processing information and assists individuals in arriving at decisions that correctly reflect a set of preexisting preferences (Lau and Redlawsk 2006; Popkin

1994). Cues such as party identification, ideology, endorsements, and social networks (Downs 1957; Kahn and Kenney 2002; Norrander 1986; Steger 2007; Stone, Rapoport, and Atkeson 1995) provide the necessary information to evaluate and inform opinion formation and candidate preferences without having to invest limited resources to learn about political actors. In general, during periods of normal politics, people rely heavily on directional motivation (DiMaggio 1997; Nickerson 1998; Wason 1968).

Even during elections, a time that we think of politics as creating an extraordinary spectacle, routine politics is often the norm because the process of campaigning is designed to stimulate directionally motivated reasoning. At a very basic level, campaign politics focuses on activating predispositions of party, ideology, and group, reminding voters who they are and where they belong politically (Berelson, Lazarsfeld, and McPhee 1954; Brader 2006; Campbell et al. 1960; Gelman and King 1993; Lewis-Beck et al. 2008). Campaigns attempt to energize their supporters by creating enthusiasm around candidates and motivating their team members to mobilize, participate, and support the party standard-bearer (Brader 2006). In this way, many voters make a standard decision based upon their partisan affiliations and predispositions (Downs 1957; Gelman and King 1993).

That does not mean that elections do not convey information or that voters are necessarily unresponsive to it (Alvarez 1999; Lau and Redlawsk 2006). The state of the economy, in particular, has been repeatedly shown to matter in election outcomes and voter decision making (Lewis-Beck and Stegmaier 2007). However, even when the economy is weak, voters tend to filter that information through a partisan lens (Bartels 2002; Campbell et al. 1960; Conover, Feldman, and Knight 1987; Ladner and Wlezien 2007). At the same time, it is worth noting that when campaigns happen in conjunction with extraordinary events – for example, in 1932 during the Great Depression – the election context may magnify social disruptions associated with the catastrophe, setting the stage for critical realignments. With the exception of these rare moments, most elections represent periods of normal politics, with clear partisan politics around typical debates that fit easily with voters understanding of the world, making directional motivation cognitively easy.

EXTRAORDINARY EVENTS AS POLITICAL CONTEXT

Extraordinary moments, in contrast to periods of normal politics, provide a very different context for the transmission of political information. Catastrophes are known in the policy world as focusing events because they command attention of the masses and elites alike, and often force people to confront social and political issues that are new or had been previously ignored (Baumgartner and Jones 2009; Birkland 1997, 2006; Kingdon 2002). Disasters are often sudden, are relatively uncommon, and produce unexpected outcomes (Birkland 2006). Unlike with routine politics, where policy makers attempt to manipulate the salience of an issue strategically, catastrophes define both the timing and level of public salience. Policy makers, the media, and the public become aware of them at roughly the same time (Birkland 2006:2). The unexpected and shocking nature of the event leads to widespread attentiveness, making it both personal and collective.

Extraordinary events offer the general complexity of ordinary politics, but in an environment where nearly everyone is attentive. In this circumstance, elite ability to spin the story is limited by the unfolding sequence of the catastrophe (Bennett, Lawrence, and Livingston 2007; Schiffer 2009). Eyewitness accounts from journalists and others on location combine with a clear linear progression of events in the story to help citizens construct a reality that is not easily dismissed, even if that reality is inconvenient for leaders. This linear progression of the story in the media is important because experimental evidence suggests that people make more accurate judgments about responsibility when a story is presented from beginning to end (Hastie, Penrod, and Pennington 1983; Pennington and Hastie 1986). During extraordinary moments, such as 9/11, Hurricane Katrina, the Oklahoma City bombing, or the *Challenger* Space Shuttle explosion, the events of the crisis structure the narrative available to journalists and elites, thereby reducing the potential to manage or control the story. Instead, viewers themselves can place events and actions in temporal context, including the actions or inactions of government and its leaders.

For the public, unexpected calamities induce anxiety that stimulates a different type of information processing than we see during periods of normal politics (MacKuen et al. 2010; Marcus, Neuman, and MacKuen 2000). Decades of research across multiple academic disciplines reveal that humans are biologically hard-wired to respond to surprising or shocking stimuli – particularly if that stimulus is negative or threatening (Fiske 1980; Lang 2000; Marcus, Neuman, and MacKuen 2000; Newhagen and Reeves 1992; Schützwohl and Borgstedt 2005; Shoemaker 1996). In this sense, shock operates the same as anxiety by triggering the brain's "surveillance system" (Meyer, Reisenzein, and Schützwohl 1997; Shutzwohl and Borgstedt 2005). The surveillance system, once activated, encourages attentiveness and appraisal of new information (Marcus, Neuman, and MacKuen 2000). Individual attentiveness is critical to what makes collective crises influential because attentiveness is a necessary condition for receiving information.

Catastrophes and other types of crises are natural stimulators of the surveillance system. Indeed, research shows that individuals appear, uniformly, to learn about and respond to such events (Page and Shapiro 1992; Prior 2002). For example, those who felt anxious following 9/11 watched more television than those who did not (Huddy et al. 2005), and those who sought information about potential threats and risks post-9/11 reported greater interest in all news, and negative news in particular (Hoffner et al. 2009). Prior (2002) shows that after 9/11, knowledge about the War on Terror was widespread among the public, including rather detailed knowledge about how anthrax infects the body. In short, citizens can and do learn political information when it is necessary, relevant, and easily accessible.

Extraordinary events, then, generate surprise and anxiety, and these emotions lead individuals to search for information to understand the causes of discrepant events in order to return to a state of normal processing (Hewstone 1989; Meyer 1988; Meyer et al. 1991; Shoemaker 1996; Weiner 1985, 1995). This information processing strategy is known as accuracy-based motivated reasoning (Kunda 1990). If their investigation reveals nothing of personal relevance or shows the event to fit with prior expectations about catastrophes, the briefly attentive public may return to their normal mental processes rather than encode new information and adjust opinions. On the other hand, if the nature of the crisis leads to both shock and a sense of personal relevance, then the need to form a causal story to explain events and determine accountability is great. Therefore, emotions associated with catastrophes are an important precursor to attribution because certain types of emotion disrupt the normal or routine processing of information and spur efforts to identify causes of unexpected outcomes.

Later in this chapter, we outline an individual-level model that shows how the context of an extraordinary moment shapes the processing and acceptance of political messages. Central to the model is the emotion-laden, affective assignment of blame. Our argument draws heavily upon the insights from the theory of affective intelligence, which highlights how emotion augments reasoning rather than circumvents it (Marcus, Neuman, and MacKuen 2000; see also Brader 2005; MacKuen et al. 2010; Valentino et al. 2008, 2009). The key to understanding opinion in extraordinary times lies in recognizing how heightened salience and emotional stimulation alter how people process framed political messages following a disaster. Political scientists have explored the implications of affective intelligence for a number of different attitudes or contexts, including elections and campaigns (Brader 2005, 2006; Marcus, Neuman, and MacKuen 2000), citizen knowledge and information seeking (Valentino et al. 2008), citizenship (MacKuen et al. 2010), and terrorism (Huddy et al. 2005; Merolla and Zechmeister 2009), but they have not explored its implications for forming attributions of blame for unexpected negative events, such as catastrophes. Examining the importance of emotion in the formation of attributions following catastrophic events affords a new venue for testing, extending, and developing theories related to affective intelligence. However, to understand when emotion is likely to alter the processing of information, we need to trace how epochal events reach the public and influence both the information environment and the emotional state of individuals paying attention to the news coverage.

MEDIA COVERAGE AND THE INFORMATION ENVIRONMENT IN EXTRAORDINARY EVENTS

At the root, epochal events fall far from normal experience. Most become media spectacles with all the emotion and qualities of high-drama storytelling, including a cast of heroes and villains. Unexpected and catastrophic incidents force people to confront the reality of external threats to their well-being and to confront their own mortality, particularly when they identify or empathize with those affected.

Because of these characteristics, natural and man-made catastrophes hold special status in the formation of public opinions – their impact on the public psyche is unparalleled by day-to-day news events. But these events also bring politics to the forefront, as public officials respond to catastrophes and the news media search for answers for why such events occurred.

Media create the initial framework for understanding extraordinary events as they convey information to the public from those closest to the catastrophe – victims, first-responders, and local officials. Local media and journalists on the scene serve up eyewitness evidence along with frequent and repeated updates of breaking information. As events unfold, national and local news organizations join forces to seek out reactions of elites and experts well beyond the scene, including state and national government officials. From the first moments of a disaster, the news media frame its context as they organize and convey information to the public. Framing occurs when journalists select visual images, elite quotes, or journalistic commentary to highlight some aspects of an issue or event while downplaying others (Chong and Druckman 2007b, 2007c; Entman 2003). These frames provide the information necessary to create causal stories that explain the realities of life or life events (Gamson and Modigliani 1987, 1989; Tuchman 1978) and promote "particular definitions and interpretations of political issues" (Shah et al. 2002).

Media framing of extraordinary events has a predictable quality because journalists draw from a set of standard operating procedures and stock scripts to help them manage in challenging circumstances. Coverage of extraordinary events typically follows three distinct phases. The initial phase occurs while the event is actively unfolding; during the second stage, immediately following the initial, active phase, journalists investigate the causes of the event and correct any factual errors that occurred during the initial reporting stage; and in the third stage, the news media seek to bring perspective to the event and place it in a broader social and political context (see Graber 2005:131–4).

During the first phase of coverage, the news is dominated by the need for factual knowledge, but causal stories often emerge as a way to sort out the meaning of emerging facts. As Graber (2005:133) notes, "pressure for news encourages reporters and public officials alike to speculate about a disaster's causes." At the same time, journalists, limited by time, circumstance, and resources, are unable to put together a broader, thematic analysis specific to the crisis, so they turn to a set of routine catastrophe storylines to make sense out of the chaos (Shoemaker and Reese 1996). Unlike in normal times, in the wake of catastrophe, journalists are more likely to exercise an independent voice and less likely to simply index elite stories, because part of their scripted role is to investigate and report on the causes of the disaster.

During the active phase of coverage, news stories tend to highlight the chaos, fear, and suffering that arises directly from the crisis placing the nature of the event as the central causal agent of pain and suffering. Stories highlight the experiences of victims during and after the event and of first-responders, as well as the challenges of keeping order in the wake of chaotic events (Tierney, Bevc, and Kuligowski, 2006). During the second and third phases of coverage, journalists turn to more penetrating questions of why the catastrophe occurred. In these phases, they begin to seek opinions from technical experts and political elites. During the third phase of coverage, causal stories related to government failure or government success are most likely to emerge. It is also during this phase that political elites begin efforts to "shape political fallout from the event" (Graber 2005:133). However, elites are providing reactions after the media have already at least partially framed unexpected events and after citizens have already formed a set of initial impressions and opinions. The sequencing of coverage phases makes it more difficult for elites to reframe the drama.

Journalistic investigations in the second and third phases tend to follow two lines of inquiry. One is why the disaster happened and the other is how effectively government officials responded in the aftermath. For example, in the wake of 9/11, journalists questioned whether we knew about threats from Al Qaeda in advance and whether warning signs were adequately heeded by government officials (Elliot 2002; Risen 2001). Of course, local, state, and national government's absence of response in the early days following Katrina was a major and compelling story, as were questions about President Bush and FEMA Director Brown's absence of leadership from the outset (Revkin 2005; Shane and Lipton 2005). Media evaluations of government response in disasters include not only the direct responsiveness to victims of a catastrophe, but the quality of leadership exhibited by key political figures, such as presidents, governors, and mayors. In crises, the public and media look to political leaders for reassurance and a means of reducing anxiety (Bucy 2003; Merolla and Zechmeister 2009). When leaders fail on this dimension, it is remarked upon in the press.

During each phase of coverage, media actively frame the information provided to the public. Although multiple frames are common at the outset of any catastrophe, frames and causal stories rise and fall in the media as the frames are winnowed to one or a few dominant frames. It is through identifying the relative dominance of frames that it becomes possible to predict how the catastrophe will ripple through the political world. Frames and their associated messages, in normal and extraordinary times, can have both "volume," which stems from sheer repetition, and "strength," which stems from credibility (Chong and Druckman 2007a). Because of the 24/7 news cycle, facts and frames of extraordinary events are frequently repeated, especially in the first few hours and days of coverage, making volume unusually high. Credibility, or strength of frames, is often determined by their correspondence to observable conditions. Disasters attract eyewitnesses, chief among them journalists. When journalists or others bring personal, eyewitness accounts of events, the framing associated with them is especially strong.

The final and perhaps most important attribute of media coverage to which we call attention is the pervasive use of emotional primes that naturally arise in the context of catastrophes. An *emotional prime* is any aspect of news coverage that serves to trigger certain emotions such as shock, disgust, sadness, joy, or anger. Such aspects are primes in the sense that the triggered emotions prepare the receiver to process information in particular ways. In a catastrophe, many of the emotional primes intensify the anxiety and attentiveness of the public. Even in normal times, it is common for television news organizations to use "sensationalistic" devices known to lure viewers, such as dramatic music, quick cuts between scenes, and emotional visual footage (Fischoff 2004; Vettehen, Nuijten, and Peeters 2008). Televised coverage of catastrophic and extraordinary events lends itself to such devices.[1] Reporters in the field rely primarily on available eyewitnesses

[1] There is a broad literature that examines, experimentally, the effects of sensationalist devices on attention, emotion, and memory. See, among others, Grabe, Lang, and Zhao 2003; Graber 2005; Lang et al. 2007; Shoemaker 1996. See especially Vettehen, Nuijten, and Peeters 2008.

who report on their personal experiences, a device known to increase the credibility and emotional impact of the coverage (Vettehen, Nuijten, and Peeters 2008). Animated visuals, particularly of emotional human faces, are stirring emotional primes for viewers (Simons et al. 2000; Wild, Erbs, and Bartels 2001). TV, in particular, is a powerful medium of communication influencing both the least and most educated in similar ways (Jerit, Barabas, and Bolsen 2006). Whether intentional or simply a byproduct of the nature of disaster coverage, the result is the same: emotionally evocative coverage and a public that is riveted by the story. As a package, these devices create emotionally compelling stories that engage the attention of viewers and encourage connections between the media messages and the feelings generated from them (Grabe, Lang, and Zhao 2003; Graber 2005; Lang et al. 2007; Shoemaker 1996; Vettehen, Nuijten, and Peeters 2008).

Recent research points to neurobiological reasons why visual images in news media are such powerful stimulators of attention and vicarious emotion. The human brain is equipped with a mirror neuron system (MNS) that reacts to observed actions and emotions of others as if we were experiencing them ourselves (Enticott et al. 2008; Molnar-Szakacs 2011). Magnetic resonance imaging (MRI) studies show that observers display the same neural activity patterns associated with performing actions or feeling emotions that they observe in actors, and that this neural activity is generated preconsciously and involuntarily (Molnar-Szakacs 2011). As a result, emotional mirroring serves as a basis for social cognition and empathy (Enticott et al. 2008; Molnar-Szakacs 2011). Empathy is essentially a vicarious emotional response in which one recognizes the plight of others and can imagine oneself in those circumstances (Eisenberg and Fabes 1990; Eisenberg et al. 1991). The activation of the MNS is one of the reasons that when we see a smiling face, we begin to smile ourselves, and that when we see a face in distress, we also begin to feel a sense of distress. Disaster coverage is rife with the types of images likely to create mirrored emotions of anxiety and distress that encourage attentiveness to media (Hoffner et al. 2009; Zillmann, Taylor, and Lewis 1998). Moreover, empathetic mirroring appears to be stronger when observing those who share the same cultural or social identity (Molnar-Szakacs 2011). This suggests that when media coverage shows victims of a catastrophe to be members of one's own social group, the emotions felt in response to the

catastrophe may be especially strong. Likewise, it suggests that catastrophes with human victims are much more powerful than environmental catastrophes (such as forest fires or oil spills) that present few
images of human suffering.

PUBLIC REACTIONS: AFFECTIVE ATTRIBUTIONS OF BLAME IN TIMES OF CRISES

An extraordinary event and the media coverage surrounding it create
an emotional environment that encourages attentiveness and the formation of causal explanations. The combined pressures for media
outlets to fill the airwaves to satisfy a voracious public and the need
for politicians to manage blame following a high-profile incident naturally create an environment that is favorable to spawning multiple
causal claims. As with normal politics, many extraordinary moments
produce multiple frames to explain and justify events and outcomes.
Although extraordinary events may be quickly winnowed to only one
frame, as occurred the Gulf of Tonkin (Zaller 1992) or 9/11 (Merolla
and Zechmeister 2009), it is also common to observe multiple persistent frames, as occurred after Hurricane Katrina and the Oklahoma
City bombing. A multiple frame environment is particularly complex
because it provides many cues from which individuals can pick and
choose. Explaining the choices they make depends upon understanding whether their information search is *directionally motivated*, in
search of answers that are consistent with existing beliefs, or *accuracy
motivated*, in search of the answers that are most consistent with facts
of the event, regardless of existing beliefs (Kunda 1990). We argue
that when extraordinary events trigger shock and anxiety for individuals, the strategy of directionally motivated reasoning for many
gives way to accuracy-motivated reasoning. In contrast to directional
motivations, where individuals actively (although unconsciously)
apply biases to the reception and processing of information, accuracy-
oriented motivations discourage the application of biased processing
and encourage the unbiased reception and processing of information
(DiMaggio 1997; Kunda 1987, 1990; McAllister, Mitchell, and Beach
1979; Tetlock 1983).

Prior research shows that media framing and priming influence
opinions by altering the set of considerations brought to mind about

an issue, by altering the weights given to various considerations, or by offering persuasive messages (Chong and Druckman 2007a, 2007b, 2007c; Zaller 1992). However, not everyone is susceptible to the effects of framing. Motivated reasoning normally plays a strong role in sorting out competing messages (Lavine, Lodge, and Freitas 2005). Those with strong prior opinions or predispositions tend to select self-reinforcing information, evaluate information in a biased fashion, or simply resist and filter countervailing information (Chong and Druckman 2007a; Kunda 1987, 1990; Zaller 1992).

Why people adopt certain causal stories rather than others has captured the attention of scholars in several fields. Early studies in social psychology explored how individuals construct explanations of the motivations or behaviors of others around them as a function of individual cognition and motivation (Crittenden 1983; Weiner 1995). Later scholarship, particularly in sociology, took a broader approach by exploring how social context shapes attributions to one's self and others (Howard and Pike 1986). This line of inquiry expanded to include attribution of blame for events or outcomes (Guimond, Begin, and Palmer 1989; Hewstone 1989).

Studies of blame attribution in political science have focused almost exclusively on either the effects of external stimuli, such as framing and media messages (for example, Iyengar 1991), or on internal characteristics such as predispositions and political sophistication (see for example, Gomez and Wilson 2003, 2008; Haider-Markel and Joslyn 2001). The two branches of scholarly research rarely examine how the one interacts with the other. Our argument breaks new ground by showing how discrete emotions that stimulate the brain's surveillance system moderate predispositions during the process of assigning blame.

Of course, motivated reasoning also applies to blame attribution. Sharp and Joslyn (2001), for example, found that predispositions stemming from socialization and past experiences, along with gender and age, influenced attribution of the societal problem of rape to pornography. Rudolph (2003a) found clear evidence of partisan rationalization in the formation of economic evaluations (see also Gomez and Wilson 2003). Iyengar (1991) found that in addition to framing, characteristics such as political ideology and partisanship shaped attributions for crime, terrorism, poverty, racial inequality, and unemployment. Taken as a whole, this body of research highlights how causal attribution is a normal and often unconscious mental process where attributions are formed easily and automatically out of preexisting judgments.

We argue, however, that in extraordinary times, the process of assigning blame is different because the costs versus benefits associated with directionally biased reasoning, compared to the costs versus benefits of accuracy-based reasoning, increase. When this happens, individuals rely more heavily on contemporaneous information to form opinions, and the combination of the media context and an individual's emotional state determine the magnitude of the effect. By combining the rich body of research on emotion and information processing, particularly from the literature on affective intelligence (Brader 2006; MacKuen et al. 2010; Marcus 2000; Marcus, Neuman and MacKuen 2000; Valentino et al. 2008, 2009) and the literature on motivated reasoning (Kunda 1987, 1990; Lodge and Taber 2005; Taber and Lodge 2006), we offer a theory of affective attributions to explain patterns of attributions in public opinion following epochal events. *Affective attributions* are those formed from the combined effects of emotions generated by the catastrophic event and the cognitive processing of new information pertaining to it. During catastrophic times, anxious citizens increase their likelihood of learning new information that has the power to update key political opinions.

Recent studies of emotion and attribution of blame find that emotion is related to causal attribution, but the pathway of influence is unclear. Malhotra and Kuo (2009) argue and find that strong emotions, measured as an index of anger and sadness, increased reliance on party cues when assigning blame ranks to different political leaders following Hurricane Katrina. Haider-Markel, Delehanty, and Beverlin (2007) demonstrate that a strong emotional response to Hurricane Katrina, measured as an index of shock, sadness, and anger, increased three different attributions of blame, one to national government rather than state government, and two attributions suggesting that the reason that national government was slow was that the victims were poor or black. The use of emotion indices in both studies makes it difficult to parse out how specific emotions influence attributions. Recent research into the links between emotion and political attitudes other than attributions finds that that sadness, anger, and shock operate differently to produce different outcomes, something that our theoretical argument distinguishes (Valentino et al. 2008, 2009).

Affective attribution occurs when emotion-provoking events such as disasters or catastrophes alter the incentives for different types of motivated reasoning and prompt a switch, albeit automatically and unconsciously, to accuracy-based motivated reasoning. Specifically, accuracy motivations encourage individuals to seek and appraise a broad range of information, even information that runs counter to predispositions (see Kunda 1987, 1990). Such motivations are likely when individuals believe that accurate evaluation is necessary to fulfill personal goals or needs. Experimental research shows that even when subjects are faced with circumstances that trigger both directional and accuracy-based motivations, those with accuracy-based motivations process information with greater depth than those with only directional motivations (Kunda 1990). Likewise, anxious individuals are more likely to seek balanced information when they have personal reasons for doing so (Valentino et al. 2008, 2009) and when individuals assess risky and uncertain situations to determine whether they are threatening (MacKuen et al. 2010; Marcus, Neuman and MacKuen 2010). MacKuen et al. (2010:441) note that "[w]hen people are in risky and novel circumstances, they are likely to be better off engaging in deliberative mechanisms, and thoughtful consideration, in order to handle the uncertainty."

When disasters strike, individuals become attentive to the emotionally charged coverage of the event, creating a connection between themselves and the victims. They feel a sense of empathetic anxiety for victims and a sense of concern for what the disaster might mean for themselves or for loved ones. In this way, the event becomes personally relevant, prompting the need to identify potential threats and attribute blame. But because catastrophes reveal actions, events, and outcomes that are unusual in day-to-day life, typical processing strategies designed to classify them quickly and attribute blame are unavailable. Attempting to apply standard processing routines to novel events increases the risk of making errors in judgment – potentially costly errors given the state of potential danger. In addition, the usual avenues that one draws upon for heuristics-based processing may be absent in the early phase of disaster coverage because first-person accounts and journalists' direct experiences dominate the news. Local officials and rescuers are typically unknown to the broader national audience and are unlikely to stimulate clear partisan or predispositional cues. As a result, the audience is faced with a cafeteria of framed messages and speculations offered by journalists that are backed with credible eye-witness evidence. Because of the sheer volume of information available across multiple media outlets, the information costs associated with accuracy-based motivations decline. For the emotionally engaged, careful assessment of a broad range of information yields greater confidence, thereby resolving anxiety through attributions. In short, directionally motivated reasoning gives way to accuracy-motivated reasoning for those driven by an anxious response to the event.

This means that in a media environment in which frames are relatively consistent across outlets and backed up by compelling episodic evidence, the acceptance of dominant frames should be high, *even when they run counter to predispositions* (Chong 1996; Chong and Druckman 2007a). In the case of 9/11, where a one-message environment dominated, attribution of blame focused on an external stimuli and led to policy preferences that favored reducing civil liberties and an increased trust in the leaders of government, even among Democrats (Merolla and Zechmeister 2009). However, if the message environment offers multiple frames or causal messages, individuals are likely to gravitate toward attributions that are congruent with predispositions. At the same time, feelings of anxiety should attenuate the strength of this effect for individuals because of their increased attentiveness to highly credible, persuasive information in the media combined with a need to assess threatening events fully and accurately. Individual variation in the strength of directional motivations should depend upon individuals' level of anxiety. For those made most anxious, we should see greater acceptance of frames with high volume and credibility, including those inconsistent with predispositions.

To sum up, several factors combine to stimulate the affective acceptance of causal attribution frames offered in the media following a catastrophic moment. First, attentiveness opens up a mechanism for political information to reach those who are normally inattentive to politics. Second, anxiety primes them not only to seek out information, but also to *receive* and *accept* the information provided (MacKuen et al. 2010; Marcus, Neuman, and MacKuen 2000; Valentino et al. 2009). The result, at the individual level, is greater collective agreement with dominant causal frames. At the aggregate level, when clear attribution frames dominate the media, the result is greater uniformity of opinions for those made anxious by the catastrophe, thus providing an individual-level mechanism that supports societal-level punctuations in political attitudes and preferences for policy. Dominant causal messages are a necessary but insufficient condition to produce widespread public agreement about attributions of blame. Emotion is a necessary ingredient for causal stories to transcend individual predispositions.

AFFECTIVE ATTRIBUTIONS AND THEIR CONSEQUENCES FOR POLITICAL OPINIONS

Attributions, once formed, are consequential for a wide variety of other public opinions, especially opinions about leaders and public policies. Causal stories highlight particular problems and suggest avenues of resolution (Stone 1989). Therefore, acceptance of dominant causal stories that arise from catastrophes is quite consequential for individual attitudes. These causal attributions, ascribed broadly as is common following a major catastrophe, can become an engine for political change. Although scholars have long recognized that catastrophes produce punctuated political change (i.e., Baumgartner and Jones 2009; Birkland 1997, 2006; Kingdon 2002), little is known about the micro-level processes that support them (Wood and Doan 2003). Affective attributions generate support around dominant causal stories and might serve as one such microfoundation. Therefore, we need to understand not only how causal attributions are formed following a catastrophe, but also how they influence other types of political opinions.

An anxious and receptive public is fertile ground for the creation of a nationally shared understanding of political problems and potential solutions. Epochal events shape public evaluations of government and policy through attributions of blame and credit that arise naturally from elite and journalistic assessments of unfolding events. Indeed, for the politically inattentive, catastrophes offer a rare (although unsought) glimpse of government and its leaders in action. Political actors and government agencies that rarely receive attention from the public are thrust onto the public stage as the media assess questions of responsibility for the catastrophe. During normal politics, government goes about its work with little notice from the public. In times of crisis, however, the public becomes acutely aware of the functions of government as a byproduct of seeking information about extraordinary events, and this acceptance of information alters opinion.

Causal attributions can point to failures in leadership that subsequently influence evaluations of elected officials. They can also point to failures in the structure and function of government, leading to calls for changes in policies or institutions as a way to avoid future crises. Because our focus in this chapter is abstract and general, we lump together several different types of political opinions, including evaluations of leaders, government institutions, and policy solutions. We do so because the process through which disasters shape these general types of opinions is the same. However, in any given disaster, the set of actors and events defines the relevant set of political opinions to examine. For example, in regard to the subject of our case study, Hurricane Katrina, the relevant elected officials include President George W. Bush, Governor Blanco, and Mayor Nagin, thus we might wonder how causal attributions of blame map onto each of their evaluations. However, following 9/11, the relevant leaders included Mayor Giuliani, Governor George Pataki, and President George W. Bush. Likewise, relevant policy opinions following Katrina involve institutions and procedures related to disaster management, whereas relevant policy opinions following 9/11 pertain to laws and institutions related to terrorism. Regardless of the differences in the specific political opinions, we argue that an overarching process can guide predictions of specific opinions in any post-disaster period. In this section, we elaborate a general framework for how the context that emerges around an extraordinary event and the emotions that it stimulates and the attributions that it facilitates lead to political consequences.

Figure 2.2 presents a graphic representation of the various paths of influence. It is worth noting that, when applied to specific cases, this model could represent the formation of wholly new opinions about political actors, institutions, or policies that were previously unknown to the individual. But it could also represent the process through which existing opinions are updated. In the latter case, the prior opinion would serve as a type of predisposition. In either case, however, political opinions are an outcome of affective attributions, and both attributions and emotions have direct, mediating, and conditional effects. Arrows with a plus or minus in this model indicate areas where we predict specific directional effects. For example, we expect

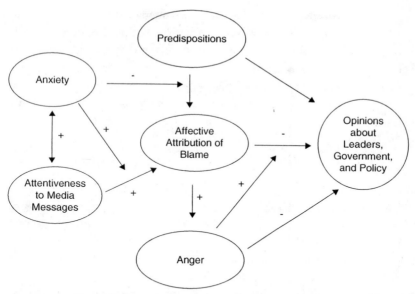

FIGURE 2.2. Causal Linkages in Opinion Formation during Extraordinary Events.

that attention to the media messages in catastrophes raises anxiety, at least at the outset, and increased anxiety leads to heightened attention to messages. Likewise, we expect anxiety to attenuate the effects of predispositions when making attributions. And we expect attributions of blame to reduce favorability ratings of leaders deemed as responsible and to shape preferences for punitive policies that target actors deemed responsible for the catastrophe.

Arrows without a directional sign are situations where we cannot predict, a priori, a directional effect. We cannot know, for example, the targets of media attributions in a given catastrophe, so we cannot predict how predispositions might shape them. If the target is a Democrat, then those with Democratic predispositions would be less likely to accept the attribution, but those with Republican predispositions would more easily accept the attribution. However, in both cases, the anxiety associated with the event should attenuate that link; hence the negative sign on the arrow represents the conditional path of influence that flows from anxiety. In contrast, anxiety *increases* the chances that messages with high volume and credibility will be accepted, so the conditional arrow is given a positive expectation.

Finally, note the role of the emotion anger in this figure. It serves as both a direct and conditioning effect on political opinions and is an important catalyst that helps translate attributions into opinions about political actors or policies. The path from attribution to anger has not been explored in political science thus far, but represents a potentially robust mechanism through which epochal events shape political outcomes.

AFFECTIVE ATTRIBUTIONS AND THE ANGER–PUNISHMENT LINK

Thus far, we have focused on the central role played by the emotions of shock and anxiety in opening individuals to causal stories and frames in the media, and these attributions certainly have direct influences on how leaders and government are evaluated. But acceptance of particular causal stories provides targets for another emotion, anger, which also has consequences for evaluation of government and policy preferences.

Anxiety and anger are increasingly seen as distinct negative emotions by political scientists (Druckman and McDermott 2008; Huddy, Feldman, and Cassese 2007; MacKuen et al. 2010; Marcus et al. 2006; Petersen 2010; Redlawsk et al. 2007; Steenbergen and Ellis 2006; Valentino et al. 2008), psychologists (Lerner and Kelter 2000; Lerner et al. 2003), and neuroscientists (Carver 2004; Davidson 1995; Davidson et al. 2000; Spezio and Adolphs 2007). For example, political scientists have shown that feelings of anger, as opposed to feelings of anxiety, about the national economy led to lower evaluations of President Ronald Reagan (Conover and Feldman 1986). Merolla and Zechmeister (2009) found that when manipulating threat in an experimental design, threat produced little anger but significant anxiety. Their findings suggest that these emotions arise from distinct sources. In other research, where both emotions were considered simultaneously, Huddy, Feldman, and Cassese (2007) demonstrated that anger reduced the perception of the risk of the Iraq War and resulted in more support for the war and military intervention. Anxiety, however, did the reverse: It increased the individual's perception of risk and reduced support for the Iraq War.

We, like others, argue that anxiety and anger are discrete emotions that operate in different ways to shape opinions (see especially Huddy,

Feldman, and Cassese 2007 and Valentino et al. 2008). The underlying theoretical reason for these distinct effects is that individuals' opinions are formed in the context of specific situations. Their personal emotional reaction is based upon their perceptions and understandings of the complexity of the world. Surprise at unexpected novel events stimulates the emotion of anxiety (Schützwohl and Borgstedt 2005). The response to the anxiety is a search for information to appraise the situation and understand its causes (MacLeod and Mathews 1988; Marcus and MacKuen 1993; Marcus, Neuman, and MacKuen 2000; Mathews and MacLeod 1986; Mogg et al. 1990; Valentino et al. 2008; Williams et al. 1997). In this way, individuals are open to new information that may result in attributions of blame that are inconsistent with their predispositions. Anger, on the other hand, is an action-oriented emotion and does not motivate thoughtfulness (Bodenhausen, Sheppard, and Kramer 1994; Lerner, Goldberg, and Tetlock 1998; Lerner and Tiedens 2005; Tiedens 2001; Tiedens and Linton 2001; Valentino et al. 2008). Rather, it is focused on acting upon prior judgments of responsibility (Fiddick 2004; Haidt 2003; Petersen 2010; Weiner, Osbourne, and Rudolph 2011). Social psychologists repeatedly show in laboratory experiments that anger stems from causal attributions for unjust and negative outcomes (Rudolph et al. 2004). When individuals attribute blame to someone who could have controlled or prevented the negative outcome, they feel angry (Averill 1983; Betancourt and Blair 1992; Rudolph et al. 2004; Weiner, Graham, and Chandler 1982; Weiner et al. 1987; Weiner, Osbourne, and Rudolph 2011). Petersen (2010: 358) describes anger as a "moral emotion" that moderates attitudes and behaviors toward specific individuals, such as a leader or candidate, or toward groups, such as criminals (Lerner, Goldberg, and Tetlock 1998; Petersen 2010) or terrorists (Huddy, Feldman, and Cassese 2007). Therefore anger, unlike anxiety, stems from judgments of who is at fault and intensifies when the negative event is seen as unjust (Clore and Centerbar 2004; Ortony, Clore, and Collins 1988; Shaver, Kirson, and O'Connor 1987; Smith and Ellsworth 1985; Weiss, Suckow, and Cropanzano 1999). Consequently, feelings of anger lead to a desire to punish violators who precipitated the unexpected event or crisis.

The information gained about the unexpected and unusual event through the attribution process leads to clear targets of responsibility and, hence, targets of anger. Anger can be expressed fully only when it has a target in which to channel the emotional energy. Importantly, this suggests that anger happens after cognition or explanation; it is an outcome of attribution. By recognizing this fact, it is clear that anger should have both direct and conditioning effects on political opinions. This also helps explain why anxiety and anger are positively related but why they have different effects on the formation of opinions. An individual experiences a shock, which launches a process of affective attribution of blame. If the scan of information used in making the attributions reveals that the unjust actions of certain parties or groups are to blame, the attributions also result in anger and a subsequent desire to punish those responsible. In this case, there is an observable correlation between anxiety and anger, but the paths through which they influence political evaluations differ.

This distinction is a departure from recent work that argues that these emotions are positively correlated, but tap different feelings from the same stimulus (Huddy, Feldman, and Cassese 2007; MacKuen et al. 2010; Petersen 2010). Although the extraordinary event may initially produce anxiety, anger comes later and is stimulated by the attributions process. *Blame cognition*, the recognition of blame that comes from affective attribution, is fundamental to both the origins and focus of anger. It directs anger when the fault is seen as avoidable and when the negative event is seen as unjust. In addition, anger serves to heighten the connection between blame and evaluations. Because anger is an action-oriented emotion, it enhances the desire to "act" on attributions through translating them into lower evaluations of leaders as well as stronger preferences for punitive policies. The conditional effects of anger are likely to be especially strong for policies that are directed at the causal agents of the crisis. In later chapters, we test the claim that the emotions of anger and anxiety operated distinctly in shaping opinions following Hurricane Katrina and test the degree to which anger enhances the effects of affective attributions.

SUMMARY AND CONCLUSIONS

Periods of normal politics regularly are disrupted by periods of extraordinary politics in which unexpected events dominate the media and make us question our understanding of the orderliness and predictability of the world around us. The lack of predictability raises our awareness and induces anxiety, which leads us on a quest for answers as to why the event happened, how it happened, and how best to create policies and rules to reduce the risk that it will happen again. Through this process, we form attributions of blame that can trigger additional emotions, such as anger, that have independent effects on our evaluations of government and leaders and our policy preferences.

Our model makes a number of theoretical contributions, most notably expanding our understanding of how predispositions interact with the media context in the formation of political attributions. At one level, this model of how individuals form opinions from the joint effects of information and emotion applies to both extraordinary and normal times. The affective intelligence literature clearly shows that anxiety alters mental processing of information and, at the individual level, anxiety could occur for many different reasons that are unrelated to catastrophes. What is unique about our model is the recognition that the nature of an extraordinary event creates a particular type of environment that is likely to trigger affective attributions of blame that are politically relevant, and this process is widespread in society. Unexpected events create an anxious environment where many people are open to new information and where information is provided in such a way that they can sift through it and make conclusions about blame and responsibility. This happens in an information environment that discourages simple indexing of elite arguments. Journalists along with local officials and victims dominate the narratives, whereas elite interpretations of events are reactive and secondary to the magnitude of the disaster. It is the combination of the media context and the emotional triggers that makes politics in extraordinary times different. Our work brings to the forefront these regularities.

3

The Media Message Environment and the Emotional Context of Hurricane Katrina

In this and subsequent chapters, we draw upon the theoretical argument presented in Chapter 2 to form specific testable predictions about public opinion following Hurricane Katrina. To do so, we begin with a careful evaluation of the political context and media message environment that surrounded the catastrophe. A systematic analysis of the media context of Hurricane Katrina reveals how the nature of coverage and journalistic norms contributed to the emotional engagement of the public and highlights how the media environment created a set of causal frames for interpreting the progression of events. Specifically, we answer the following questions: How was the crisis framed and portrayed in the media? How were emotional primes used to engage the interests of citizens? Which causal stories dominated the coverage? Was coverage similar across televised news outlets or did the mix of causal stories presented depend upon the choice of networks? The answers to these questions set the stage for later chapters because media framing and attributions of blame provided the necessary information for the public to construct an understanding of the causes of the crisis.

MEDIA DATA

We evaluated the causal attributions and emotional magnitude of televised media coverage from two independent perspectives: first, an analysis of video segments from two network evening news programs,

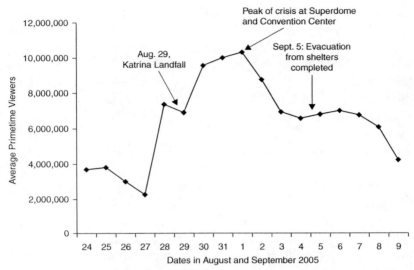

FIGURE 3.1. Average Primetime News Viewers Based on Nielsen Ratings for FNC, CNN, and MSNBC, Combined.

The Fox Report with Shepard Smith on FNC and *News Night* with Aaron Brown on CNN; and second, an analysis of all attributions in the printed transcripts from five evening news broadcasts: *ABC World News Tonight*, *The NBC Nightly News*, *The CBS Evening News*, *CNN Special Report*, and *The Fox News Hour*.[1] We coded news segments from video broadcasts for nineteen days during and after the storm, from August 27, 2005, two days before the storm hit land, through September 14, 2005. According to viewership information, this time frame represents the period during which the public was most attentive to cable news coverage (see Figure 3.1). Printed transcripts of the broadcasts were coded from August 27 through October 1 to provide a greater time horizon to determine the persistence of causal attribution frames. When we compare or combine results from video and transcript coding, we restrict the transcript data to the same time period as for the coded video data.

---

[1] Printed transcripts of *The Fox Report* with Shepard Smith were not available, so we used the next-closest evening news broadcast in terms of broadcast time and viewership, *The Fox News Hour*.

We focused on coding televised media because it is the preferred source for crisis information, especially in the early phase of a disaster, when the media offer up-to-the-moment reports accompanied by arresting visual images (Althaus 2002; Graber 2005; Piotrowski and Armstrong 1998; Robinson 2010; Van Belle 2000). For coding video broadcasts, we selected CNN and FNC because they were the news channels most frequently selected as a primary news source by our respondents, a finding consistent with other surveys taken immediately after the storm.[2] Coding full video broadcasts in addition to print transcripts permits us to evaluate the combined emotional impact of the visual and verbal content that the public was likely exposed to during the early weeks of the catastrophe. The units of analysis were the news segments within each broadcast, but we also recorded each explicit and implicit attribution within each news segment (see Appendix B for full coding details). For video coding, trained coders watched each segment multiple times to assess the magnitude and valance (positive/negative) of emotional primes. In addition, they coded the content of visual cues in each segment during the first hour of each broadcast. Taken together, the analysis of 504 video and 1,170 transcript segments provided a comprehensive picture of the media context surrounding the storm.

PUBLIC ATTENTIVENESS AND MEDIA SELECTION
FOLLOWING HURRICANE KATRINA

Public awareness of catastrophes is typically quite high, yet only a small proportion of the American population ever directly experiences a disaster. Instead, most people learn about extraordinary events through televised newscasts and other media reports. Attention to news coverage spiked dramatically during Hurricane Katrina as people sought information about quickly changing events. Nielsen ratings showed substantial

[2] In a Pew survey conducted on September 6, 2005, 31 percent reported turning to CNN, 22 percent to FNC, 14 percent to ABC, 12 percent to NBC, and 8 percent to CBS. This was a telephone survey of 1,103 respondents conducted by Princeton Survey Research Associates International for the Pew Research Center for the People and the Press, September 6–7, 2005. Survey results retrieved August 17, 2011, from the iPOLL Databank, Roper Center for Public Opinion Research, University of Connecticut: http://www.ropercenter.uconn.edu.proxy.lib.fsu.edu/data_access/ipoll/ipoll.html.

increases in viewership following Hurricane Katrina, with cable news tripling its normal number of viewers (see Figure 3.1). Networks also drew record audiences for primetime news programming, particularly for their primetime specials covering the storm's aftermath.[3]

A national *CNN/USA Today* survey conducted by Gallup about ten days after the storm hit New Orleans reported that 96 percent of respondents followed the coverage of the catastrophe somewhat or very closely.[4] In our survey, fielded one month later, just over 94 percent of respondents reported paying at least some or a great deal of attention to coverage of the storm. Only 4 percent paid little attention and a scant 2 percent paid no attention at all. This type of intense attentiveness is characteristic of large-scale disasters as individuals become dependent on media for information (Ball-Rokeach and DeFleur 1976; Beaudoin 2007; Fischoff 2004). To put this in context, attentiveness to Katrina was much higher in comparison to attentiveness to government affairs. According to the American National Election Studies (ANES) of 2004, 68 percent indicated that they followed government affairs most (28 percent) or some (40 percent) of the time, while 22 percent indicated only now and then and 10 percent indicated that they followed such news hardly at all.

Prior to Hurricane Katrina making landfall, news outlets mobilized scores of journalists to report on the preparations for the storm and its impending impact (Sylvester 2008). Consequently, national news organizations had reporters, photojournalists, and staff with remote satellite trucks embedded in key areas hit by the hurricane, allowing the public to experience, firsthand, the aftermath of the disaster. Given the enormous capability of cable news channels to bring up-to-the-minute reports from locations within the disaster area, it is not surprising that television was listed as the primary source of coverage

---

[3] A *USA Today* online story of television audience ratings reported that major networks devoted nine specials or weekly newsmagazine programs to Hurricane Katrina, with *Dateline*'s special garnering 12.2 million viewers (Levin 2005; *USA Today* 2005). This more than tripled the share of primetime viewers of FNC, the top cable channel, with 4.1 million viewers.

[4] The survey results reported here were obtained from searches of the iPOLL Databank and other resources provided by the Roper Center for Public Opinion Research, University of Connecticut. Survey by Cable News Network, *USA Today*. Methodology: Conducted by the Gallup Organization, September 8–11, 2005, and based on 1,005 telephone interviews. Sample: national adult (Gallup/CNN/*USA Today* 2005).

for most respondents in the Hurricane Katrina study. Fully 75 percent of respondents used television as their primary source, but nearly all (95 percent) watched at least some televised coverage of the catastrophe. For the 25 percent who looked beyond television for their primary source, 8 percent relied on newspapers, 8 percent turned to the Internet, and 9 percent obtained most of their news through radio or word of mouth. Among those who had seen at least some coverage of televised news, most selected cable news, mostly CNN (33 percent) or FNC (19 percent). Far fewer selected one of the major networks – ABC (11 percent), CBS (6 percent), or NBC (9 percent) – or the alternative cable channel, MSNBC (4 percent). The remainder of respondents reported turning to local news for most of their coverage. Although we asked viewers our question a month after the storm, the distribution of sources is quite similar to news viewership reports from a Pew survey conducted on September 6, where 31 percent reported turning to CNN, 22 percent to FNC, 14 percent to ABC, 12 percent to NBC, and 8 percent to CBS.[5] The breadth of attentiveness and the concentration of attention on national news create an opportunity for framed media messages to penetrate the collective American psyche.

EMOTIONAL PRIMES IN COVERAGE OF HURRICANE KATRINA

Television, as the primary media mode, delivered powerful emotional primes to a riveted audience, including scenes of dramatic rescues from rooftops, distraught citizens begging for help, visibly emotional reporters, and shocking scenes of destruction and death.

An *emotional prime* is defined as any aspect of the coverage that triggers fundamental human emotions – especially shock and anxiety – thereby encouraging emotion-based processing of accompanying or subsequent information. Emotional primes in televised news coverage stem from a variety of features, including the nature of still or moving visuals; the facial expressions of journalists or other individuals featured in the coverage; and elements of video production such as quick-cuts between scenes, handheld camera shots, and dramatic music (Fischoff 2004; Lang et al. 2007; Vettehen, Nuijten, and Peeters 2008).

Coverage of Hurricane Katrina, from the beginning, stimulated a sense of heightened anxiety due to its unexpectedly large and

---

[5] See note 2 for details of the survey.

threatening nature. News anchors frequently and urgently announced that an unprecedented category 5 storm was bearing down on a braced but fearful Gulf Coast. A sense of anxiety continued to permeate broadcasts as journalists embedded in areas directly hit by the hurricane provided ongoing and dramatic coverage of the catastrophe in progress. However, the most emotionally evocative coverage came after the levees broke, flooding large sections of New Orleans and devastating property and lives.

Emotions ran high among television reporters, with many breaking down on the air, showing visible emotion in their facial expressions, words, and body language. Journalists, stretched to their breaking point by the combination of the disaster and the intractable working conditions, were unable to hide from viewers their personal shock, pain, desperation, and anger as they waited alongside victims for aid to arrive (Fisher 2005; Kurtz 2005). Reporters and news administrators describe covering the aftermath of Katrina as far more difficult than any crisis they had covered previously, including 9/11, because of the incredible devastation to basic civil infrastructure (Sylvester 2008).

As a result, reporters in New Orleans were forced to rely heavily on localized eyewitness accounts and interviews with local officials and residents to convey the facts of the disaster to the public (Fisher 2005; Sylvester 2008). Fifty-four percent of video segments we coded on CNN and FNC contained visuals of victims of the storm, many of whom were visibly distraught. The frequent use of ordinary citizens to convey the nature of the disaster through their personal experiences was emotionally compelling because experimental research shows evidence that emotional arousal is strongest in response to news stories with quotes from a layperson (Vettehen, Nuijten, and Peeters 2008). In part, this is because layperson accounts are typically embedded in an episodic frame where the focus is on individual experiences rather than broader thematic evidence (Iyengar 1991). Analysis of the TV news transcripts for five major networks revealed that nearly half (48 percent) of all segments used an episodic frame when presenting information about the storm.[6] This type of coverage serves as a

---

[6] In contrast, Barnes et al. (2008) found much less evidence of episodic coverage of Hurricane Katrina in an analysis of over 750 articles appearing in August and September in two major newspapers, the *Washington Post* and the *New York Times*. Fewer than 10 percent of articles were framed from an episodic perspective.

strong emotional prime because the display of emotional facial expressions encourages affective engagement among viewers (Simons et al. 1999, 2000; Wild, Erbs, and Bartels 2001), while the mirror neuron system triggers a sense of emotional empathy for those on the screen (Eisenberg et al. 1991; Enticott et al. 2008; Molnar-Szakacs 2011).

In the days following Katrina, journalists were especially likely to focus on threatening and disturbing stories of "armed thugs," riots, looters, and the deplorable and dangerous conditions in New Orleans. Such stories fit easily into the disaster script that highlights the breakdown of law and order following catastrophe. Consider the language selected for the voiceover that accompanied video footage of victims at the New Orleans Convention Center:

The New Orleans Convention Center has been described by many as the hurricane shelter from hell. Now there is explicit evidence of that. Very disturbing photographs supplied to CNN show four dead people who had apparently been mutilated.... It is not known how these people died, but the source says it is apparent that, at some point, they had been physically abused (Gary Tuchman, CNN national correspondent, *CNN Daybreak*, September 9, 2005).

The unexpected and gruesome images spawned feelings of shock, anxiety, and disgust. Although it was later revealed that some of the dramatic stories of crime were exaggerated or inaccurate (see Tierney, Bevc, and Kuligowski 2006), the public had already been exposed to the emotion-laden images and words that left indelible impressions of the catastrophe.

Among the most significant anxiety-provoking primes are those that connect the catastrophe to personally relevant outcomes. Following Katrina, reporters made it clear that even viewers far outside the Gulf region had something to fear from the storm by identifying how the economic consequences of the storm would touch the lives of all Americans through gas, food, and other commodity prices: "When energy companies rushed to shut down refineries and offshore drilling platforms, the price of oil shot up. When the Port of New Orleans shut down, a number of other commodities, ones that you might not expect, were affected" (Charles Gibson, *ABC Evening News*, August 29, 2005). Likewise, stories about the resulting gas shortages and substantial increases in gas prices were prevalent, with newscasts frequently showing long lines of frustrated, angry people at gas stations

(Bamberger and Kumins 2005). Personalizing the risk factors associated with the hurricane and generalizing harm beyond the directly affected area are important characteristics of the coverage because Meyer (1988) argues that part of the mental processing that occurs in the wake of shock is an appraisal of the personal relevance of the shocking stimuli. In the case of Katrina, the media continued for many weeks to connect the storm to more general economic threats.

To assess systematically the extent to which viewers were likely to encounter strong emotional primes, we coded video news segments for the content of their visual images and assigned a subjective score for the degree to which the segment, overall, was visually and emotionally stimulating. Coders rated 76 percent of segments as having visual emotional primes, and, of those segments, a majority (at least 51 percent) were unambiguously negative, 13 percent were unambiguously positive, and the remaining 36 percent contained offsetting or neutral emotional primes.

Although nearly one-quarter of all segments lacked any visual emotional primes, this did not mean that they lacked any emotional prime. Instead, in most, the emotional prime was verbal. In these types of segments, viewers were most likely to encounter a visual of the news anchor's face or perhaps a visual of "talking heads" – elites commenting on the event. Despite the emotion-neutral visual, many news anchors used language that was emotionally evocative. Indeed, among the 24 percent of segments that had no visual emotional prime, 47 percent of them contained a verbal emotional prime. In all, only 13 percent of segments on CNN and FNC lacked any type of emotional prime during the first two weeks of the storm.

Consistently, studies show that stories with negative video images are much more emotionally arousing than those without them (Brader 2006; Lang, Newhagen, and Reeves 1996). Coders recorded the topics of each image present in each segment and we categorized these into low-stimulation and high-stimulation images. Highly stimulating emotional imagery included close-up shots of damage and destruction, scenes of rescue, images of dead and dying humans, images of dead or suffering animals, images of people rioting and/or committing crimes, and images of victims suffering and/or begging for help, as well as victims celebrating emotional reunions. Low- and nonstimulating visuals included "talking heads," visits to storm-damaged areas by political elites, visuals of charts and graphs, and visuals of previous storms, as well as a variety of other emotionally benign visuals, such as pets and people waiting in shelters.

Nearly three in five segments (57 percent) on both channels contained at least one "high-emotion" image in the segment, and most of the images shown were negative in valance. Positive valance images – such as victims reuniting with family and celebrating their safety or high drama rescues – appeared in only 20 percent of the segments on CNN and FNC, while negative images appeared in 52 percent. Moreover, the average number of negative high-emotion images per segment was .75 (the range was zero to five per segment), which was significantly higher ($p|t|<.05$) than the average number of positive images per segment, .20 (the range was zero to two per segment), based on a difference of means t-test.

Both qualitative and quantitative assessments of post–Hurricane Katrina coverage highlight the emotional qualities of the coverage with ample primes to trigger a sense of empathy for the plight of the victims and personal anxiety over the potential broader economic effects of the storm.

AFFECTIVE ENGAGEMENT OF THE PUBLIC

How did viewing the emotion-laden coverage affect the public? We draw upon the survey responses from our national survey following Hurricane Katrina to answer this question. In doing so, we provide a descriptive overview of several key variables that are important to our hypothesis tests in later chapters.

We have argued that discrete emotions like shock and anxiety stimulate attentiveness to information about the storm. At the same time, we recognize that increased attentiveness to shocking and emotionally provocative scenes should reinforce and deepen emotional reactions (see Figures 2.1 and 2.2). It is impossible to tease out the reciprocal nature of this relationship in cross-sectional data collected a month after the event because we cannot measure the initial level of attentiveness sparked by the shock of the event – we only have measures based on retrospective reports of attentiveness to coverage in general. Nevertheless, at a minimum, we expect to see a positive correlation between attentiveness and emotion. Given the nature and frequency of emotional primes in media coverage, we also anticipate that those who were most attentive felt the greatest emotional impact of the storm. At any rate, both attentiveness and surveillance-triggering emotions are necessary conditions for the receipt of framed political information embedded in coverage of the catastrophe.

We measure shock empirically through a survey question, asking respondents whether they felt shocked by "what happened in New Orleans after Hurricane Katrina." For those who answered "yes," we asked a follow-up question to determine the intensity of their feeling. Respondents were asked whether they felt "slightly," "somewhat," or "extremely" shocked. Nearly one-third of all respondents (31 percent) felt extremely shocked, whereas 23 percent felt somewhat shocked. Thirty-seven percent, however, did not feel shocked at all and 8 percent felt only slightly shocked.

A sense of fear or anxiety in the wake of major crises is common, although feelings of personal vulnerability are generally limited to those who are more closely connected to the tragedy either through personal familiarity or personal contact and closeness to victims. Following 9/11, for example, those in urban areas close to the areas of attack felt a greater sense of fear of terrorism than those in rural areas and more physically distant (Huddy et al. 2005). This was true in the case of Hurricane Katrina as well. When respondents were asked whether they felt afraid as a result of what had happened in New Orleans, only 22 percent of respondents reported any feeling of fear, with only 8 percent indicating they were extremely afraid. Although nearly one-quarter of respondents indicated that they were at least slightly afraid, fear was concentrated among minorities, those most proximate to the storm, and those with personal connections to storm victims. Therefore, we turn to sources of anxiety likely to affect a broader swath of the public.

Anxiety for those distant from a catastrophe can take various forms, such as fears of future disasters or concerns that the current disaster will indirectly affect them or the nation (see Huddy et al. 2002, 2005). After Katrina, media played an important role in generating this anxiety by emphasizing the broad economic ramifications, particularly those related to oil and gas production and those related to the massive costs of rebuilding the areas damaged by the storm. Concern over what Hurricane Katrina might mean for the national economy was relatively common among respondents. We asked respondents to indicate whether they were "concerned" that the recent hurricanes (Katrina and Rita) would "cause a nationwide economic recession." Fully 72 percent indicated they were somewhat (33 percent) or very (39 percent) concerned; only 28 percent of respondents expressed little or no concern.

It is important to note that the wording of the question for our survey was chosen to draw out the affective component of the economic evaluation by asking about *concern* that Hurricane Katrina would lead to a nationwide recession rather than asking about the *likelihood* of a recession. Although economic concerns in the wake of major events are at least somewhat rooted in cognitive evaluations, it is the emotional component of anxiousness or worry about the national economy that helps to drive attributions of blame and other political opinions. Nevertheless, the response to this question contains both affective and cognitive components because the respondents must evaluate the likelihood of recession as part of assessing their concern over it. However, prior research does suggest that anxiety magnifies estimates of risk (Huddy, Feldman, and Cassese 2007; Huddy, Khatib, and Capelos 2002), so even the cognitive assessment of likelihood elicited by this question is driven partly by emotion. As a result, we believe that the affective component sufficiently dominates this measure to allow us to use it as an indicator of the public's emotional response to the storm in this and later chapters. In addition, we include a measure of political knowledge in our models to control for cognitive skills.

Table 3.1 shows that attentiveness is positively related to the emotion variables, shock and concern. Given the relatively small number of cases in the "not very attentive" (3 percent) and "not at all attentive" (5 percent) categories, we pool them to simplify the presentation. This yields three categories of news attentiveness to compare with emotionality: inattentive (8 percent), somewhat attentive (35 percent), and very attentive (57 percent). Likewise, to simplify presentation, we present relative frequencies for only the top and bottom categories of the emotion variables for each level of attentiveness. The means of shock and concern across attentiveness levels are derived from the full scale of each emotion variable, however, and the range of each variable is 0 to 3, with higher values indicating greater emotionality.

TABLE 3.1. *Emotional Engagement by Level of Attentiveness*

	Not Attentive	Sig.	Somewhat Attentive	Sig.	Highly Attentive	Sig.
Shocked						
Not shocked	54%	a, b	39%	a, c	34%	b, c
Extremely shocked	21%		23%	c	39%	c
Mean	1.00	a, b	1.35	a, c	1.64	b, c
(SE)	(.17)		(.07)		(.06)	
N	58		324		586	
Concerned about Economy						
Not at all/not too concerned	42%	b	38%	c	21%	b, c
Very concerned	26%	b	25%	c	48%	b, c
Mean	1.67 (.14)	b	1.77	c	2.21	b, c
(SE)			(.06)		(.04)	
N	57		324		585	

Notes: Data are weighted to population proportions by age and sex.
[a] $p < .05$, difference between inattentive and somewhat attentive.
[b] $p < .05$, difference between inattentive and very attentive.
[c] $p < .05$, difference between somewhat attentive and very attentive.

It is clear from the table that the level of shock and concern was greatest among those who were highly attentive to news coverage.[7] Both variables show a monotonic increase as the level of attention increases, consistent with our expectation that the two variables are positively correlated. The differences in average emotion across categories are statistically significant, meaning that it is unlikely we would see these differences by chance alone. The percentage of somewhat attentive respondents who were extremely shocked was 23 percent, considerably lower than the 39 percent of highly attentive viewers who reported feeling extremely shocked. We see a similar pattern for the variable "concern." The proportion of those who felt very concerned about the economy nearly doubled as we move from the lowest category of attention to the highest category of attention. Only 26 percent

---

[7] Data are weighted to reflect the gender and age of the U.S. population. Significance tests are based on two-tailed difference in proportions tests or difference of means tests.

of those who were inattentive felt very concerned about a recession compared to 48 percent of those who were highly attentive.

Although not reported in the table, our survey data suggest that televised coverage of the storm's aftermath generated stronger emotional responses than other sources of media. Sixty-five percent of people who watched television as their primary source of news indicated that they were shocked by what had happened in New Orleans compared to only 57 percent of those who used print or other media as their primary source ($p|t|<.05$). Likewise, 77 percent of those who turned to TV reported being at least somewhat concerned over the economy while only 60 percent of those using other sources felt similarly concerned ($p|t|<.01$). These patterns in the data are precisely what we would expect to see following the hurricane if the emotionally charged media coverage is engaging the public affectively. Those most attentive are the most shocked and concerned about the storm, and we see stronger emotion among those using the source of media that delivers the strongest forms of emotional primes. It is worth noting that most respondents who chose print, the Internet, or radio as their primary source for news about the storm also reported watching at least some television, so the comparison is biased toward finding no differences.

Finally, because Hurricane Katrina had important racial dimensions, we examine the relationships among race, attentiveness, and emotion. In general, we expect coverage of victims of any disaster to stir an empathetic response from viewers, but when the victims of the storm have a clear social or racial identity, we expect empathetic emotional engagement to be especially strong. In the case of Hurricane Katrina, visuals of victims acted as a social identity cue because the primary victim group in New Orleans was black. According to the 2000 census, 67 percent of New Orleans residents were African Americans and most of the victims seen on television appeared to be poor and black (Bartels 2006; Bobo 2006; Huddy and Feldman 2006b; Sweeney 2006). Not surprisingly, a survey during the fall of 2005 showed that nearly all blacks (93 percent) expressed some sympathy toward those left behind in New Orleans and they were more likely than whites to express sympathy for those left behind (Huddy and Feldman 2006b).

Table 3.2 shows clear differences in both attentiveness and anxiety based on race. The top part of the table examines differences in strong engagement by race, while the bottom section of the table examines

TABLE 3.2. *Attention and Emotion, by Race (Std Errors)*

	White	Sig.	Black	Sig.	Other	Sig.
Percentage in Highest Category						
Very attentive	54%	a, b	73%	a, c	58%	b, c
Extremely shocked	28%	a, b	42%	a	40%	b
Very concerned	32%	a, b	66%	a, c	45%	b, c
Means (SE)						
Attentiveness	2.44 (.03)	a	2.60 (.08)		2.47 (.08)	a
Shocked	1.44 (.05)		1.58 (.13)		1.64 (.13)	
Concerned	1.92 (.04)	a	2.47 (.08)	a, c	2.09 (.10)	c
N	725		136		114	

Notes: Data are weighted to population proportions for age and sex. "Other" includes Asians, Hispanics, and other minorities.
[a] $p < .05$, difference between white and black.
[b] $p < .05$, difference between white and other.
[c] $p < .05$, difference between black and other.

differences in the mean level of engagement. Among blacks, 73 percent reported being very attentive to coverage of Katrina, compared to only 54 percent of whites and 58 percent of other minorities. Thus, the proportion of blacks who had high exposure to the combined racial and emotional primes was much greater. In this light, it is not surprising to find that blacks were also significantly more likely than whites to report feeling extremely shocked about what had happened in New Orleans and very concerned that Katrina would affect the national economy.

We also see that blacks, on average, are more concerned about the economy. However, the mean level of shock did not differ statistically between the two groups. At first glance, this seems surprising, especially in light of the higher proportion of blacks in the "extremely shocked" category. However, we attribute this finding to the historical experiences of blacks with government and government aid. We note that on all of our other measures of emotion – including anger, disappointment, and fear – that blacks were significantly more emotional than whites. Thus, the overall picture of emotional engagement across race suggests greater attentiveness and empathetic engagement by those who share social identity with the primary victim group.

Overall, the proportion of the population who is emotionally primed to receive the types of messages presented in the media, particularly stories of cause and blame, is quite high. Nevertheless, it is also important for our purposes that there is some variation in emotional engagement because this allows us, in later chapters, to gain leverage on how differing levels of emotion stimulated by the storm coverage influence attributions of blame and other opinions about government and policy.

MEDIA, POLITICS, AND BLAME FOLLOWING HURRICANE KATRINA

A central contention of Chapter 2 is that emotions such as shock and anxiety make individuals more receptive to information offered in conjunction with the emotional primes. Therefore, the final bit of context we need in order to form specific hypotheses about blame attributions and political opinions in later chapters is an understanding of the causal attributions that dominated the news in the days and weeks following the storm. We focus on the three general causal frames to which journalists typically turn when covering catastrophic events: (1) "nature of the catastrophe" frames that identify the unusual and overwhelming nature of the event; (2) "societal breakdown" frames that center on how the crises lead to widespread lack of compliance with norms and laws of society; and (3) "blame" frames that identify a human or governmental causal agent. At the core of each frame is a causal attribution to one or more agents responsible for the suffering and pain that occurred during the disaster.

Analysis of Media Coverage of Hurricane Katrina

News segments, defined as distinct stories within each of the five networks' evening newscasts, were coded for overall tone and content and for a predefined list of specific attributions of credit and blame associated with each of the key causal frames (see Appendix C for details). Attributions could be implicit, meaning implied by tone or leading statements or questions from reporters, or they could be explicit, such as direct statements by national officials that, for example, state leaders were to blame for the lack of aid. Each explicit attribution, both statements of blame and credit, were coded to determine the target of the attribution; the valance of the attribution (positive or negative); and any "reason," evidence, or justification given for the blame statement. This allowed us to identify and categorize attributions into broader thematic frames of blame that were common throughout the coverage. In total, we coded 1,170 segments during the time period, with 2,893 explicit statements attributing credit or blame, averaging 2.47 attributions per segment.

The results indicate that attributions were quite common in news coverage of Hurricane Katrina, with 77 percent of segments making at least one attribution of blame or credit. Segments without attributions (23 percent) were usually reports summarizing facts about the catastrophe.[8] Among all segments, most (63 percent) contained at least some negative attributions of blame, with 39 percent containing only negative attributions. Negative attributions addressed outcomes such as the slow response of government, the lack of basic necessities such as food and water, the devastation to property and livelihoods, and the reasons the levees failed.

Thirty-eight percent of all segments contained one or more positive attributions of credit. The common topics of positive attributions were the heroic efforts of individuals and groups during the crisis, such as the outpouring of support for victims from society as a whole, the dramatic rescues by the military, and the support to victims given by residents in neighboring areas. Only 14 percent of all segments contained exclusively positive attributions. The remainder of those containing positive attribution contained both positive and negative attributions, so most positive attributions were offset by negative attributions within the same segment.

"Nature of Catastrophe" Frame

In the context of Hurricane Katrina, news framed as the "nature of the catastrophe" conveyed the message that the hurricane was overwhelming, and as a result, no one could address the onslaught of problems accompanying the crisis. It was the unusual size and scope of this storm that caused pain and suffering, not people. In this frame,

---

[8] Seventy-two percent of segments without attribution were classed as "information," with most of the remaining classed as human interest or introductory or closing remarks to a broadcast.

government officials and residents along the Gulf were both victims struggling to cope in impossible circumstances.

Early in the coverage cycle, journalists dubbed Hurricane Katrina a "monster storm" because of its enormous size – over one thousand miles wide – and 175-mile-per-hour wind speed (CNN 2005c). Journalists, weather experts, and political elites frequently referenced the size and nature of the storm as the reason for the physical devastation and the difficulty getting assistance to hard-hit areas, especially New Orleans. In fact, of the 737 transcripts containing negative attributions, 41 percent contained at least one explicit or implicit attribution directing attention to the overwhelming nature of the storm.

Attributions of blame to nature had especially high volume during the first few days as the storm approached. Eight-five percent of segments in the days prior to and just after landfall (August 27–30) contained at least one, but this dropped to only 25 percent of segments for the remaining period.

The personal stories from victims of the power of the storm and the visual images of physical damage to property and civil infrastructure lent credibility and strength to the "blame nature" frame. Those in government who sought to explain why it was so difficult to aid victims of the storm strongly favored the "blame nature" causal frame. Both state and national leaders emphasized that the magnitude of the storm presented insurmountable problems for government. Even prior to the storm, Louisiana Governor Kathleen Blanco declared that. "I have determined that this incident will be of such severity and magnitude that effective response will be beyond the capabilities of the state and the affected local governments (CNN 2005c: 16). Department of Homeland Security Secretary Michael Chertoff, in a public address on September 3, 2005, employs this frame in this way:

I want to just say that words cannot describe what one witnesses with one's own eyes when you actually see the devastation caused by Mother Nature, a Mother Nature that has been anything but maternal.... We are throwing all of the capabilities and assets of the United States into this effort. This is a daunting challenge. I guess I would say this is probably the worst catastrophe or set of catastrophes certainly that I'm aware of in the history of the country, a devastating hurricane followed by a second devastating flood (Chertoff 2005).

The frame highlights that despite a full-out effort by the government, the conditions of the catastrophe were simply impossible to overcome.

The same message permeated President Bush's New Orleans Jackson Square speech on September 15, in which he emphasized the overwhelming nature of the combined disasters of the hurricane and the levee failure (CNN 2005b). Although he publicly claimed responsibility for the slow response of government, he also partially excused it in light of the nature and scope of the catastrophe.[9]

"Societal Breakdown" Frame

The "societal breakdown" frame focuses attention on how citizens' adherence to norms and laws governing behavior break down during disasters and the resulting consequences for the rescue efforts. Sociologists and communications scholars demonstrate that media coverage frequently perpetuates myths about behavioral transgressions of victims prior to and after the impact of a disaster (Fischer 1998; Stock 2007; Tierney, Bevc, and Kuligowski 2006; Wenger and Friedman 1986). Victims are portrayed as making irrational decisions about evacuation, panicking in the face of crisis, and devolving into anarchic and criminal behavior (Fischer 1998; Stock 2007; Tierney, Bevc, and Kuligowski 2006). However, in part, the focus on societal breakdown after Katrina stemmed from reporters' firsthand experiences with the storm. Journalists directly witnessed the chaos in New Orleans during the first few days after the storm and personally experienced the fears associated with being cut off from the rest of the world (Fisher 2005; Sylvester 2008).

NON-EVACUATION FRAME. The societal breakdown frame was reflected in reports of the public ignoring government orders to evacuate. During Hurricane Katrina, tens of thousands of people remained in New Orleans rather than heeding mandatory evacuation orders given by Mayor Nagin and Governor Blanco. News interviews with individuals who decided to stay behind were a hallmark of pre-disaster coverage. Some stayed behind due to lack of money, resources, a place to go, or transportation, while others stayed behind to protect their homes and personal belongings from crime (Elder et al. 2007). Still others doubted the storm would hit with full force or hoped that the path of the hurricane would veer away from the city.

---

[9] See McGraw (1990:121) for the distinction between elite justification and elite excuses. Although Bush took responsibility, he offered mitigating circumstances to partially offset the blame.

Some of the reasons given by individuals for their choice to remain in New Orleans became fodder for media debate and gained considerable traction later as the public and the media questioned whether New Orleans Mayor Nagin had done all in his power to evacuate the needy. For example, several news outlets noted that Nagin waited longer than officials in other coastal cities and counties along the Gulf Coast to give evacuation orders and that instead of commandeering school and public transit buses to evacuate those who did not have access to personal transportation, he sent them to the Superdome (ABC News 2005b; Russell 2005; *Seattle Times* 2005; Thomas 2005). Thus, this frame offers a somewhat mixed attribution. On the one hand, the frame directs blame toward citizens for their own irrational and noncompliant behavior in the face of a grave emergency, but later the media focus shifted to highlighting that noncompliance was at least partly the fault of poor implementation of evacuation plans by local government.

Regardless of the reasons for public noncompliance, the number of people in need of rescue or assistance following the storm was staggering. The need quickly outstripped available resources stored in the shelters and the supplies of first responders. Although 80 percent of the population of New Orleans evacuated, the challenges in meeting the needs of the remaining population were insurmountable for several days after the storm.

Although the attribution of blame for human suffering to noncompliance with evacuation orders never dominated TV coverage, it did appear frequently in the first days after the storm. On average, 28 percent of negative attribution segments during the days prior to and just after landfall (August 27–30) contained this attribution. The average dropped considerably for the remaining days in our coding period (August 31–October 1), down to 10 percent, as the media shifted focus to other attribution targets. In all, 12 percent of segments with negative attributions contained either implicit or explicit references to residents ignoring evacuation orders as a cause of human suffering. However, the volume and strength of this attribution were highest early in the storm when viewership was also at its peak, so the attribution is very likely to have been part of the stories heard by those tuning in.

CRIMINAL BEHAVIOR. The second "societal breakdown" frame emerged early in the coverage and focused on the panic and looting in the wake of catastrophic events. These stories are consistent with the standard script that the media uses for disaster coverage (Stock 2007; Tierney, Bevc, and Kuligowski 2006; Wenger and Friedman 1986). Many journalists reported stories of theft, rape, and murder in the Superdome and the New Orleans Convention Center (Gugliotta and Whoriskey 2005; Lipton et al. 2005; MacCash and O'Byrne 2005; McFadden and Blumenthal 2005; Treaster and Kleinfield 2005). Although later reports would show the looting and crime reports to have been grossly overstated and, in some cases, wholly inaccurate, those tuning in as the storm unfolded were exposed to strong frames emphasizing the breakdown of society following the breach of the levees (Tierney, Bevc, and Kuligowski 2006). In this frame, pain and suffering in the affected area were attributed to the behavior of those affected by the storm. A good example of this type of frame is embodied in the quote from Aaron Brown, opening his newscast on August 31, just days after the storm:

Good evening, again, everyone. It became clear today that the Gulf Coast is facing the type of crisis we expect to see in a developing country, not the richest country in the world. It is a natural disaster combined with some very human misbehavior. Police in the city of New Orleans, 1,500 of them, have now been called off their search-and-rescue work to simply deal with the lawlessness in the city. Things spiraling, it appears, towards some sort of chaos (*CNN Newsnight* with Aaron Brown, August 31, 2005).

Overall, 19 percent of segments with negative attributions attributed blame to crime or criminal behavior, but the greatest focus on this frame came just a few days after the storm, when the media reported a flurry of rumors about lawless gangs roaming the streets, shooting at supply helicopters, and killing at will in the shelters. On September 1, more than half of all news segments (53 percent) and two-thirds of news segments with negative attributions (68 percent) contained at least one attribution of blame to criminal behavior.

Government-Centered "Blame Game" Frames

Government blame frames are common following catastrophes because the news media and the public turn to government for solutions. In the aftermath of Hurricane Katrina, government blame frames were front and center throughout the coverage, especially as days passed without aid arriving to those stranded inside New Orleans.[10] In contrast to the "overwhelming nature" frame or the "societal breakdown" frame, the "blame game" frame locates the cause of pain and suffering after the storm with government and its agents. News accounts highlighted the expectations that the public held for government performance and searched for explanations for why government failed to meet those expectations. Media blame frames are a normal stage in the cycle of covering extraordinary events (Graber 2005), and political elites are willing players as they try to excuse or justify negative outcomes (McGraw 1990, 1991). Blame framing emerges strongly in the second and third phases of coverage. Once the initial events of the crisis have passed and journalists have time to step back and reflect on why the catastrophe occurred, they seek to understand both the proximate and societal causes of the event (Graber 2005).

Journalists' questions about government failures were unusually intense, as reporters on the ground and in the studio demanded to know why the response was so slow (see CNN 2005c; Fisher 2005; Kurtz 2005). Fisher (2005) notes: "It's not clear whether the news media were liberated by the Internet era's emphasis on opinion and personality, or whether the particulars of this story demanded a more confrontational approach, but from 'Nightline' to 'Fox News Sunday,' from the front pages of the Los Angeles Times to the blogs on the Web site of New Orleans' Times-Picayune, reporters got in the faces of the authorities." However, this aggressive and independent voice is consistent with our theoretical understanding of how journalists operate during extraordinary events as they investigate the causes of disaster.

Analyses of the televised transcripts show that most negative attributions of blame targeted government and government agents.[11] Among all segments, 42 percent contained at least one negative attribution of

---

[10] Our media data from CNN and FNC show that 65 percent of CNN coverage and 56 percent of FNC coverage focused solely on New Orleans and only 15 percent of CNN coverage and 24 percent of FNC coverage had no mention of New Orleans. Also see the Pew Research Center for Excellence in Journalism (2005), which also notes that New Orleans was the primary location for news coverage of Hurricane Katrina.

[11] Attributions of blame toward government include a wide range of actors and agencies at all levels of government as well as generic attributions to "government" that do not specify a level, actor, or agency. See Appendix C for specific coding of this variable.

blame directed toward government, and among the 737 segments that contained negative attributions, 63 percent contained an attribution of blame directed toward government. In contrast, nature, the next most common attribution in the media, appeared in only 41 percent of segments. The dominance of the "government blame" frame is not surprising, as government is seen, fundamentally, as the protector of citizens in times of crisis. Therefore, when crises become unmanageable, journalists and citizens seek plausible explanations based on their understanding of the prescribed roles of government in society.

Hurricane Katrina, like many catastrophes, required responses from more than one level of government, and therefore it is common for journalistic blame frames to include more than one target. We explore the two most common blame frames that emerged in coverage following Katrina: the national government blame frame and the federalist blame frame. The former is a relatively straightforward frame that arises from public and media expectations that the national government should take a central role in aiding citizens in times of epochal crises. Blaming the president and the national government is a simple attribution that is generally plausible on the surface (Gomez and Wilson 2001, 2003). The federalist blame frame, however, requires more complex attributions of blame because it highlights how multiple levels of government play a role in disaster response. As a result, the response of one level of government may hinge, fundamentally, on the actions of actors at other levels of government. The federalist frame offers a convenient avenue for political elites to shift blame and excuse their role in negative outcomes (Maestas et al. 2008).

NATIONAL GOVERNMENT BLAME FRAME. The attribution of blame to the national government was the most prevalent among all negative attributions to government; 71 percent of government-blame segments contained at least one attribution focused specifically on the performance of the national government.[12] Forty percent of government-blame segments contained at least one attribution of blame directed toward government in general without identifying a particular level of government. However, the generic government attributions were most

---

[12] The attribution count included both implicit and explicit attributions of blame directed toward the president or his surrogates, FEMA and Director Brown, DHS and Director Chertoff, the military, or other national government representatives.

often included in segments that also contained specific blame attributions to the national government, thus strengthening the national government attribution frame. Sixty-two percent of the segments blaming government in general also contained an attribution blaming the national government.

Journalists, along with victims and local officials, expressed shock and anger at the absence of aid, especially in New Orleans. Well-known and high-profile reporters such as Anderson Cooper, Joe Scarborough, and Tim Russert grilled public officials with disbelief and visible anger about the federal response to the storm (Kurtz 2005), while public officials railed at FEMA for its slow and sometimes even absurd responses to requests for help (Thomas 2005). Political leaders and pundits from both parties focused their blame on the slow response by the federal government and especially the director of FEMA, Michael Brown (Benjamin 2005). Even FNC, widely believed to be biased in favor of the Bush administration, was highly critical of the national government's efforts (Kurtz 2005). Our data confirm this perspective.

Tough questions about the national government's response arose quickly in the coverage cycle as the situation in New Orleans became more desperate. In an interview on September 1, Soledad O'Brien (CNN) questioned Department of Homeland Security Secretary Michael Chertoff about the absence of federal assistance: "The president this morning...said that a lot of help is coming. Many people would say why is it *coming*? Why three days after the disaster is it not there already?"(CNN 2005c:60, emphasis added). She proceeded to hammer Chertoff with a series of questions implying that national government was to blame for errors and ill preparation, particularly given that officials knew well in advance of Katrina that a category 3 storm could cause widespread destruction in New Orleans.

Although political elites from the national government, especially the White House and the executive branch, attempted to deflect blame by focusing on the nature of the storm and the role of lower levels of government in the outcome, they had little ability to spin the story. The linearity of events and the eyewitness accounts of suffering that were highlighted in the media exposed a wide gap between official reports that government was responsive to the disaster and the realities that existed on the ground in New Orleans.

STATE AND LOCAL BLAME IN A FEDERALIST CONTEXT. The national government bore the brunt of media criticism; however, other levels of government did not escape unscathed. State government was blamed in 22 percent of segments and local government was blamed in 36 percent of segments. This is not entirely surprising, as crisis management in the United States is largely a federal endeavor and therefore an essential contextual feature for understanding government response to Hurricane Katrina and media coverage of the disaster (see Schneider 2005, 2008). Local and state officials are charged with providing the first line of response following a disaster, with the national government providing government assistance to local and state authorities. After 9/11, this chain of command was clearly codified in the National Response Plan adopted by the Department of Homeland Security in December of 2004. The plan, however, had a fundamental problem that was highlighted in the Hurricane Katrina crisis. In the days after Hurricane Katrina, there was no local government infrastructure because it had been destroyed by the catastrophe, preventing a local – let alone a coordinated – response (Griffin 2007). Because communication systems between local and state government were unavailable, the ordinary chain of command was not possible. Governor Blanco was unable to bundle needed federal requests because she had no clear information from local authorities about what was needed. This led to an uncoordinated rescue effort for the first four days after the hurricane, reducing its effectiveness (U.S. House 2006).

In the intense media-rich information environment following the storm, the incentives for politicians to diffuse blame to other actors were high. The federalist nature of the disaster response offered ample opportunities for cross-level and cross-party fingerpointing. With New Orleans engulfed in water, the blame game quickly became both political and partisan, something duly noted with frustration by journalists. Conservatives, Republicans, and surrogates for the president directed blame toward New Orleans' Democratic Mayor Nagin and Louisiana's Democratic Governor Blanco. Democrats and liberals, including Governor Blanco and Mayor Nagin, directed blame toward the White House; FEMA and its director, Brown; and DHS and its director, Chertoff. The stories featuring political fingerpointing and journalistic dissection of the political blame game were prominent in the news media, especially during the second week after the storm (Pew Research Center 2005). However, there was considerable confusion in the media pertaining to the responsibility of different levels of government and errors in factual reporting of government actions. For example, a *Washington Post* article reported that part of the problem was that Governor Blanco had not declared a state of emergency even after the storm had hit and destroyed New Orleans (Roig-Franzia and Hsu 2005). This erroneous fact was picked up by other news outlets, including *Newsweek*. Only later did the *Washington Post* issue a correction that Governor Blanco declared an emergency on Friday, August 26, two days before Katrina hit (Roig-Franzia and Hsu 2005).

Eventually, on September 13, half of a month after Katrina hit, Bush took responsibility for the federal response to the storm in a White House press release, but when he did so, he made clear that the federal government was but one of the responsible actors: "Katrina exposed serious problems in our response capability at all levels of government, and to the extent that the federal government didn't fully do its job right, I take responsibility" (CNN 2005c).

The joint pattern of national and state/local blame appearing in many segments reveals a bias in the blame game toward blaming national government. Often, interviews with political elites took the form of competing attributions, where government officials pointed fingers at one another in an effort to redirect blame for the tragic events in New Orleans (Maestas et al. 2008). Because the "blame game" involved elite attempts to diffuse blame to different levels of government, we most often see attributions of blame to the state and local level in the same segment as attributions of blame directed at national government. Sixty-one percent of attributions of blame to state or local government occurred in a segment that also attributed blame to the national government. In contrast, only 35 percent of segments blaming the national government also blamed the state or local government.

Attributions by Television Source

Thus far, we have shown that several frames and their accompanying attributions of blame were prevalent, overall, in the media. But did public exposure to frames depend upon which network they selected?

TABLE 3.3. *Percentage of All News Segments Containing Implicit or Explicit Attributions of Blame, Transcript Segments*

	All	Network	CNN	FNC
National government	44	42[b]	44	52[b]
State government	14	10[a, b]	16[a]	23[b]
Local government	23	16[a,b]	30[a]	30[b]
Nature/size of storm	41	43	41	38
Failure to evacuate	12	12	13	10
Crime/criminal behavior	19	20	22	15
N	737	369	216	152

[a] $p < .05$, difference between network and CNN.
[b] $p < .05$, difference between network and FNC.
[c] $p < .05$, difference between CNN and FNC.

In short, the answer is no. Although there were slight differences across news networks, attributions of blame associated with all three of the major frames were part of the coverage for all networks. For example, on location coverage of Hurricane Katrina by Shepard Smith, the well-trusted primetime news anchor for FNC, made it clear to the public that he viewed government as failing its citizens. Years later in an interview, he stated the following:

That there were people in great need and no leadership was emerging to help them was beyond reason to me. That was all the perspective I needed. Everybody wanted to make this a partisan thing, but it was a failure on all levels that I never could have dreamed of.

Indeed, Smith reportedly ignored talking points from the network in favor of covering what he saw as the facts of the situation on the ground (Ricchiardi 2010).

However, there were some minor differences in the mix of stories across networks (see Table 3.3).[13] For example, FNC had more segments with attributions to national government compared to network news ($p|t|<.05$), but FNC was also more likely than other major networks (ABC, CBS, and NBC) to cover the failings of state and

---

[13] We combine all three national network newscasts due to their similarity in format and in coverage. Although there are some differences in the proportions of attributions among ABC, CBS, and NBC, none are statistically significant by conventional standards.

local government. Although FNC appears to have more frequently directed blame toward state government than CNN (23 percent of segments compared to 16 percent), this difference is not statistically significant. CNN and FNC attributed blame to local factors at roughly the same rate – 30 percent of segments compared to only 16 percent for network news. Thus, those watching cable news were more likely to see the story that Louisiana Governor Kathleen Blanco failed to call for help in the critical hours following the storm or that Mayor Nagin and local officials did a poor job evacuating residents before the storm.

We also found little difference in the proportion of blame assigned to the overwhelming nature of the storm or the "societal breakdown" frame. Cable stations and network newscasts attributed blame to non-compliance with evacuation orders at the same rate, around 10 to 12 percent. Post-storm crime and criminal behavior received greater attention, with FNC having the lowest rate of only 15 percent of all negative segments while CNN had the highest with 22 percent, but the difference was not statistically significant. The overwhelming nature of the storm was the only frame that was a close competitor, in terms of volume, to the national government blame frame.

To summarize, viewers tuning into national or cable news broadcasts would have seen much the same story – a story of chaos and destruction that was largely the fault of Mother Nature and government, although some blame targeted victims as well. The volume and strength of blame frames that focused on all levels of government were great, with only relatively small and substantively uninteresting differences among networks.

Timing of Attributions

Finally, we examine whether attributions from all three frames were visible early in the coverage cycle, when viewer attention and emotion was at its highest. Timing is important because in later chapters, we assume that the public was exposed to each of these frames. This assumption is most tenable if we demonstrate that these frames emerged during the active phase of the crisis, when viewership was double or triple its normal size. Recall that cable news viewership was more than double its average from August 29 through September 3,

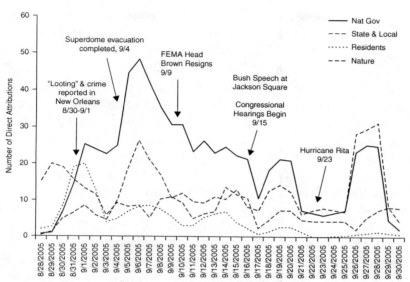

FIGURE 3.2. Count of Attributions of Blame on All Networks, Three-Day Moving Average.

while other accounts place viewership of national news broadcasts at triple their normal audience (see Fisher 2005). Viewership began to decline and level off after the peak of the crisis at the New Orleans Superdome and the Convention Center, but viewership was still well above average between September 4 and 9. Viewership did not return to normal levels until around September 9. Therefore, at the aggregate level, the exposure to diverse attributions of blame would have occurred in the early part of the crisis, when viewership was extraordinarily high.

Figure 3.2 charts the time path of the "volume" of attributions of blame over time. In this analysis, the units of analysis are the explicit attributions made by speakers in the newscasts that we analyzed, whether those speakers were journalists, residents, or elite spokespersons. Volume is defined as the three-day moving average of explicit attributions of blame from each of the causal frames. This measure picks up the repetition of the attributions within and across segments. For visual simplicity, we collapsed together attributions to state and local government and we collapsed together the "societal breakdown" attributions.

The dynamic patterns of attribution coverage roughly follow what is typical of catastrophic events, with the "nature of the crisis" frame dominating the initial coverage, quickly followed by the "societal chaos" frame, and these two frames quickly giving way to stories dominated by blame frames. By September 1, just a few days into the storm, attributions of blame to the national government and its agents exceeded all other attributions and kept climbing to reach a peak on September 6, the day after shelter evacuations were finally completed. At this point, average viewership of cable news remained around 7 million viewers during primetime – almost double the normal level of viewership – while viewership of national network news was still easily triple. Blame attributions declined over time, dropping off substantially after President Bush's Jackson Square speech on September 15, 2005. Here Bush accepted responsibility for failures in the aftermath of the storm. But he and his surrogates also cited the nature of the storm as an excuse and noted the role that state and local government played in the crisis. Consequently, "nature of the storm" attributions and state and local government attributions both increased around the time of the speech.

Although coverage of Hurricane Rita crowded out coverage of Katrina for a few days in late September, Rita also offered a new opportunity for comparing storms and rehashing the attributions of blame for Katrina in light of the performance of state and local officials in Texas. Notably, New Orleans mayor Nagin faced especially strong criticism for how he handled the approach of Rita to New Orleans as he closed the city to those hoping to return after Katrina. Because the attributions of blame are related to his treatment of Katrina victims, these are included in the negative local attribution counts and lead to the strong spike in negative local attributions late in the month.

SUMMARY AND CONCLUSIONS

In Chapter 2, we identified several preconditions necessary for catastrophes to influence broader public opinions about government and its leaders. A catastrophe must stimulate public engagement, not only cognitively but also emotionally. We have shown in this chapter the wide array of emotional primes that occurred frequently in coverage of Hurricane Katrina and its aftermath. We have also demonstrated that the public was highly attentive to coverage, particularly televised coverage. Moreover, those attentive to coverage were also likely to feel strong emotions of shock over conditions in New Orleans and concern over the broader consequences of the storm. Yet we also see variation in levels of both attentiveness and emotionality – variation that we can use to help explain why some might be more receptive to coverage than others as we test our theory.

For extraordinary events to influence opinions, they must also offer clear attributions of political blame. Debate about causal responsibility and the assignment of blame in the media is a natural part of how news coverage evolves following extraordinary events (Graber 2005). As we have shown in this chapter, the media implicated actors at multiple levels of government, along with Mother Nature and the victims themselves. The resulting cacophony was fertile material for the public to use in forming causal attribution and connecting those attributions to broader evaluations of government and leaders, topics we turn to in the next few chapters. As we highlight in subsequent chapters, we expect these attributions to influence evaluation of the elected leaders at the federal, state, and local levels of government who were in charge of handling the crisis; more broadly, we anticipate that these attributions influenced the level of confidence in the institutions of government.

4

Affective Attributions

Assigning Blame during Extraordinary Times

The general argument from Chapter 2 highlights how emotional responses following catastrophe opens the public to absorbing and accepting framed messages attributing credit or blame. Shock and anxiety encourage people to seek an accurate understanding of the world to assess the level and source of potential threats. Therefore, they encourage people to set aside predispositional biases when evaluating information about an anxiety-producing event. The purpose of this chapter is to test the core proposition of our theory of affective attribution by examining how attributions were evaluated by the public following Hurricane Katrina. In the previous chapter, we established that the media offered a menu of blame stories, particularly in the early days when the public was most attentive. The overwhelming majority of the public (94 percent of our sample) saw at least some televised coverage of Hurricane Katrina, so the likelihood of exposure to the blame frames that we have identified is high. Finally, the media messages about attribution of blame were convincing partly because of the clear sequence of events and partly because they were delivered by credible sources and backed with compelling visual images. This means that individuals needed some mechanism to evaluate the competing claims in the media, and we contend that this depends, fundamentally, on both their predispositions and their affective engagement with the story.

From a research standpoint, this type of a multimessage environment creates an ideal context for us to test whether emotion moderates the effects of predispositions on opinion. In a single-message environment, where pundits and elites agree, it is hard to separate the effects of emotion from elite and media cues. In a multimessage environment, we can identify the independent and moderating effects of emotion because there are multiple credible messages that are potentially persuasive to individuals.

PUBLIC AGREEMENT WITH BLAME FRAMES

Did the public agree with the dominant frames presented in the media? Evidence from surveys suggests that they did. A national poll released on September 15, just over two weeks past the storm, shows that all levels of government and victims were deemed culpable for the aftereffects of the storm, with the federal government getting most of the blame (Birkland and Waterman 2008). The CBS News/*New York Times* polls asked, "In New Orleans, after the Hurricane, hundreds of thousands of people were unable to evacuate the flooded city and they lacked food, water, and shelter. Who would you say was the most to blame for those conditions?" Twenty-nine percent indicated that the federal government, Bush, or FEMA was to blame, 20 percent blamed city government or Mayor Nagin, 12 percent blamed Louisiana State government or Governor Blanco, 12 percent blamed the residents of New Orleans, 12 percent blamed all levels of government, and another 9 percent indicated they didn't know.[1]

In our national survey, we asked respondents their level of agreement with a set of attribution statements, each of which expressed a different causal frame that was offered across all media outlets. Four of the attribution questions asked respondents to indicate on a seven-point scale, ranging from strongly disagree to strongly agree, how much they agreed with each of the following statements:

- "The damage from Katrina was so overwhelming that no government could have adequately responded to it." (Nature of the Storm frame)

---

[1] Poll conducted by CBS News/*New York Times*, September 9–13, 2005, and based on 1,167 telephone interviews. The sample was national adult with an oversample of blacks. An oversample of African Americans was conducted for this poll for a total sample of 211 African Americans. Results are weighted to be representative of a national adult population.

- "The human suffering in New Orleans was the result of too many people ignoring the evacuation orders." (Societal Breakdown–Non-evacuation frame)
- "First responders and rescuers could have entered New Orleans more quickly if crime and violence had not broken out." (Societal Breakdown–Crime frame)
- "The U.S. National Government knew Katrina was coming but did not adequately prepare to respond." (National Government Blame frame)

We asked respondents their level of agreement with each rather than pitting explanations against one another so that we could identify whether respondents agreed with multiple statements or just one statement. Among our respondents, 99 percent agreed with at least one of these attribution statements, while 93 percent agreed with multiple statements. This is consistent with what we would expect based on the attribution-rich media environment from the outset of the storm. In the early days, when most people tuned in, the media offered all of these frames across all major news outlets. Only later, after viewership dropped off, did the stories about causes other than government failures drop in prominence.

We also asked an additional question with a four-point response scale that locates blame for the national government's response time with the failure of the state to call for enough help. Respondents were asked whether "state failure to call for help" had "no effect," "little effect," "some effect," or "a great deal of effect" on how quickly the national government responded to the situation in New Orleans (Federalist Blame frame). This measure taps whether the federalist structure of disaster response provides a mechanism for shifting blame for the performance of one level of government to another. In this case, blame is shifted from the national government to the state government. Seventy-seven percent thought that the actions of state government had either a "great deal of effect" (46 percent) or "some effect" (31 percent) on the national government's response time.

Tables 4.1 and 4.2 show the percentages of respondents in each category for these five attribution frames. One of the more striking features of Table 4.1 is the high level of polarization in the public. For each of the seven-point attribution items, the majority of cases

TABLE 4.1. *Distribution of Public Responses to Attributions of Blame, in Percentages*

	National Government	Nature of the Storm	Societal Breakdown: Crime	Societal Breakdown: Non-evacuation
Strongly disagree	8	12	6	4
Disagree	21	31	24	17
Somewhat disagree	6	6	5	6
Neither agree nor disagree	4	3	7	4
Somewhat agree	13	14	14	19
Agree	26	24	31	31
Strongly agree	22	10	13	18
N	952	956	936	957

Note: Data are weighted to population proportions by age and sex.

TABLE 4.2. *Distributions of Responses of Belief that State Failure Had an Effect on National Government Response Time, in Percentages*

	State Failure to Call for Help
No effect	11
Little effect	11
Some effect	31
Great deal of effect	46
N	791

Note: Data are weighted to population proportions by age and sex.

fell in the bottom-two and top-two categories. Very few respondents expressed neutral or weak feelings about the causal statements. Among the middle-range choices on the scale, weak agreement was more common than neutral or weak disagreement. It is also worth noting that there were generally fewer "strongly disagrees" than "strongly agrees," with the exception of the attribution to nature. Likewise, the "national government blame" frame and the two "societal breakdown" frames had a greater proportion of respondents in the "agree" categories than in the "disagree" categories, indicating that the attribution frames in the media had fairly broad support among the public.

Interestingly, if you pool all the "agree" responses ("somewhat agree," "agree," and "strongly agree"), the causal story that received the highest percentage of agreement was the failure to evacuate, with 68 percent of respondents at least somewhat agreeing with this statement. This story was followed closely by the government failure statement, at 61 percent. However, the "national government blame" frame had more in the "strongly agree" category than other attributions, suggesting that this attribution aroused more intense feelings. The "state blame" frame is not directly comparable because of the difference in answer scales, but 46 percent of respondents indicated that they believed that state failure to call for help had a "great effect" on the national government's slow response in New Orleans. Despite the widespread coverage of the overwhelming nature of the storm, the "nature-of-the-storm" attribution item had the fewest respondents in the "strongly agree" category and the smallest percent of agreement overall. In part, we believe this stems from the survey question's wording, which excuses government, something respondents seemed loath to do. However, we also believe this result stems from the fact that this frame, while strong and credible in the first few days of the storm, later became an elite excuse and justification that was not credible to journalists or the public.

Table 4.3 demonstrates that there is a partisan element to the acceptance of causal attributions, a theme we will return to later in this chapter as we develop specific hypotheses.[2] Democrats were much more likely than Republicans to agree that the national government was to blame. Eighty-two percent of Democrats at least somewhat agreed with this attribution frame compared to only 39 percent of Republicans (differences of proportions test, $p|t|<.001$). The national government blame frame resonated as credible with Democrats, who were already skeptical of the Republican Bush administration, and

[2] Party was measured using a two-part question. The first asked respondents to indicate whether they thought of themselves as a Democrat, Republican, independent, or something else. The second part of the question asked Democrats and Republicans whether they were strong or weak. For independents, we asked whether they leaned toward the Republican or Democratic party. For the small percentage who did not respond to this question, we used political ideology as a proxy for partisanship. Party categories include those who claim to be independents but lean toward one of the parties. The category "independents" includes both strict independents and those who associate with neither major party (i.e., third-party supporters).

TABLE 4.3. *Agreement with Attributions by Partisanship, in Percentages*

	Democrat	Independent/ No Major Party Affiliation[c]	Republican	N
National government[a]	82	61	39[*]	952
Federalist (state failure)[b]	75	72	83[*]	791
Nature of the storm	37	44	65[*]	956
Non-evacuation	62	66	77[*]	957
Crime	52	56	66[*]	936

[*] $p < .05$, difference of proportions test between Democrats and Republicans.
Notes: Data are weighted to population proportions for age and sex.
[a] Percentage within party who somewhat agree, agree, or strongly agree.
[b] Percentage within party who thought state failure had "some effect" or a "great effect."
[c] Category includes those who rated themselves as "independent" or "other" and those who said "don't know" when asked about party identification.

the media portrayal served to reinforce their attitudes. Conversely, the national government blame frame was less likely to resonate with Republicans, who held long-standing positive evaluations of Bush and his administration. The opposite pattern emerges for the state blame frame, but it is weaker. Seventy-five percent of Democrats indicated that they thought state failure to call for help had at least some effect on the response time, compared to 83 percent of Republicans ($p|t| < .05$). The smaller difference for the state blame frame may be due to the fact that the state's Democratic governor, Kathleen Blanco, was largely unknown before the storm and had no national reputation as a leader, positive or negative, so all information about the state government and its leadership came in the context of storm coverage.

Republicans were more likely to agree with any blame frame other than the national government blame frame. The percentage of Republicans who agreed with the state blame frame, the nature-of-the-storm frame, and the two societal breakdown frames were at or above 65 percent, compared to the 39 percent who agreed with the national blame frame. Likewise, for each frame other than the national blame frame, the percentage of Republicans agreeing with the frame exceeded the percentage of Democrats. The alternative stories – such as state failure to call for enough help, the societal breakdown frames, and the nature-of-the-storm frame – did not conflict with strongly held partisan predispositions and offered a means of diverting blame from national government and the Bush administration.

This is a pattern that we would expect in a multiple-message environment given the strong tendency among individuals to engage in directionally motivated reasoning (Lodge and Taber 2000; Taber and Lodge 2006). However, in the next section, we outline the conditions under which we would expect to see an attenuation of directional reasoning, leaving the door open to greater similarity of opinions across partisans.

EMPIRICAL EXPECTATIONS FROM THE THEORY OF AFFECTIVE ATTRIBUTIONS

If our theory of affective attributions is correct, we should see that *anxiety attenuates the strength of any partisan effects on attributions of blame, particularly for those causal frames most likely to cue party predispositions, such as the government blame frames.* Anxiety, which in this case was triggered by the catastrophic events, serves to activate an appraisal mechanism (Marcus, Neuman, and MacKuen 2000; MacKuen et al. 2010). We contend that when this happens, the goals of information processing shift from reliance on standard directionally motivated routines to a mechanism that sets aside predispositions to assess more accurately the novel and potentially threatening event. In a multimessage environment where frames are available uniformly across all media sources and presented in a way that makes them cognitively and emotionally credible, we should see high acceptance of framed messages, even when those messages run counter to predispositions. As we saw in Chapter 3, the information environment following Katrina was not conducive to a biased selection of information because the various media outlets offered the same menu of stories. The frames were strong and highly credible and their volume loud – particularly for the government-blame frames.

The specific test of our argument depends upon examining whether emotional response to the storm dampens any partisan bias in attributions of blame. The two attributions where this should be most apparent is attribution to the national and state government. The national government's preparation and response were the responsibility of

FEMA and DHS, run by an appointee of a Republican, President Bush. State government efforts were led by a Democrat, Governor Blanco, and her appointees. Partisan cues were an important part of the public dialogue, especially later in the coverage as the blame game peaked. Democrat and Republican political elites directed blame at different levels of government as a means of excusing or justifying their poor performances. The partisan nature of the debate, and the clear stances of well-known political elites, should have cued a process of motivated reasoning in the public, and there is evidence of such a process in the data presented in the previous section. However, if our argument is correct, we should see attenuated effects of partisanship for those who are emotionally engaged by the storm. Specifically we hypothesize the following:

I. In general, Democrats are more likely to agree with the national government blame frame than Republicans; however:
   a. Anxious Republicans are more likely to agree with the national government blame frame than unanxious Republicans.
   b. The level of agreement among Democrats will be relatively unchanged by feelings of anxiety.
   c. Anxious Republicans will hold opinions more similar to those of Democrats than unanxious Republicans.

Expectation *b* stems from the fact that directional and accuracy motivations for Democrats predict the same pattern of attributions. Although Democrats might also set aside their predispositions and consider current information more deeply, the outcome of this process is unlikely to be empirically observable. Therefore, we can evaluate our claim for this attribution only by examining whether anxious Republicans are more similar to Democrats (*c*) and whether unanxious and anxious Republicans differ (*a*).

The critical test for our argument is whether this expectation is reversed for the state blame frame. Because the state blame frame centers on a Democratic governor, we expect directionally motivated reasoning to encourage rejection of the attribution for Democrats. However, anxious Democrats should be motivated to seek and appraise information, even if it runs counter to their predispositions, and they should be more accepting of the information. For Republicans, we should see no empirical difference between the anxious and unanxious. Directionally motivated reasoning and affective reasoning should produce roughly the same pattern of attribution of blame for Republicans.

II. In general, Democrats are less likely than Republicans to believe that state failure to call for help had a great effect on response times in New Orleans; however:
   a. Anxious Democrats are more likely to believe that the state failure had a great effect than unanxious Democrats.
   b. We should see no difference in anxious and unanxious Republicans in their beliefs that the state was to blame for delayed national response.
   c. Anxious Democrats should hold opinions more similar to those of Republicans than to those of un-anxious Democrats.

The predictions of directional and accuracy-motivated reasoning are not quite as clear for the other nongovernmental attributions except to say that we anticipate that Republicans may have a general motivation to accept explanations such as natural causes and societal breakdown as a way of diluting blame across multiple factors and shifting responsibility to others. Table 4.3 showed a baseline difference in the level of agreement across partisans. In keeping with our expectations, we generally see that Republicans tend to agree with a broader range of attributions to sources other than the national government. For example, they are more likely than Democrats to agree with the attribution that nature was to blame (65 percent of Republicans agree compared to 37 percent of Democrats, $p < .001$), the attribution that criminal behavior was to blame (66 percent of Republicans compared to 52 percent of Democrats, $p < .001$), and that non-evacuees were to blame (77 percent of Republicans compared to 62 percent of Democrats, $p < .001$). As a result, we expect that emotion should attenuate the strength of party identification in each of these cases, with anxious Republicans and anxious Democrats holding more similar opinions than unanxious Republicans and Democrats.

EMPIRICAL MODELS AND RESULTS, ATTRIBUTIONS OF BLAME

The dependent variables to test our hypotheses, the attributions of blame, are measured using ordered categorical scales, so we test the hypotheses listed under I and II using ordered-probit models. Our three focal independent variables from our hypotheses are party identification, measured on a seven-point scale ranging from strong Democrat (−3) to strong Republican (+3); anxiety, measured as the mean of feeling shocked *and* concerned about the economy, which ranges from zero to three; and a multiplicative interaction between the two variables.

Based on our hypotheses, we expect party identification to influence the degree of support for the attribution, but the *effect* of party identification should be weaker for anxious partisans. In other words, in each case, we expect the coefficient for the interaction variable to work in the *opposite* direction of partisanship. We also include a number of controls in the model – including attention to coverage of Hurricane Katrina, socioeconomic status, demographic characteristics, and political sophistication – to ensure that our results are not spurious (full tables are reported in Appendix D).

Table 4.4 shows the coefficients for the three focal variables needed to test our hypotheses, and the results are largely supportive of our argument. Party identification has a significant effect on attributing blame in each of the five models, but those effects are attenuated when the respondent is anxious. The coefficients are indisputably significant ($p < .05$) in three of the five models, and the direction of effect is correct in all cases. The sign of the coefficient for the interaction term is the opposite of the sign of the coefficient for party identification, indicating that anxiety attenuates the effect of party identification.

Recall that party identification is coded from −3 to +3, so the coefficient for anxiety – the mean of shocked and concerned – indicates the effect for those who do not identify at all with one of the two major parties. Generally, we expected anxiety to heighten acceptance of all attribution frames, and in all but one of the models, the direct effect was positive and at least marginally significant. However, the direction of effect was unexpectedly negative for attributing blame to the nature of the storm. This result may indicate that the frame was simply not plausible in the broader multimessage environment or it may reflect a reaction to the wording of our question, which served to explicitly excuse government, something that was clearly counter to the dominant media messages.

TABLE 4.4. *Ordered-Probit Models of Attributions of Blame, Select Coefficients for Focal Variables*

	Blame Frame				
	National Government	Nature of Storm	Criminal Behavior	Non-evacuation	State Failure
Party ID (Strong Dem to Strong Rep)	−0.309***	0.165***	0.125***	0.151***	0.210***
Anxiety	0.309***	−0.111**	0.063	0.036	0.101*
Anxiety × Party ID	0.057***	−0.024	−0.035*	−0.027	−0.071***
N	919	922	902	922	763

***p < .01; **p < .05; *p < .10; two-tailed tests.

Notes: Dependent variables are the level of agreement with each attribution. The high value of the seven response categories is "strongly agree." All models were run with a full set of controls, including attention to news coverage, knowing someone harmed by Katrina or Rita, political knowledge, age, sex, race, income, and homeownership. The full model results are reported in Table D.1 in Appendix D.

Nevertheless, from our perspective the most important result in this table is that anxiety attenuates the effects of party identification, because this shows that anxiety produces the hypothesized effect. Moreover, in the two models where we expected to see the greatest difference between those who were anxious and those who were not – national government blame and state government blame – the effect is clearly significant (p < .001). Even the models for attribution to criminal behavior, the nature of the storm, and non-evacuation exhibit a pattern consistent with our argument, although the estimates for the joint effect are much smaller and just miss the cutoff for statistical significance at conventional levels. In previous chapters, we saw that anxiety prompted greater attentiveness and therefore exposure to all of the stories. But in this model, even after controlling for the effects of exposure by including the attentiveness measure in the model (see Appendix D), we still see a substantial effect of anxiety on attributions of blame.

Partisanship, Emotion, and Blame Based on Predicted Probabilities

The sign and significance of coefficients are informative as a test, but they do not explore all the implications of our theory; so, we turn to examining the substantive effects of the model through predicting probabilities of responses (King, Tomz, and Wittenberg 2000). We expected to find particular patterns of acceptance among partisans for the state and national blame frames. To assess this, we examine the predicted probabilities that a respondent would agree or strongly agree with a particular frame based on the ordered-probit models. The predicted probabilities tell us how likely it is that an individual with a particular set of characteristics and particular level of emotion would respond no lower than category 6 of our seven-point scale, meaning that he or she at minimum agrees, if not strongly, with the attribution. A predicted probability near 1.0 means that the individual is almost certain to agree, while a predicted probability of near 0 means that he or she is almost certain not to agree. When a person is estimated to have greater than a .5 probability of agreeing, we see that person as more likely than not of falling into the category of opinion that we are predicting. To obtain the predicted values of agreeing with an attribution, we set the values of all independent variables in the model to their mean or mode, then we varied the values of the focal independent variables from their low to high values to see how doing so changes the likelihood of the individual agreeing with the attributions.

The critical test, for our argument, is whether anxious partisans are more likely to accept attributions that contradict their predispositions than unanxious partisans. Thus we compare how party identification affects agreement for those who fall in the category of 0 on our anxiety scale (meaning not at all anxious) and those who fall in the category of 3 (meaning extremely anxious).

Figures 4.1 and 4.2 plot the predicted probabilities from the national government blame frame and state blame frame to examine whether the evidence supports this expectation, whereas the dotted lines around each indicate the 90 percent confidence intervals. When the confidence intervals for the two solid lines do not overlap with one another, the difference in the predicted probabilities between the unanxious and the extremely anxious is statistically significant.

The results show that the affective-based difference in predicted probabilities for accepting the attribution of blame lies with the in-party group – the group most likely to reject the attribution based on predispositional grounds alone. In the case of the national blame attribution, Republicans are the in-party and Democrats are

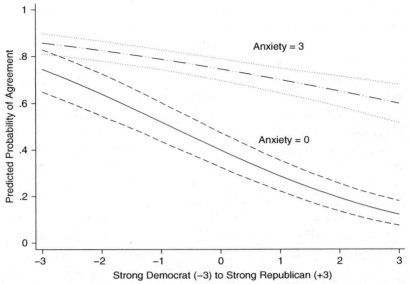

FIGURE 4.1. Effects of Party Identification on Agreement with Attribution to National Government, Conditioned by Level of Anxiety.

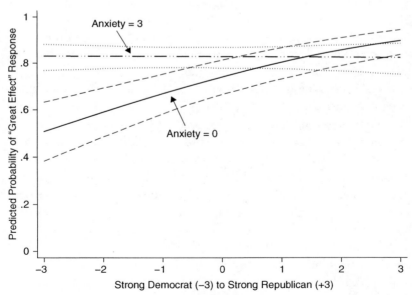

FIGURE 4.2. Effects of Party Identification on Agreement with Attribution to State Government, Conditioned by Level of Anxiety.

the out-party. Anxious and unanxious Democrats had very similar predicted probabilities of agreeing that national government was to blame, reaching over .8 at the extreme end. This similarity is expected because the strong and credible media messages serve to reinforce preexisting opinions about the Republican-run national government. However the difference between anxious and unanxious respondents becomes apparent and is statistically significant for Republicans (the confidence intervals around the two predicted probabilities diverge), indicating that anxious Republican respondents are more likely than unanxious Republican respondents to attribute blame to the national government. Overall, the line showing the predicted probability of agreement is much steeper for those who are not feeling anxious, as would be expected by partisan-motivated reasoning, and this shows that partisanship is primarily driving the likelihood. Among those who felt anxiety as a result of the storm, however, the effects of partisanship on the predicted probability of agreement are much weaker, as evidenced by the flatter line.

The same pattern emerges in Figure 4.2, which shows the likelihood of believing that the state's failure to call for help had a great effect on national government response times. There was very little difference between the predicted probabilities for anxious and unanxious Republicans because they are part of the "out-party" group for this attribution. In contrast, we see a statistically significant difference for Democrats, the in-party group for this attribution of blame. As mentioned earlier, the empirical prediction for anxious and unanxious out-party respondents is the same because motivated and accuracy approaches would lead Republicans to view state failure as an acceptable explanation. However, for Democrats, directionally motivated reasoning would lead to rejection of attribution of blame directed toward the Democratic-controlled state government, while accuracy bias that encourages evaluation and acceptance of media messages would lead to acceptance of a frame that runs counter to predispositions. In fact, among anxious respondents, the degree of support for the state blame frame is about equal for Democrats and Republicans. Only among the unanxious do we see partisan divergence in support of this attribution.

Figures 4.3, 4.4, and 4.5 show the same moderating relationship, although the differences between the unanxious and the anxious are

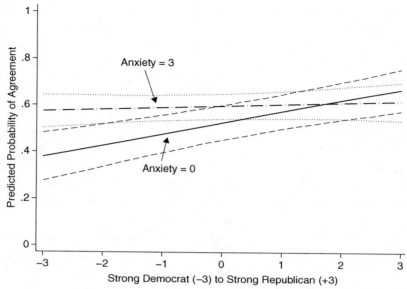

FIGURE 4.3. Effects of Party Identification on Agreement with Criminal Behavior Attribution, Conditioned by Level of Anxiety.

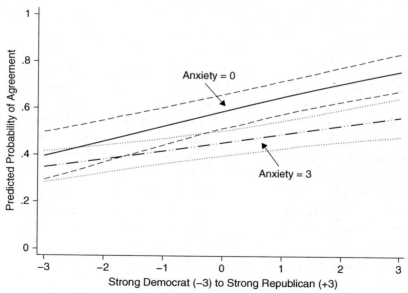

FIGURE 4.4. Effects of Party Identification on Agreement with Attribution to Nature, Conditioned by Level of Anxiety.

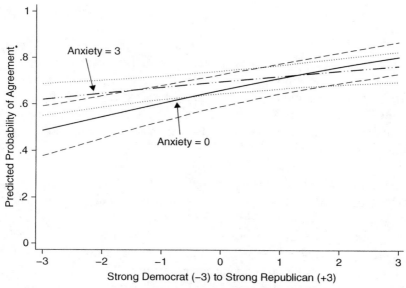

FIGURE 4.5. Effects of Party Identification on Agreement with Non-evacuation Attribution, Conditioned by Level of Anxiety.

significantly different only for the attributions blaming crime and nature. The pattern holds for blaming non-evacuation, but the confidence intervals overlap, so we cannot be sure that the two groups are statistically distinct.

It is interesting to see that for the blame-crime attribution, partisanship has no statistically discernible effect on agreement for those who were anxious. Anxious Republicans and Democrats are both more likely than not to agree with this attribution. In contrast, unanxious Democrats and Republicans differ appreciably from one another, with the predicted probability of agreeing exceeding .5 for most Republicans but not for Democrats (see Figure 4.4). The attenuation effect seems somewhat weaker for the non-evacuation attribution, but still shows statistical evidence of moderating Republican views. Because blaming nature was a common theme among those in the executive branch of the national government as a means for justifying performance, we would expect directional motivations to lead to greater agreement with this attribution. Accuracy motivations that lead to consideration of alternative stories, including those of government blame, attenuate the effects of partisan-based biases.

As a group, the findings that the effects of partisan predispositions are attenuated are noteworthy because they suggest that extraordinary events provide an emotionally based mechanism for producing greater consensus in the public. This, of course, opens the doors to significant and possibly abrupt policy change and increases the likelihood that leaders will be held accountable for their actions in subsequent elections.

Aggregate Level Effects of the Micro-Level Process

The aggregate level effect of this micro-level process can be considerable. For the government blame attributions, the scope of this effect in the context of the survey sample is quite large. Even at the lowest levels of emotional engagement, where anxiety measures 1 on a 0 to 3 scale, there are still statistically significant moderating effects on accepting the national government blame attribution (see Figure 4.6). Fully 83 percent of our sample scored 1 or higher on this measure, although there is some difference across party: 77 percent of Republicans met this criterion, as did 87 percent of Democrats. For the majority of people in both parties, emotion served to attenuate the strength of their partisan predispositions somewhat when meting out blame for the catastrophe in New Orleans.

We see the same type of results, although not quite as strong, for the acceptance of the federalism or state failure blame frame. The difference in predicting that the state government had either some or a great deal of effect on national government response time remained statistically distinct as long as the respondent scored 2 or higher on the anxiety-level measure – a condition met by 50 percent of our sample (39 percent of Republicans and 61 percent of Democrats).[3] As in the case of national government blame, this means that a large proportion of Democratic and Republican respondents moved closer to a shared meaning of what went wrong in the disaster. To be fair, there are still partisan differences in attributions of blame, but in major events about which half or more of

---

[3] Descriptive statistics for the anxiety measure (weighted): mean = 1.77, standard deviation = .88, 25th percentile = 1, 50th percentile = 2, 75th percentile = 2.5.

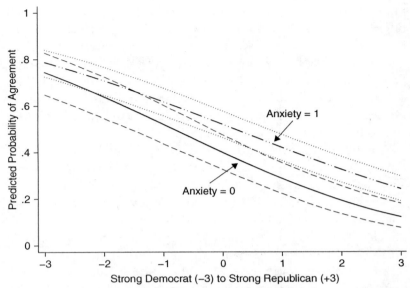

FIGURE 4.6. Effects of Party Identification on Agreement with National Government Attribution, No-Anxiety and Low-Anxiety Respondents.

the public moderate their views, the effect on aggregate opinions can be substantial, thereby driving what we observe as negative or positive "rallies" in opinions.

RACE AND ATTRIBUTIONS OF BLAME

In Chapters 2 and 3, we discussed the connections between empathy and emotional engagement and highlighted that one source of empathy stems from social or racial identity. There is no doubt that the media context of the storm placed race at the forefront, visually, and the media's focus on issues of race and class emphasized these types of cues (see Bartels 2006; Bobo 2006; Haider-Markel, Delehanty, and Beverlin 2007; Huddy and Feldman 2006b; Pew Research Center 2005). As a result, blacks and other minorities were both more attentive to coverage of the storm and scored slightly higher, overall, on our composite measure of anxiety than whites ($p|t|<.05$, two-tailed test). But it is also possible that the anxiety measures we use do not fully capture the emotional intensity or complexity felt by blacks following the storm. How did racial differences shape attributions of blame following Katrina? Did race have additional effects beyond what is mediated through emotion? Our theory clearly implies that those feeling greater empathy should be more likely to accept strong, credible stories in the media.[4] As a result, we expect to find that blacks are more likely to attribute blame to both national and state government than whites, even after controlling for party identification.

A number of studies have explored the importance of race and class on opinions about government following Hurricane Katrina, and the findings are highly consistent across studies: Blacks register stronger attributions of blame toward government than whites (Haider-Markel, Delehanty, and Beverlin 2007; Huddy and Feldman 2006b). Our findings mirror those of prior studies in this regard. Table 4.5 shows the predicted probabilities from our attribution models for blaming national government for whites, blacks, and other minorities. For ease of presentation, and because the relevant differences occur in the more extreme categories, we have collapsed the "agree" and "strongly agree" categories into one, and the "disagree" and "strongly disagree" categories into another. Blacks had a greater predicted probability of agreeing with the national-government-blame frame than whites ($p < .05$). Likewise, so did other minorities. Thus it appears that the opinions of both groups were responsive to the context of the crisis.

A similar pattern is evident in blaming the state government for failing to call for help. The probability of believing this failure had a "great effect" was .59 for blacks, but only .48 for whites. Notably, the differences in the predicted probability between whites and other minorities in this case are not statistically significant because the standard error around the difference for other minorities is quite large. Likewise, the differences in blaming the nature of the storm follow patterns we would expect, with blacks less likely than whites to excuse government because of the overwhelming nature of the storm.

---

[4] Our theoretical argument suggests that race, as an indicator of emotion, should condition predispositions in a manner similarly to anxiety. However, we cannot test the claim because our sample contains insufficient joint variation in race and party. Nearly all blacks were also Democrats.

TABLE 4.5. *Predicted Probabilities of Agreement with Societal Breakdown Frames, by Race*

	White	Black	Other Minority
National Government Blame Frame			
Agree/strongly agree	0.48	0.66	0.58 [a, b]
Disagree/strongly disagree	0.24	0.12	0.17 [a, b]
State Failure Blame Frame			
Great effect	0.48	0.59	0.41 [a]
No effect	0.11	0.07	0.15 [a]
Societal Breakdown: Criminal Behavior			
Agree/strongly agree	0.40	0.35	0.42
Disagree/strongly disagree	0.34	0.38	0.32
Societal Breakdown: Non-evacuation			
Agree/strongly agree	0.42	0.40	0.37
Disagree/strongly disagree	0.25	0.27	0.30
Nature of Storm			
Agree/strongly agree	0.28	0.25	0.38 [b]
Disagree/strongly disagree	0.48	0.53	0.38 [b]

Notes: Predicted probabilities are from models reported in Table D.1 in Appendix D with all independent variables set to median or mode. Predicted probabilities were generated using Clarify 2.1 (Tomz, Wittenberg, and King 2003).
[a] The difference between white and black is significant at p < .05, one-tailed test.
[b] The difference between white and other minority is significant at p < .05, one-tailed test.

Predicting attitudes about the societal breakdown frames based on race is a bit more complicated because blacks faced cross-pressures from group identity and media framing that focused on the behavior of the victims. Social psychologists have long been aware that the fundamental attribution error of attributing success to one's self and failures to external causes also occurs when one attributes blame pertaining to those in one's social group (Hewstone 1989). Therefore, because blacks identify with the victims who were negatively framed in these attributions, we hypothesized that blacks would be more likely to *reject* these explanations than other racial groups. However, as Table 4.5 shows, there is little difference in the views of blacks compared to whites. Whites were slightly more likely than blacks to agree that criminal behavior delayed aid following the storm, although the difference is substantively small and not statistically significant. Similarly, whites and blacks were nearly equally likely to agree that residents ignoring evacuation orders played a role in human suffering after the storm. This finding differs somewhat from Huddy and Feldman (2006b:108), who showed that blacks were much less likely to blame victims of the storm than whites,[5] but the nature of the question asked in our survey was quite different. However, there are some differences between blacks and those of other minority groups, although due to the small number of non-black minorities in our sample, the margins of error around predictions are quite large, rendering the difference statistically insignificant. The predicted probability that a non-black minority would agree with the criminal blame frame was .42, compared to .35 for blacks. Their predicted probability also exceeded that of whites, but not by a statistically significant amount.

The results from the two societal breakdown attribution models are different than we had hypothesized. Standard conceptualizations drawn from social identity and group cohesiveness theory would predict blacks to be less likely to blame victims because they share a racial and social identity. To speculate on the reason for this unexpected result, we draw upon recent research on race and framing among blacks that suggests that implicit frames or racial cues may alter black opinions in ways that differ from the standard expectations (Cohen 1999; White 2009). Specifically, Cohen (1999) argues that the application of group identity and linked fate depends on the nature of the particular portion of the black community that is perceived to be affected by the issue. Blacks not only consider whether the racial frame or cue that they receive is about blacks, but whether the cue is relevant for *all* blacks or just a subset of blacks. If victims are considered non-representative of the broader social or racial group of blacks, we may not see the same level of rejection for the "blame evacuees" or "blame crime" frame that we saw with the "blame nature" frame or with the acceptance of the "blame government" frame. This is because blacks

---

[5] Specifically, Huddy and Feldman (2006b:108) asked respondents to apportion blame for residents being trapped and for conditions after the flooding. In both cases, there was a substantial difference in the proportion of blacks and whites who apportioned blame to residents compared to other figures such as Governor Blanco, Mayor Nagin, the Bush administration, or others.

do not inherently consider those portrayed negatively as representative of their social identity.

Further, White (2007) argues that implicit racial cues are different for blacks and whites. Implicit cues for whites lead to increased racial thinking because coded visual messages or words prime racial attitudes and connect racial attitudes to evaluations of policies and candidates (Mendelberg 1997, 2001). Accordingly, terms such as "inner city" or "crime" are racialized for whites due to long-term portrayals by the media (see Gilens 1999; Gilliam and Iyengar 2000) leading racial attitudes to be primed from implicit cues. This is also the reason that George H. W. Bush's famous Willie Horton ad worked so well among whites in the 1988 presidential race (Mendelberg 1997). The visual image of a black criminal implicitly cued racial schema linking underlying racial attitudes with Bush's opponent, Governor Michael Dukakis.

However, for blacks, implicit racial cues work in a different way. Because blacks also recognize that certain words and connotations, such as crime, negatively affect opinions of the group, they reject the implicit cue of identification because the underlying meaning is not consistent with group interests (White 2007). Thus, "when an issue is linked to a marginalized subset of the in-group, the role of Black group identification in determining support for that issue is attenuated; the issue, despite the implication of its racial meaning, is treated as beyond the 'boundaries of Blackness'"(White 2007:352). When an implicit negative cue centers on a "marginal" segment of the black community, blacks reject the cue because it is inconsistent with their views about group identity and linked fate.

In the case of Hurricane Katrina, blacks responded differently to the crime frame and the non-evacuee frame, both of which implicate victim *behavior* in their plight. One interpretation is that the different response is due to the fact that these messages focus on negative aspects that blacks prefer not to associate with their own identity, thus these messages do not prime racial attitudes for blacks. Instead, for the societal breakdown attributions, blacks deemphasize their racial identity with the victims and thus identity and cohesiveness theories no longer apply, which then results in greater similarity of opinions among blacks and whites. Certainly, the possibility of differential social identity cues in the attribution process is intriguing and an avenue of research that deserves deeper consideration.

Summary

In the preceding sections, we have amassed strong evidence that at the individual level, anxiety and empathy shape attributions of blame in the wake of catastrophic events. Moreover, this process applies broadly because most people feel a sense of anxiety following a major catastrophe. The nature of the storm, the coverage of the devastation in New Orleans, and the shocking events that unfolded in the days and weeks following the storm created a *collective* environment conducive to opinion change. In turn, greater collective opinion agreement on the root cause and perhaps solutions to unexpected problems increased the odds of agreement on policy solutions – a task we take up in later chapters. But our results here are indicative of a process in which the nature of media coverage following disasters helps to circumvent normal political processing of information and encourage deliberation that transcends normal partisan filters. Events that are abrupt, shocking, and unexpected and that generate emotional anxiety and empathy are those most ripe for creating a collective environment that reaches the tipping point for problem definition. When a large portion of the public feels personally connected to a catastrophic event and worries about personal ramifications, they carefully consider information that they might otherwise filter or reject based on their usual political beliefs.

THE EMOTIONAL FALLOUT FROM ATTRIBUTION OF BLAME

In Chapter 2, we theorized that one of the products of attributions might be anger. Anger is an emotion felt in response to perceived causal control, meaning that when one perceives an actor to have been able to control or prevent a negative outcome, the observer feels angry (Averill 1983; Rudolph et al. 2004; Weiner, Osbourne, and Rudolph 2011). Anger is different from anxiety because it occurs *after* making a judgment about the reason that a negative outcome occurred, whereas anxiety can arise without any causal understanding whatsoever. This means that anger, and not anxiety, is the emotion that is enhanced when some actor or agent is held responsible for the problem. This makes anger an important and distinct political variable, because when responsibility can be determined for poor political outcomes, anger should lead to greater disenchantment with the actor. From a political perspective, anger is fully developed only when a target is identified to focus anger's energy, a point we explore more fully in subsequent chapters. In addition, anger is an action-oriented emotion, leading people to want to punish and harm those responsible for the unjust act (Rudolph et al. 2004; Weiner 1995). Anxiety, on the other hand, triggers a search and appraisal of threats in order to identify ways to avert potential harm. The sequencing runs from anxiety to causal attributions, and from attributions to anger, with anger spurring a desire to punish the transgressor. The latter part of the sequence, attribution to anger to action, has been extensively tested and supported in social psychology (see Rudolph et al. 2004; Weiner, Osbourne, and Rudolph 2011), thus although our own data are cross-sectional, we believe we are on firm ground in asserting a particular causal order.

This theoretical framework suggests a different role for anger than anxiety in the processing of information than is typically put forward, and many treat anger and anxiety as if they are part of a single dimension of negative affect or are triggered in tandem (Haider-Markel, Delehanty, and Beverlin 2007; Huddy, Feldman, and Cassese 2007). The two negative emotions might be positively related if they derive directly from the same stimulus, but this happens only if anxiety leads to attributions that foster anger. For example, the 9/11 terrorist attack caused both anxiety and anger. Initially, the attacks created anxiety, but later, once the attackers were identified, much of the public felt anger toward the terrorists and wanted to punish them. This framework is consistent with the finding by Huddy, Feldman, and Cassese (2007), where angry people wanted to punish the evildoers and saw military action as a viable approach. At the same time, however, they also found that anxious individuals had a *reduced* level of support for military action in the Iraq War and suggested that anxiety led to *risk-averse* preferences. Although we can only speculate, one possibility for this finding is that those with high anxiety had yet to clearly ascribe blame to Iraq and, in the face of anxiety, feared taking military action without fully understanding the causes.

The implication of this theoretical framework is that attributions of blame to someone or something that could have controlled or prevented the outcome should lead to anger. The best test for such an expectation would involve the manipulation of frames and information to produce anxiety and attributions. However, our data are cross-sectional so we cannot directly determine cause and effect. Instead, we are limited to testing whether there is a positive relationship between attributions and anger following Hurricane Katrina, as would be predicted by the extensive body of experimental work.

EMPIRICAL MODELS AND RESULTS, ANGER

The dependent variable for this analysis is drawn from a two-part survey question designed to tap the emotion of anger. We asked respondents an initial yes-or-no question: "Have you felt angry because of what's happened in New Orleans after Katrina?" For those who responded yes to the first question, it was followed by this question: "Are you extremely angry, somewhat angry, or slightly angry?" This provides us with a four-point scale from no anger (0) to extreme anger (3). Nearly half of respondents (49 percent) indicated that they felt no anger, 7 percent indicated that they were slightly angry, 23 percent indicated they were somewhat angry, and 21 percent indicated that they were extremely angry. Because the variable is ordered and categorical, we ran an ordered-probit model. Our focal variables were the attributions of blame to different factors discussed earlier in this chapter (nature of the storm, national government, state failure to call for help, victim non-evacuation, and criminal behavior).

Our clearest expectations are those related to attribution of blame to government entities. Society turns to government to prevent and respond to calamity during and after natural disasters, so those in government are the ones with the greatest locus of control for outcomes following a disaster. Others, such as the victims who ignored evacuation orders or who participated in rioting or looting, have locus of control for their own behavior and bear some responsibility for the broader crisis, but it is hard to construe their locus of control as broad enough to have prevented the dire situation that befell New Orleans. For example, the evacuees might have contributed to the pressures, but they were certainly not at fault for the levees breaking. Moreover, most people held multiple attributions of blame that included government blame. Only fifty-four people in the sample who subscribed to one of the societal breakdown frames did not concurrently attribute blame for the aftermath to government. Thus, we should see a strong positive relationship between agreement with attributions of blame toward government – both national and state – and the level of anger expressed by respondents. In contrast, we expect a negative relationship between attributions of blame to the overwhelming nature of the storm and anger because this attribution specifically negates government's ability to control the outcome in the face of the scale of the disaster.

We also control for the level of anxiety as well as media attentiveness. Both variables should be positively related to anger. The anxiety variable is a particularly important control because we are arguing that attributions are the source of anger and that it arises from these attributions independent of feelings of anxiety. If anxiety and anger are measuring essentially the same thing, we should see a strong and significant effect for anxiety, but should find little effect of any of the other variables in the model, particularly the attributions of blame. At the same time, we do expect a positive relationship between anxiety and anger because anxiety increases receptiveness of strong and credible frames in the media. Our attribution list, although representative of the broad and important causal frames that emerged in the weeks following the storm, may not comprehensively capture all causal attributions offered in the media. Anxiety, to the extent that it is associated with additional judgments of responsibility, would positively predict anger. Similarly, we may also find an effect of attentiveness as this speaks to the level of exposure to the strong, credible stories in the media. We also control for all the usual demographic characteristics included in other models (age, gender, race, education, income, and homeownership) as well as political knowledge, partisanship, ideology, and whether or not the respondent knew a victim of the storm a priori.

Predicted Probabilities of Feeling Anger

Table 4.6 shows the coefficients for the blame attributions, anxiety, and attentiveness; the full table of coefficients can be found in Appendix D.

TABLE 4.6. *Select Ordered-Probit Coefficients from the Model of Anger*

Attribution	Anger
Blame nature	−.119***
Blame national government	.074**
Blame criminal behavior	−.017
Blame non-evacuees	−.074***
State failed to call for help	.124**
Anxiety	.488***
Attentiveness	.138
N	653

*** p < .01; **p < .05; *p < .0; two-tailed tests.

Notes: The dependent variable is a four-category measure of how angry the respondent felt in response to what happened in New Orleans. The high-valued category is "extremely angry." See the report of full model results with all controls included in Table D.2 in Appendix D.

The results are supportive of the theoretical linkages process we have outlined in Chapter 2 and in this section: Blaming government, both national and state, increases anger. The coefficients are positive and statistically significant for both variables. To understand what these findings mean in real terms, we generated predicted probabilities from the model, holding all other variables constant at their mean or modal values. We find that when the variable "blame national government" is set to its minimum value, the combined chance of being either somewhat angry (.25) or very angry (.09) is .34. In other words, the odds that a respondent registered a high degree of anger were about one in three. On the other hand, when the "blame national government" variable is set to its maximum value, respondents have a better than 50–50 chance of feeling somewhat angry (.33) or very angry (.19) – a considerably higher chance. Attributing blame to the state's failure to call for enough help shows a very similar effect. When the state blame variable is at its minimum, the chance that a respondent would express feeling either somewhat or very angry is .36, but it is .50 when the state blame variable is set to its maximum value.

Notably, we see no effect for the "blame crime" attribution and a negative effect for attribution to non-evacuees and the overwhelming nature of the storm. The latter finding was expected – blaming nature removes the locus of control from government and eliminates a central cause for anger, that is, a perception of controllability. Interestingly, the non-evacuation frame also reduces anger, something we did not predict. One way to interpret this finding, post hoc, is that this attribution, like the attribution to nature, shifted the locus of control away from government, making the aftermath seem less controllable by anyone. This also suggests something about the measure of anger that we use: It appears to be primarily directed toward the government, not the victims. Unfortunately, we cannot disentangle whether there is something especially compelling about government blame that generates anger or whether the broad entity of nameless and faceless evacuees is a difficult target.

Interestingly, we also see that anxiety is positive and significant – those who are more anxious are substantially more angry. The predicted probability of being angry when anxiety is set to its lowest value is only .20, but this jumps to .72 when it is at its highest value. Importantly, however, we see that anxiety's inclusion does not swamp the effects of the government blame frames on anger.

With regard to other controls included in the model (shown in Appendix D), we find that that women were slightly more angry than men and that knowing a victim increased anger marginally. We find no effect of partisanship, but do find a negative relationship between greater conservatism and anger. The latter is most likely related to normative beliefs that the locus of control for outcomes should be at the personal and not governmental level, although much of this should be mediated through attributions of blame. Nevertheless, the key finding from our model is that attributions of blame to government entities resulted in increased anger and that these operated distinct from anxiety. In later chapters, we examine how anger spurs punitive attitudes, both in terms of evaluating leaders and in shaping preferences for public policies.

SUMMARY AND CONCLUSIONS

In this chapter, we have developed and tested a theory of affective attributions by applying the logic of the affective intelligence literature to the process of forming or accepting attributions of blame offered in a multimessage environment. Extraordinary events, catastrophes, disasters, and other types of crises create hyper-coverage that is permeated with stories of blame and credit. In normal times, directionally motivated reasoning such as partisan bias helps to sort out competing claims in a multiple-message environment. However, in times of crisis, emotional engagement prompts individuals to set aside biased approaches of processing in order to understand unexpected and anxiety-provoking events. The result is a weakened effect of predispositions on attributions of blame. Instead, dominant media messages structure attitudes in ways that they might not in other times.

That attributions are driven in part by affective processes is important at the societal level because elevated emotion is widespread following catastrophes. During times of normal politics, when biased directional processing is common, the public is unlikely to evaluate critically leaders from the in-group party. These results show that following a catastrophic event, reflection and attitude adjustment occur among those we would least expect: respondents confronting attributions that direct blame to leaders or governments that are of their own party. Crises provide unique moments in which partisans are willing to take a hard look at leaders regardless of their own predispositions and ask whether leaders are deserving of credit or blame.

5

Federalism in a Multiple-Message Environment

Are the Appropriate Leaders Held Accountable?

Attributions of blame play a fundamental role in the successful working of a democracy. At the heart of democratic theory is the expectation that citizens hold their representatives accountable for their behavior and for the outcomes they produce as elected leaders. V. O. Key (1966), in his seminal work *The Responsible Electorate*, posited that voters were able to make reasonable judgments regarding the success or failure of elected leaders and reward or punish them at the voting booth. Theoretically, attributions of blame serve as a key mechanism, first, for determining who is responsible for political outcomes and, second, for leveraging these judgments to hold elected leaders accountable. As such, they should play a central role in both performance evaluations and vote choice. Importantly, this implies that for democracy to function properly, citizens must appropriately connect their attributions to the responsible party or leader.

Examining this question in the context of extraordinary times is valuable because it provides a type of environment that is very different from normal politics for assigning blame and rendering judgments. Moreover, because such events often bring to the forefront political leaders who were previously unknown to the broader public, they provide an academic tabula rasa to examine how partisan cues compete with media messages of responsibility and blame in the evaluation of otherwise little-known political figures.

Although research shows that judgments regarding responsibility are commonplace in the political realm, during normal times the lack of attentiveness and motivated directional reasoning on the part of citizens tends to encourage a partisan bias. As a result, assignments of political attribution often take on a partisan flavor, crediting leaders of the same party for successes and blaming leaders of the other party for failures (Gomez and Wilson 2001, 2003; Peffley and Williams 1985; Rudolph 2003b; Tyler 1982). However, during extraordinary times the contextual environment that citizens find themselves in is clearly different, enabling citizens to engage in accuracy-based reasoning to inform and update their opinions. In this context, predispositions, which are powerful cognitive forces that frame the world in ways that make sense with preexisting belief systems, are partially suppressed, allowing people to examine the situation more carefully and make attributions of blame that may contradict their ordinary biases. We saw evidence of this process in the last chapter, where we found that attributions of blame were less tied to partisanship following Hurricane Katrina for those who were emotionally moved by the aftermath of the storm. In other words, emotional engagement allowed for greater cross-party agreement.

At the same time, it cannot simply be assumed that attributions will strongly relate to evaluations, particularly in a multiple-message environment. We saw from the media environment that there were multiple actors to blame, including various levels of government and victims themselves. The federalist nature of disaster response left lines of authority somewhat blurry in both the coverage of the storm and in the minds of the public (CNN 2005b). This complex environment with multiple actors at different levels of government could blunt the expected link between attributions and evaluations by allowing citizens to pick and choose which leaders were responsible based on predispositions rather than attributions of blame. Therefore, in this chapter we ask the following question: Do attributions influence evaluations of the performance of political actors, independent of other factors?

In addition to exploring the links between attributions and evaluations, this chapter allows us to address more complicated questions about the role of discrete emotions in the formation of political judgments. In the previous chapter, we highlighted the role of anxiety in encouraging the acceptance of attributions of blame prevalent in the media. We also demonstrated that attributions of blame toward government spawned anger in respondents. In the second half of this chapter, we introduce the emotion of anger into the analysis of evaluations.

In Chapter 2, we argued that anger plays a distinct role in shaping how attribution influences evaluations directly and indirectly. The analysis in this chapter tests the specific empirical implications of this argument in the context of Hurricane Katrina. The chapter begins with an overview of the evaluations of leaders, examines the direct effects of attributions of blame, then turns to examining the direct and conditional effects of emotions.

EVALUATIONS OF THE PERFORMANCE OF LEADERS DURING HURRICANE KATRINA

There is ample evidence that Hurricane Katrina was a force in shaping public opinions about leaders, particularly evaluations of President Bush. His approval ratings, already in decline, showed an additional drop following the storm (Langer 2005). However, Bush was only one of three key leaders judged by the media and the public – Louisiana's Governor Blanco and New Orleans' Mayor Nagin were the other two. Both the state and local leaders were key figures in the disaster, and the national media interviewed them repeatedly before, during, and after the storm. As a result, people far outside of their home state and city came to know them and hold opinions about their performance in preparing for the storm and handling its aftermath.

How did they fare in public opinion compared to Bush? Our survey asked respondents, "Now I'd like to know how you think government and government officials responded in the first few days after Hurricane Katrina hit. For each, please tell me whether the performance was excellent, good, only fair or poor." Table 5.1 shows the frequency of responses for each leader and reveals striking similarity across all three. A large majority of respondents felt that all three leaders' performance in response to the crisis was only fair or poor. Tellingly, very few people lacked opinions about these individuals, despite the fact that two of the three had no national presence prior to the storm. The "don't know" responses for Bush accounted for only 3 percent. Only 10 percent replied "don't know" for Blanco and 9 percent for Nagin. Even though nearly all of our respondents resided outside of New Orleans and the State of Louisiana, most could still form some type of evaluation of each leader's performance. This suggests that the information available in the news coverage of the crisis was sufficient for most respondents to evaluate these leaders. In normal

TABLE 5.1. *Evaluations of Leader Performance in the First Few Days after the Storm, in Percentages*

	President George W. Bush	Louisiana Governor Blanco	New Orleans Mayor Nagin
Evaluation (all)			
Poor	42	39	40
Only fair	31	36	30
Good	20	21	23
Excellent	7	4	7
N	981	876	888
Evaluation Democrats			
Poor	63	28	29
Only fair	25	43	35
Good	9	25	26
Excellent	3	4	10
N	410	375	386
Evaluation Republicans			
Poor	16	53	56
Only fair	33	29	22
Good	38	15	17
Excellent	13	3	5
N	355	336	334
Evaluation Independents			
Poor	50	38	37
Only fair	33	36	31
Good	13	22	24
Excellent	4	4	8
N	189	165	168

Notes: Ns are unweighted; relative frequencies are weighted by age and sex.
Party categories include those who claim to be independents but lean toward one of the parties. The category "independents" includes both strict independents and those who associate with neither major party (i.e., third-party supporters).

political circumstances, it is likely that very few citizens beyond the borders of Louisiana would be aware of Governor Blanco or Mayor Nagin, let alone hold clear opinions about them as leaders (Delli Carpini and Keeter 1996).

At first glance, the overall evaluations suggest very little variation in the perceptions of each executive; however, when we consider the predisposition of partisanship, we see rather large differences. The similarities in opinions across the three leaders mask important subgroup differences. This is important because party identification provides a powerful cue for shaping presidential and gubernatorial approval (Cohen and King 2004; Howell and Vanderleeuw 1990; Orth 2001). Following Hurricane Katrina, media and elites provided clear cues to the public about the partisanship of each of the primary leaders (NPR 2005; Ruddy 2005). Therefore, we expect Democrats to be more likely than Republicans to hold more negative views of the Republican president and to hold more positive views of the Democratic governor and mayor. Likewise, we expect Republicans to be more likely than Democrats to have more positive views of the Republican president and have more negative views of the Democratic governor and mayor. The bottom portion of Table 5.1 shows that the data are quite consistent with these expectations. Republicans were much more favorable to Bush and much less favorable to Democrats Blanco and Nagin. Conversely, Democrats were much more favorable toward Blanco and Nagin than the Republican Bush. Independents in all cases were in-between the evaluations of Democrats and Republicans.

However, partisanship is only one part of the story, because as we saw in the last chapter, some individuals attributed blame in ways that ran counter to their party identification. Did the attributions of blame that we identified shape evaluations independent of party identification? If so, this suggests that even though the media environment cued party identification of leaders, it also provided alternative information that helped the public to connect the dots from catastrophic outcomes to the leaders deemed responsible.

ATTRIBUTIONS AND THE ASSIGNMENT OF POLITICAL RESPONSIBILITY

Research in the area of economic voting provides the strongest support for the theory that citizens are sensitive to attributions in the assignment of political responsibility. Beginning with Key (1966) and formalized more clearly in the works of Fiorina (1981) and Kramer (1971), economic voting theory argues a reward–punish decision-making framework for voters. When voters' personal economic situation and/or the national or state economic situations are worse off, voters punish the incumbent officeholder. Likewise, when voters' personal economic conditions and/or the national or state economic conditions are better, voters reward the incumbent officeholder. This theory has gained a great deal of support at the executive level, especially at the presidential level, but also at the gubernatorial level, using both individual and aggregate data (Atkeson and Partin 1995, 1998; Chubb 1988; Fiorina 1978, 1981; Kiewiet 1981; Kinder and Kiewiet 1978, 1981; Niemi, Stanley, and Vogel 1995; Rudolph 2003b; Stein 1990; Weatherford 1978).

More recent debates in this literature have provided a more nuanced understanding of how responsibility interacts with institutional context. For example, scholars have combined responsible party government theory with economic voting theory to determine whether clarity of responsibility increases the assignment of political responsibility (Anderson 1995; Leyden and Borrelli 1995; Lowry, Alt, and Ferree 1998; Powell and Whitten 1993). These scholars argue that when states or nations divide power among institutions, as happens in federal systems, and different parties control different institutions, then determining who is responsible for policy outcomes is less clear (Gomez and Wilson 2003; Sundquist 1988). Federalism and divided government make it more difficult for voters to assign blame, make judgments of leaders, and vote in a manner consistent with normative democratic theory. Comparative studies across nations (Anderson 1995, 2000; Powell and Whitten1993) and across the American states (Leyden and Borrelli 1995; Lowry, Alt, and Ferree 1998) also find support for this argument.

None of these studies, however, had direct measures of attribution. When attribution is considered, it has an important mediating effect on accountability. Indeed, research shows that there is a stronger relationship between economic evaluations and vote choice when government or societal factors are seen as responsible (Abramowitz, Lanoue, and Ramesh 1988). When the president is directly attributed with responsibility for national economic conditions, economic evaluations have strong effects on presidential vote choice and presidential approval (Gomez and Wilson 2003; Kinder and Mebane 1983; Lau and Sears 1981; Peffley and Williams 1985; Rudolph and Grant 2002; Tyler 1982). Similar effects are seen at the state level, where state economic conditions influence gubernatorial support when clear attribution of blame can be made to state government responsibility (Arceneaux 2005; Atkeson and Partin 2001; Rudolph 2003a; Stein 1990).

Research in other policy areas also shows that attribution of credit and blame influence evaluations and the vote choice (Arceneaux and

Stein 2006; Iyengar 1989; Marsh and Tilley 2009). In a recent study in Ireland and Great Britain, Marsh and Tilley (2009:129–30) find that when citizens believe that government is responsible for the performance of the economy, health care, taxes, education, and the general standard of living, it influences their vote choice. But when they do not believe that government is at fault for these outcomes, such results do not influence citizens' vote choice. Similar results are found for disaster management on vote choice (Arceneaux and Stein 2006).

For our case, this body of literature suggests that public evaluations of leaders should be tied to both an understanding of the lines of authority and to an understanding of government's culpability for pain and suffering following the storm. In prior chapters, we saw that multiple causal stories or frames were offered in the media, and these were either accepted or rejected by individuals as explanations for the tragic circumstances in New Orleans. We argue that these types of attributions were then used by individuals to assign responsibility to leaders and that we can observe this through examining the relationship between attributions and evaluations of leaders. Therefore, we expect that those who agreed that the national government was to blame will evaluate President Bush more poorly than those who disagreed with that attribution. Likewise, those who believed that the suffering in New Orleans resulted from the state failing to call for sufficient help should evaluate Governor Blanco more harshly than those who did not.

MULTIPLE MESSAGES, FEDERALISM, AND ASSIGNMENT OF RESPONSIBILITY

Although we expect government blame attributions to influence evaluations of those same government leaders directly, we also argue that alternative blame attributions, including blame attributions to other levels of government, can serve to excuse leaders or mitigate their responsibility. Assigning responsibility for political and policy outcomes is more complex in a federalist system because some power belongs primarily to the national government, some power belongs primarily to the state government, and some power is shared between federal and state governments. Theoretically, federalism enhances both citizen representation (Beer 1978) and government accountability

(Madison 2010) by allowing voters to select leaders at the local, state, and federal level. The advantage to voters is that multiple points of access increase their likelihood of representation. One problem with federalism, however, is that although it provides more opportunities for citizens to get what they want, it can potentially muddy the waters and make it more difficult for citizens to know who is responsible. There are two major reasons for this lack of clarity. First, it may be inherent to a federalist structure in which power is often shared among different levels of government. Citizens may be unaware of the lines of authority or mistakenly believe that one level of government is responsible when the authority lies with another.

This was certainly true in Hurricane Katrina. We asked respondents to our survey to indicate who they believed to be responsible for ordering the National Guard troops to respond to the disaster. The correct answer is the state government, but only 54 percent of respondents were aware of that fact. Twenty-nine percent believed it was either the president's or FEMA's responsibility, incorrectly locating this responsibility at the national level.[1] Eighteen percent admitted that they did not know which level was responsible. Therefore, we expect that perceptions of responsibility toward the state government will lead to lower evaluations of Governor Blanco and higher evaluations of President Bush. However, perceptions that responsibility belonged to President Bush or FEMA should result in lower evaluations of President Bush and higher evaluations of Governor Blanco. At the top of Table 5.2, we find that this expectation is well founded, as the table shows the strong effects of the perception of responsibility on evaluations. This table shows the mean value of the evaluation measure for each of the three relevant leaders. The scale ranged from 0 (poor) to 3 (excellent); therefore, lower values indicate more negative evaluations. When respondents believed that the state governor was responsible for calling up the National Guard, they evaluate Governor Blanco the least favorably of the three leaders. In contrast, President Bush receives the highest mean response in this category. However, for those who incorrectly believed that

[1] We combined FEMA and President Bush because theoretically both involve the executive branch. In empirical models that included them separately, we see the same effect.

the national executive branch held the authority to order troops into the area, President Bush's evaluation was considerably lower (p < .05). Interestingly, the evaluations of Mayor Nagin mirrored those of Governor Blanco. This makes some sense if we think that respondents who believe that the national government is responsible vindicate both of the lower-level officeholders.

A second and equally important way in which federalism creates problems for assignment of responsibility relates to how elites use institutional fuzziness to shift blame from one unit or actor to another. Leaders, when faced with negative economic or social events, seek to explain or justify their actions to deflect public blame (McGraw 1990, 1991). When leaders at different levels of government or different political institutions have overlapping and shared powers, they can direct blame away from themselves and toward other plausible responsible powers. The media analysis revealed many instances of blame shifting among national, state, and local elites (Maestas et al. 2008). This is not surprising, as crisis management requires the coordination of local, state, and national players, making federalism an important consideration in the blame game. However, in the case of Katrina, the difference in party control among levels of government contributed to cross-level finger-pointing in a way consistent with motivated reasoning. In fact, the strong role that predispositions such as partisanship play in evaluation of leaders creates additional barriers to attributing blame. In a federalist structure, a potential strategy that leaders can employ to dodge blame is to pin responsibility on opponent party leaders at other levels of government.

The analysis of media coverage in the month following Katrina showed that although the national government received prominent attention and blame, errors made by state and local government authorities were brought to light as well. President Bush and his allies frequently pointed fingers at state and local government while Democrats, including Mayor Nagin and Governor Blanco, vocally criticized the Republican administration and President Bush.

Are these types of blame shifts effective? Might attributions of blame to other levels of government or even to factors outside of government *improve* evaluations for some political actors? We suggest it is possible. To be clear, this is different from the usual causal path, where attribution of blame toward a leader has a direct effect on his or

TABLE 5.2. *Mean Evaluations of President Bush, Governor Blanco, and Mayor Nagin*

	Mean Evaluation of President Bush	Mean Evaluation of Governor Blanco	Mean Evaluate of Mayor Nagin
National Guard Activation[a]			
State responsible	1.01 (524)	.72 (497)[#]	.80 (500)*
President/FEMA responsible	.77 (264)	1.11 (240)[#]	1.25 (245)*
State Government Failed to Call for Enough Help[b]			
No effect	1.03 (93)	1.33 (88)	1.42 (87)
Very little effect	.74 (80)	1.18 (77)	1.11 (76)
Some effect	.99 (218)	.99 (203)	1.05 (208)
Great effect	.89 (374)	.59 (358)[#]	.71 (360)*

Notes: [#] The difference between Blanco and Bush is p < .05. * The difference between Nagin and Bush is p < .05.

Notes: N is the unweighted observations in parentheses. Means are weighted to reflect age and sex in the population.

[a] Means for each leader are within categories for responses to the survey question asking which actor is responsible for activating the National Guard. We pooled responses assigning activation power to FEMA or the president because both are national-level agents.

[b] Means for each leader are within categories for responses to the attribution to the state's failure to call for help.

her evaluations. Rather, we are asking whether assignment of blame to causes *other* than the leader *enhances* their evaluations.

We see hints of support for this hypothesis in Table 5.2 when we compare the mean evaluations of Bush, Blanco, and Nagin, but the evidence is somewhat mixed. The mean evaluation of Governor Blanco dropped monotonically and significantly as we expected, but the results for both President Bush and Mayor Nagin were inconsistent, moving both up and down in response to increased attribution to state government. Mayor Nagin's, however, more closely resembled Governor Blanco's results. As noted earlier, because Nagin was part of the state hierarchy structure in terms of disaster management, he was likely tarred with the same brush as Governor Blanco. In addition, he was directly responsible for communicating local needs to state officials and thus was an integral part of the state's apparatus for dealing with the crisis. Thus, spillover from the attribution of state government is logical within a shared disaster management framework. In all, the table is supportive of a direct link between attributions of blame and evaluations, with spillover between state and local officials. It does not provide clear support that attributing blame toward the state improves evaluations for national leaders. However, we have not yet controlled for key factors such as the remaining attributions of blame and partisanship. The former is especially important because we know that many tended to blame both state and national officials simultaneously. Therefore, we cannot fully accept or discard our working hypothesis about the cross-leader attribution effects based on this simple analysis. We turn to a fuller test of this in the next section.

Given our theoretical framework, we hypothesize the following:

I. Individuals who more strongly agreed that national government was to blame:
   a. hold lower evaluations of President Bush and
   b. hold higher evaluations of Governor Blanco and Mayor Nagin.
II. Individuals who thought state government failure to call for help had a greater effect on national government response time will:
   a. hold lower evaluations of Governor Blanco and Mayor Nagin, and
   b. hold higher evaluations of President Bush.

It is also possible that attribution of blame to nongovernment sources such as the nature of the storm or the behavior of victims before and after the storm offered convenient targets for politicians to shift blame. Indeed, after the storm hit, elites from both parties at all levels of government pointed to the overwhelming nature of the storm as a reason for their inability to render aid (see Chapter 3). Therefore, we expect:

III. Individuals who more strongly agree that the overwhelming nature of the storm was to blame will:
   a. hold higher evaluations of President Bush, Governor Blanco, and Mayor Nagin.
IV. Individuals who more strongly agree that victim behavior was to blame will:
   a. hold higher evaluations of President Bush and Governor Blanco.

We offer a slightly different prediction for Mayor Nagin, however. Many journalists in the first days following the storm focused on the large number of people who remained in shelters in Louisiana. This attribution, however, as noted in Chapter 3, is potentially double-barreled because of Mayor Nagin's missteps in preparing evacuation from the city. So, acceptance of the causal story that pain and suffering in New Orleans stemmed from too many people ignoring evacuation orders may also correlate with believing that Mayor Nagin did a poor job in emptying the city. Thus, although we expect that blame for the non-evacuation of the city will potentially reduce negative evaluations of Bush and Blanco, it may increase the negative evaluation of Nagin:

  V. Attribution of blame toward non-evacuees will lower evaluations of Mayor Nagin because he was the authority in control of the evacuation process in New Orleans.

We begin by examining a simple two-variable contingency table to explore the relationship between attributions of blame and evaluations of leaders (see Table 5.3). Recall that nearly all of our respondents (99 percent) agreed with one of the primary attributions, and 94 percent agreed with multiple statements. However, by comparing the attribution measures for each respondent, we can determine whether the respondent held a dominant frame. These dominant frames should correlate with leadership evaluations in ways that are consistent with our hypotheses. We focus on the four items that used the identical agree-disagree scale so that we can generate a new variable to indicate which if any of the frames dominated for each respondent. The rows in Table 5.3 show the groupings of respondents who held different dominant attribution. For example, the first row shows the mean evaluations of Bush, Blanco, and Nagin for respondents who had greater agreement that the national government was to blame compared to any of the other three attributions (blaming nature, blaming criminal activities, and blaming non-evacuees). The percentage of respondents who fell into each grouping is listed in the first column in parentheses. This shows that blaming the national government was the dominant frame in our sample, with 24 percent of people agreeing more with this frame than all others. Another 22 percent placed the highest blame with the national government attribution but assigned equal blame with one or more additional attributions. Taken together, the national

TABLE 5.3. *Mean Evaluations of Bush, Blanco, and Nagin by Dominant Attribution Frame*

	Mean Evaluation of President Bush	Mean Evaluation of Governor Blanco	Mean Evaluation of Mayor Nagin
Dominant Attribution Frame (Percent of Respondents)			
Blame U.S. gov't most (24%)	.30 (213)	.95 (201)	1.13(208)
Blame nature of storm most (8%)	1.43 (67)	.74 (64)	.79 (64)
Blame criminal behavior most (9%)	1.16 (74)	.75 (67)	.97 (72)
Blame non-evacuees most (12%)	1.29 (103)	.73 (98)	.76 (97)
Blame U.S. gov't and another source equally (22%)	.55 (195)	1.08 (181)	1.08 (182)
Blame multiple sources equally, *but not* U.S. gov't (21%)	1.48 (187)	.72 (177)	.76 (171)
Blame all four equally (4%)	.89 (33)	1.38 (31)	1.56 (30)

Notes: N is in parentheses. The dominant attribution frame was determined by comparing the level of agreement for each attribution to determine which had the greatest level of agreement. Categories are mutually exclusive and exhaustive.

government receives almost a majority of dominant attributions. However, we also see that just over half of the public held a dominant frame that placed blame outside of the national government.

We turn our attention to examining whether attribution patterns were consequential for leader evaluations. We expect that those who believed the national government was most to blame will evaluate President Bush negatively, but we also hypothesize that acceptance of the other attributions might improve Bush's evaluations as he is let off the hook for the negative outcome in New Orleans. These results are consistent with our hypotheses. People who blamed national government were the least favorable toward President Bush, with a mean evaluation of only .30. His evaluation increased slightly to .55 ($p < .001$) when we consider those who assigned equal blame to the national government along with another attribution, and the evaluation improved to .89 (p < .01) for the small group of individuals who equally agreed with all four attributions (p < .10).[2] However, it is clear that Bush's evaluations are the strongest when the dominant attributions focus on causes outside of the national government.

Conversely, Governor Blanco and Mayor Nagin receive the highest marks when individuals agreed with the attribution of blame to the national government and the lowest marks when the primary frame was something other than that. Those who held a dominant frame that blamed nature or the residents of New Orleans held lower evaluations for state and local leaders than for Bush. These results may hint at federalist effects similar to those we saw in earlier tables. Because the governor and mayor were proximally closer to the victims and responsible at a very direct level for evacuating the area and securing it immediately after the storm, their evaluations were lower when these were the primary frames. However, it is unclear why they should be lower when the nature of the storm was the dominant frame. At the same time, the table clearly supports our primary expectation that blame shifts among levels of government influence evaluations. When the U.S. national government was seen as culpable for not getting aid in quickly after the storm, we find the president was punished more in his evaluations than state and local leaders. It appears that primary frames have consequences for public opinion toward leaders and that individuals differentiate among attributions and use that information to form judgments of responsibility.

EMPIRICAL MODELS AND RESULTS

The bivariate results are suggestive, but do the attributions have expected effects after we control for all attributions and include other plausible controls? Table 5.4 shows select coefficients from an ordered-probit model that tests the hypotheses that we outlined earlier in the chapter.[3] We used an ordered-probit analysis because our dependent

---

[2] Difference-of-means tests were used to compare each group to the baseline of those who blame national government the most. Probabilities are based on two-tailed significance tests.

[3] We include a dummy variable in the models in this chapter for those whose response to the national guard knowledge question that they "don't know" because that is a viable and honest response on a political knowledge question and it has been shown that the option "don't know" captures personality traits (Mondak 2001).

TABLE 5.4. *Select Ordered-Probit Coefficients from Models of Evaluations of Leaders*

	President Bush	Louisiana Governor Blanco	New Orleans Mayor Nagin
Blame nature	0.119***	0.130***	0.084***
Blame national government	−0.212***	0.154***	0.118***
Blame criminal behavior	0.050*	0.031	0.006
Blame non-evacuees	0.012	−0.022	−0.062**
State failed to call for help	−0.085*	−0.366***	−0.278***
Deploy guard, correct answer (state)	0.055	−0.249**	−0.259**
Party ID (strong Republican is highest)	0.157***	−0.056**	−0.034
Angry	−0.168***	−0.043	−0.037
Anxiety	−0.081	0.049	0.096
N	637	606	609

***p < .01; ** p <. 05; *p < .10, two-tailed tests.

Notes: Dependent variables are four-point evaluations of performance during Hurricane Katrina. See report of full model results with all controls included in Table E.1 in Appendix E.

variable – leader evaluation – is a four-category ordinal variable. The primary categories in the model mirror the five attributions that we examined in Chapter 4 and the respondents' knowledge about the lines of authority in calling for National Guard troops. Of course, an important control in our model is partisanship because, as Chapter 4 demonstrated, there is a partisan component to attributing blame, and we also know that it has a strong influence on evaluations. We discuss and compare coefficients in the first section of results, then turn to an examination of predicted probabilities to better assess the substance of our findings. The predicted probabilities are especially helpful in teasing out the relative contribution of partisanship and attribution to the evaluation of leaders. Table 5.4 also shows coefficients for anxiety and anger, but we hold off discussing them until later in the chapter when we elaborate on the role of emotion in evaluating leaders.

The full table of results with all controls included is presented in the appendix to this chapter. We controlled for several alternative causes, including political knowledge, political ideology, education, gender, race, socioeconomic status, and age. We also controlled for factors specific to the context of this time period, such as whether the respondent knew a victim of the hurricane and whether he or she was attentive to news about Hurricane Rita, a storm that battered Texas only one month after Katrina. The latter serves an important control because the media used Rita as a comparison case for Katrina. Bush was lauded as responding much better to Rita than to Katrina, so respondents attentive to coverage of Rita may have positively updated their evaluations of the president. However, Governor Blanco and Mayor Nagin were negatively compared to the performance of Texas state and local officials. We have no other a priori expectations about the controls, except in regard to ideology, because of its close correlation with partisanship, and for the race variable. Ideology is coded so that a higher score represents a more conservative respondent, so we expect a positive relationship for Republican Bush and a negative relationship for Democrats Blanco and Nagin. Mayor Nagin, a black mayor, was very visible in coverage, so social identity may shape evaluations. In addition, most of the victims portrayed in the media were black. As in Chapter 4, we may see additional effects of race if this variable captures a degree of empathy and emotion not picked up in our other variables. However, given that we have included attributions and emotion in our models, we may not see significantly different attitudes between blacks and non-blacks.

Attributions of Blame Results

Generally, with regard to our attribution variables, we find strong support for our hypotheses. For each executive, blaming nature works as expected by providing some amount of political cover. Holding constant other attributions and controls, individuals who agree more strongly that nature was to blame were more likely to evaluate leaders positively. The results, consistent across all three leaders, suggest that their strategy of emphasizing the overwhelming nature of this particular disaster was effective in justifying and excusing the outcome. For President Bush, this strategy was especially helpful because blaming nature helped to offset the negative effects of blaming the national government. It is worth noting that although blaming nature and blaming the national government are inversely related, 36 percent of those who agreed that the national government was to blame also agreed with the attribution related to the nature of the storm. As a result, for a considerable number of people, blaming nature blunted the impact of blaming the government. Likewise, blaming nature helped to offset the attributions of blame to state and local officials as well. Our results seem to indicate that when leaders can convince Americans that they are faced with unusually challenging circumstances, they become sympathetic characters worthy of support, not villains to be punished.

Not surprisingly, greater agreement with the blame national government attribution had a negative effect on evaluations of President Bush, but importantly it had a positive effect on evaluations of both Governor Blanco and Mayor Nagin. This, clearly, is a federalism effect: Blaming one branch of government reduces the impact on evaluations to other levels of government. We also see additional evidence of the effect of federalism through the variable tapping knowledge about lines of authority in disasters. Those who knew that the state executive is in charge of deploying National Guard troops held lower evaluations of both Blanco and Nagin. We hypothesized that these would affect Blanco, but not Nagin. However, it seems that respondents do not clearly distinguish between state and local officials. The effect of this variable for President Bush was positive, as we predicted, but it was not statistically significant. The bivariate results that we saw earlier in the chapter showing that Bush had lower evaluations when respondents believed that FEMA was responsible for activating the National Guard do not emerge as strongly after we control for attributions and other factors.

However, we did not see the same clear federalist pattern in evaluations for the state blame attribution. We hypothesized that the state's failure to call for help would negatively affect Governor Blanco and Mayor Nagin, and it did. Importantly, the leader most hurt by this attribution was Governor Blanco, but Mayor Nagin's support also dropped precipitously. We expected this due to his position in the chain of command for disaster management. But we also expected Bush to benefit from assignment of blame to the state level. The coefficient for Bush is negative, but weak, with only marginal significance ($p < .10$). Thus, it appears that he did not reap positive benefits from state attributions of blame as we expected, but he was not really hurt by them either. This may be due to the fact that he was the ultimate leader in this scenario and so could not benefit from state failures that were largely borne out of the crisis and the lack of infrastructure. As the pinnacle leader, perhaps he should have known that the state needed help regardless of whether local leaders called. Most importantly, the pattern of coefficients across attributions of government and nature supports our claim that blame shifts help excuse leaders' actions.

We turn now to an examination of the effects of the societal breakdown attributions. Overall, blaming the residents of New Orleans for the part that they played in the chaotic aftermath had little effect on leader evaluation. The coefficients were near zero, and only two were statistically significant. For Bush, blaming criminal activity after the storm led to an increase in positive evaluations, but the same attribution had no effect for Governor Blanco or Mayor Nagin. On the other hand, blaming non-evacuees had no effect on Bush or Blanco, but negatively affected Mayor Nagin. The latter effect was expected because Nagin came under fire for failing to use all available means to empty the city before the storm hit.

Independent and Combined Effects of Party Identification and Attributions

One of the facets of Hurricane Katrina that makes it an especially potent case is that leaders at different levels of government were from different political parties. In the last chapter, this permitted us to see how emotion reduced the connection between party and blame attribution at both the state and the national level. In this chapter, this aspect allows us to examine the relative size of the effects of partisanship and blame attributions. Theoretically, partisanship should work to maintain higher evaluations of in-party members even when they are attributed with blame, and we see evidence of this in the coefficients presented in Table 5.4. Partisanship, in this case, is a seven-point scale ranging from strong Democrat to strong Republican. Respondents who score higher on this variable are much more likely to evaluate Republican President Bush positively and much less likely to evaluate Democratic Governor Blanco positively. Party identification was negative but insignificant for evaluations of Mayor Nagin. Media cues pertaining to party seemed to be slightly stronger for Blanco than for Nagin, which may account for this difference. For Bush and Blanco, though, partisanship played a clear role in evaluating performance, and the effect was strongest for President Bush, the political figure with whom the public was most familiar prior to the storm.

Was partisanship more important than blame attribution in determining evaluations? The answer to this question speaks to the broader interpretation of the role of extraordinary events in society. If blame attributions substantially influence evaluations, compared to party identification, then our argument that catastrophes serve as a mechanism of generating collective consensus is more compelling. In Tables 5.5 and 5.6, we report the predicted probability of evaluations of all three leaders based on the full model reported in Appendix E.

To generate the predicted probabilities, we held constant the values of all independent variables in the model and then varied the values of partisanship and blame attribution agreement. In this way, we can see how the acceptance of attributions in conjunction with the powerful predisposition of party alters blame judgments. For each leader, we compare four archetype respondents: RD is for strong *Republicans* who strongly *disagreed* with the listed attribution of blame, RA is the designation for strong *Republicans* who strongly *agreed* with the attribution, DD represents strong *Democrats* who strongly *disagreed* with the attribution, and DA is for strong *Democrats* who strongly *agreed* with the attribution. We can compare the relative effects by comparing the predicted probabilities across archetypes. For example, the difference between archetype RA and RD shows the effect of the blame attribution, holding party identification constant at strong Republican. However, comparing RA and DA shows the effect of partisan difference, holding constant blame attributions. For each row, the evaluation category that has the highest-valued predicted probability is the predicted survey response from the archetype individual. For example, in the case of evaluations of President Bush, a strong Republican who strongly disagreed that nature was to blame for the destruction in New Orleans, would have been most likely to respond "fair" to the survey question evaluating the president's performance.

We begin by focusing on attribution to the overwhelming nature of the storm, because it affected performance measures the same way for each leader. Disagreement, or rejection of the attribution, led to lower evaluations of President Bush, Governor Blanco, and Mayor Nagin, whereas agreement or acceptance of the attribution led to higher evaluations. In each case, the predicted probability is highest in the "fair"

TABLE 5.5. *Predicted Probabilities of Evaluations of Bush, Blanco, and Nagin, by Party and Attribution to Nature*

	Evaluation of President Bush			
	Excellent	Good	Fair	Poor
(RD) Strong Republican, strongly *disagree* nature to blame	.03	.17	.46	.34
(RA) Strong Republican, strongly *agree* nature to blame	.08	.36	.43	.13
(DD) Strong Democrat, strongly *disagree* nature to blame	.00	.04	.26	.70
(DA) Strong Democrat, strongly *agree* nature to blame	.01	.13	.43	.43
	Evaluation of Governor Blanco			
(RD) Strong Republican, strongly *disagree* nature to blame	.00	.07	.33	.60
(RA) Strong Republican, strongly *agree* nature to blame	.03	.22	.45	.30
(DD) Strong Democrat, strongly *disagree* nature to blame	.02	.12	.40	.46
(DA) Strong Democrat, strongly *agree* nature to blame	.06	.31	.44	.19
	Evaluation of Mayor Nagin			
(RD) Strong Republican, strongly *disagree* nature to blame	.02	.14	.32	.52
(RA) Strong Republican, strongly *agree* nature to blame	.06	.25	.36	.33
(DD) Strong Democrat, strongly *disagree* nature to blame	.03	.19	.34	.44
(DA) Strong Democrat, strongly *agree* nature to blame	.09	.30	.35	.26

Notes: The predicted probabilities were generated using Clarify 2.1 (Tomz, Wittenberg, and King 2003) and the full models in Table E.1 in Appendix E with all other values set at their median or mode. Party ID comparisons were made by setting the seven-point party ID variable to 1 for strong Democrat and 7 for strong Republican. Attributions of blame to nature were set to their minimum and maximum values.

or "poor" category. The chance that a strong partisan respondent from either party would evaluate any of the leaders as "good" or "excellent" was quite small. However, we also see that that Republicans, overall, had higher predicted probabilities of evaluating Bush positively compared to Democrats, as we would expect. The predicted probability

TABLE 5.6. *Predicted Probabilities of Evaluations of Bush, Blanco, and Nagin, by Party and Attribution to National Government*

	Bush Evaluation			
	Excellent	**Good**	**Fair**	**Poor**
(RD) Strong Republican, strongly *disagree* national government to blame	.18	.45	.32	.05
(RA) Strong Republican, strongly *agree* national government to blame	.01	.16	.46	.37
(DD) Strong Democrat, strongly *disagree* national government to blame	.04	.24	.47	.25
(DA) Strong Democrat, strongly *agree* national government to blame	.00	.03	.25	.72
	Blanco Evaluation			
(RD) Strong Republican, strongly *disagree* national government to blame	.00	.05	.27	.68
(RA) Strong Republican, strongly *agree* national government to blame	.02	.20	.45	.33
(DD) Strong Democrat, strongly *disagree* national government to blame	.00	.09	.36	.55
(DA) Strong Democrat, strongly *agree* national government to blame	.04	.29	.45	.22
	Nagin Evaluation			
(RD) Strong Republican, strongly *disagree* national government to blame	.01	.10	.28	.61
(RA) Strong Republican, strongly *agree* national government to blame	.06	.25	.36	.33
(DD) Strong Democrat, strongly *disagree* national government to blame	.02	.14	.31	.53
(DA) Strong Democrat, strongly *agree* national government to blame	.09	.30	.35	.26

Notes: The predicted probabilities were generated using Clarify 2.1 (Tomz, Wittenberg, and King 2003) and the full models in Table E.1 in Appendix E with all other values set at their median or mode. Party ID comparisons were made by setting the seven-point party ID variable to 1 for strong Democrat and 7 for strong Republican. Attributions of blame to national government were set to their minimum and maximum values.

that a strong Democrat (DD or DA) would assess Bush's performance as poor exceeded the probability that a strong Republican (RD or RA) would do so by a margin of at least two to one. In fact, the probability that a strong Democrat who disagreed with the blame nature attribution would evaluate Bush as poor was an impressively high .70.

Importantly, Table 5.5 shows that the substantive effects of attribution of blame are sizable. Attribution of blame to nature appropriately increases or decreases the predicted probabilities for Bush's performance levels, but the effect is greatest for strong Democrats. When strong Republicans disagree strongly with the blame nature frame, they have a .34 chance of evaluating Bush poorly, but when they agree strongly with the blame nature frame, those odds drop to only .13, a difference of .21. Strong Democrats who strongly disagree with the blame nature frame have a .70 chance of rating Bush's performance as poor, but when they blame Mother Nature, that chance drops to .43, a difference of .27.

Because Governor Blanco and Mayor Nagin are Democrats, we expect to see that strong Democrats are more favorable to them than strong Republicans, but we also expect to see agreement with the attribution to nature to have a smaller effect for them than for Republicans. In other words, the differences in probabilities for DD and DA types should be smaller than the difference between RD and RA types. The second and third sets of probabilities in Table 5.5 show that this is indeed the case. Democrats who disagree with the blame nature frame were .27 more likely than Democrats who agreed with it to evaluate Blanco poorly. The gap for strong Republicans was slightly greater, at .30. The pattern is the same for Mayor Nagin, although less pronounced. Strong Democrats who strongly disagree with the blame nature frame had a .44 chance of rating Nagin poor, while strong Democrats who strongly agree with the blame nature frame had only a .26 chance of rating Nagin poor, a difference of .18. This, however, is the same sized difference as observed between Republicans who agreed and disagreed and statistically indistinguishable. The less-pronounced results for Mayor Nagin stem, no doubt, from the weaker effects for party identification in the model.

Table 5.6 examines the same type of comparisons, but focuses on differences in agreement with the national government blame attribution. This table shows the probabilities for each executive's evaluation for strong Democratic and strong Republican respondents when respondents fall at the minimum and maximum for the blame national government attribution. We hypothesized and found that those who accepted this frame were more likely to punish President Bush but reward Governor Blanco and Mayor Nagin. Blaming the national government led to a direct link for evaluating the president and, indirectly, justified the difficulties that state and local leaders had in responding to the crisis.

The first set of evaluation probabilities shows that strong Republicans who strongly disagreed with the attribution were substantially more likely to see President Bush in a favorable light than those who strongly agreed. Republicans who disagreed had only a .05 chance of evaluating Bush's performance as poor, while those who strongly agreed had a .37 chance. Notably, when the national government blame frame is rejected by strong Republicans, there is a .63 probability that they rate President Bush's performance as "good" or better. In fact, the most likely survey response for this category was "good." In contrast, strong Republicans who accepted the attribution were only .17 more likely to rate his performance "good" or "excellent," and the predicted response category for this group was "poor."

Strong Democrats who strongly disagreed with national government blame frame had only a .25 chance of evaluating Bush as "poor." This value is much larger than for strong Republicans (RD), but strong Democrats (DD) had many reasons to dislike Bush even before Katrina hit. Indeed, the most likely response for a strong Democrat who disagreed with the frame was only "fair." But, accepting the blame the national government frame shifted the most likely response category from "fair" to "poor." Agreement with attribution of blame for strong Republicans shifted the expected categorical response from "good" to "poor."

These results suggest an important role for attributions in dampening the power of predispositions, especially in crisis conditions. The intense information environment enables citizens to interpret facts and make judgments, even when those judgments go against their predispositions. Once an attribution is accepted, responsibility judgments of punishment are forthcoming and harsh, even when the target is someone typically admired.

Under the probabilities for Bush, we examine the effects of the same blame question for Governor Blanco and Mayor Nagin. In this case, however, blaming the national government had a positive influence on their evaluations. The more that respondents' blamed the federal government, the less likely they were to rate the performance of state and local officials "poor." The results in Table 5.6 show that strong

Democrats who strongly agree with the blame the national government frame were much less likely to evaluate Blanco's performance as "poor," the predicted probability being only .22. Strong Democrats, however, who strongly disagree with the frame were most likely to evaluate her performance as "poor," with a probability of .55. Strong Republicans who rejected the blame the federal government frame were most likely (.68) to evaluate the governor as "poor," but those who agree with the frame have only a .33 chance of rating her "poor." The results for Mayor Nagin are very similar to those for the governor. The difference between strong Democrats who strongly disagree and strongly agree with this attribution is .27, whereas it is .28 for strong Republicans. Attributions of blame clearly influence attitudes even for strong partisans.

Other Results

In terms of controls not presented in the tables, we find that conservatives are more favorable to President Bush, but ideology makes no difference in evaluations of Governor Blanco or Mayor Nagin. Greater attentiveness to Hurricane Rita led to more positive evaluations of President Bush, but made no difference to the evaluations of Blanco or Nagin. More educated individuals were likely to evaluate Bush more negatively, but education did not matter for Blanco or Nagin. Gender positively influenced evaluations of Blanco and Nagin, but not Bush.

Race also played a role in shaping evaluations of leaders. African Americans had a special connection to the storm given that visuals from the storm cued racial identity, particularly in New Orleans. Research on group identity demonstrates that group cohesiveness influences preferences for public policies, candidates, and other opinions (Chong and Rogers 2005; Federico and Luks 2005; Gay 2004; Haider-Markel, Delehanty, and Beverlin 2007; Huddy and Feldman 2006a, 2006b; Sigelman and Welch 1994; Stets and Burke 2000; Tate 1993). In this case, group identity and greater sympathy for in-group victims leads to an increased awareness of the situation and to more negative evaluations of government leaders. Blacks, however, focused their resentment – independent of their attributions, knowledge, and emotion – on President Bush. Blacks were about one-sixth, or .19, more likely to evaluate Bush's performance as "poor" than non-blacks. They, however, did not hold different evaluations of Blanco or Nagin than other minorities or whites.

DIRECT EFFECTS OF ANXIETY AND ANGER ON EVALUATION

Early on, we focused on how anxiety produced by the storm affected opinions. In this chapter, we highlight the theoretical importance of anger in regard to punishment and its difference from anxiety. In Chapter 2, we outlined the differences between the two emotions and explained why anger and anxiety operate distinctly on public opinions. Anxiety serves to trigger an affective process of evaluating and accepting information, whereas anger serves to catalyze blame into actions. Psychologically, evaluations are a means of rewarding and punishing leaders. The emotion of anger prompts a desire to punish and therefore should influence evaluations. This effect should be observable and distinct from anxiety in empirical models of evaluation. Following Hurricane Katrina, evaluations of leadership, particularly that of President Bush, present a clear target for the public's feelings of anger and we should find that citizens who feel greater anger are more likely to want to punish those responsible. Anxiety, in contrast, does not have obvious implications for evaluations. Anxiety is associated with preferences for risk-averting actions (Huddy, Feldman, and Cassese 2007), but evaluation does not fit into a risk-averse framework. We cannot clearly say that someone who is anxious should hold more or less negative opinions of his or her elected leaders. Of course, anxious people on a search for more information in this particular context would have encountered negative information about all three actors, but they also encountered offsetting information excusing the actors. Therefore, we argue theoretically that anxiety should have no influence on evaluation given that attributions of blame are controlled for in the model. Rather, we expect anxiety to work through attributions of blame while anger operates more directly. We include anxiety in our models to demonstrate how these emotions operate differently and to strengthen the evidence for our theoretical argument. Thus, with regard to emotion we hypothesize:

VI. Citizens who expressed more anger over what happened in New Orleans are more likely to punish more severely and reduce their overall evaluations of elected leaders.

VII. Citizens who expressed more anxiety should not be any different from citizens who express no anxiety on their overall evaluations of elected leaders.

Table 5.2 presented the coefficients for anger and anxiety for all three leaders. Recall that anger is measured on a four-point scale ranging from not angry (0) to extremely angry (3). As we expected, the model results showed no effect on anxiety for any of the executive leaders, and we see that only the model for President Bush had a statistically significant coefficient for this variable. The lack of an anger effect for Blanco and Nagin is not surprising. The mayor was the only actor who appears responsible for failures before the storm, and he and the governor were unable to respond after the storm because of the storm's overwhelming destruction to infrastructure and communications. Therefore, neither anger nor anxiety influences evaluations of the state and local government's performance. However, for Bush, we see strong effects for anger. We find that the predicted likelihood of a poor evaluation for Bush increases .20 when we move from not at all angry to extremely angry. Respondents who were not angry had a predicted likelihood of .32 of rating Bush as poor, but this increased to .51 among respondents who felt extremely angry at what happened in New Orleans.

CONDITIONAL EFFECTS OF ANGER ON EVALUATION

In the general theory that we outlined in Chapter 2, we argued that we should see a more nuanced effect of anger.[4] Petersen (2010) suggests that anger is an action variable, thus we argue it should serve to enhance one's desire to "act" on attributions by translating them into lowered evaluations. In other words, anger should condition the application of blame attributions by strengthening the connection between attributions and punishments. This means that anger should augment the effect that blaming the national government had on the evaluations

---

[4] We also considered whether anxiety worked in a similar way as in Chapter 4, but found no significant results, and thus do not present these models. Although the theoretical expectations regarding anxiety also suggest that it may have both direct and interactive effects by reducing the influence of partisanship in evaluations, there is no evidence of such moderation in evaluations. This seems to indicate that anxiety works primarily through moderating partisanship during the assignment-of-blame phase, and the blame attributions carry forward to evaluations. However, there is no evidence of a direct or interactive effect of anxiety on attributions. We do, however, take up this issue again when we examine policy preferences in Chapter 7, where we see separate direct and interactive effects of anxiety in preferences for policy.

TABLE 5.7. *Comparing Coefficients across Performance Models of Bush with and without the Angry Interaction*

	Evaluate Bush	Interaction: Evaluate Bush
Blame nature	.119***	.119***
Blame national government	−.212***	−.171***
Blame crime	.050*	.048*
Blame evacuees	.012	.008
State failed to call for help	−.085*	−.099*
Deploy guard correct answer	.055	.058
Angry	−.168***	.024
Anxiety	−.081	−.088
Partisanship	.157***	.156***
Angry × Blame National Government		−.042**
N	637	637

***p < .01; **p < .05; *p < .10; two-tailed tests.

Notes: Dependent variables are four-point evaluations of performance during Hurricane Katrina. See report of full model results with all controls included in Table E.2 in Appendix E.

of President Bush. To test this, we ran a model that included the direct effect of anger and the multiplicative interaction of anger and blame toward the national government, as well as all of the controls discussed earlier.[5]

Table 5.7 shows the results for all of the primary independent variables of interest for the original Bush performance evaluation model and for the interactive models. First, it is important to note that our attribution variables are largely unchanged. This is true for "blame nature," "blame crime," "blame evacuees," and "state failed to call for help." There is a small dampening of the "blame national government" effect, but not very much given that the interaction with anger is also negative, indicating that it bolsters the negative effect of the blame attribution. The net effect of blaming the national government is greater among those most angered by events in New Orleans.

To better visualize the effects of anger and attribution on evaluations of Bush, we present a comparison of the effect of attributing

[5] We also tried a fully interactive model, where angry was multiplied by all of the attributions. The coefficients and model parameters were largely the same, but the standard errors were increasingly problematic due to multicollinearity.

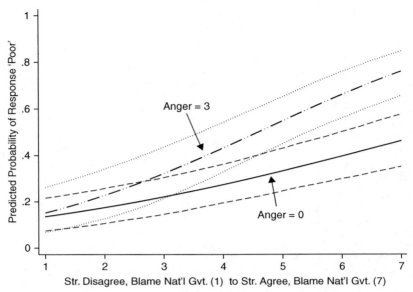

FIGURE 5.1. Effect of Attribution of Blame to National Government on the Probability of a "Poor" Evaluation of President Bush, Conditioned by Level of Anger.

blame to national government for non-angry and very angry individuals. In Figure 5.1, we graph the predicted probability that a respondent would rate President Bush's performance as "poor" – the bottom of the evaluation scale. The top line in this graph is for individuals who scored the top value on our angry measure, meaning they rated themselves as "extremely" angry. The bottom line predicts probabilities for those who expressed no anger in response to what had happened in New Orleans. All other variables, including attributions and party identification, were held constant across the two groups. In many cases, we are interested in the effect on the tail of the distribution, so we must also estimate the standard errors at each point to know when an emotional person is different from a non-emotional person (Brambor, Clark, and Golder 2006). The solid lines represent the point estimates of the effects and the dotted lines represent the 90 percent confidence intervals around each solid line. When the dotted lines for each solid line do not pass over each other, it means there are significant differences between very angry and non-angry people.

It is clear from the graph in Figure 5.1 that interaction between anger and blaming the national government is quite strong. Anger is a powerful catalyst for transforming blame attribution into political evaluation. For respondents at the low end of the attribution scale – those who disagree that national government was to blame – there is little difference in the chance of evaluating Bush's performance as "poor." They are equally unlikely to do so. But, as we move up the scale, we begin to see separation between those who were angry and those who were not. This difference is not statistically significant until the level of blame attribution reaches 5, which is the first score on the measure that indicates agreement with the blame frame. But among those who agree at any level (5, 6, or 7), angry attributors are much more punitive in their evaluations than non-angry attributors. It appears that the anger emotion is strongly linked to the desire to punish responsible actors and consequently interacts with the "blame government" attribution.

SUMMARY AND CONCLUSIONS

Overall, the results in this chapter make several important points. First, performance evaluations of elected leaders are influenced directly by attributions of blame. Attributions that are directly tied to the leader's role as executive are strongly related to their performance, whereas attributions that are tied to circumstances reduce blame. Blaming nature increased evaluation of all executive actors, while blaming the national government was negatively associated with poorer evaluations of Bush but better evaluations of Blanco and Nagin. Failure of the state government largely influenced the state and local executive and generally had no effect on Bush. These results suggest that citizens in a federal system are able to disentangle differences in responsibility across levels of government and lay blame appropriately once they make judgments. When one places blame on particular components of the story (that is, the national government, nature, or victims), that attribution has a direct influence on government leaders. When people believe that government or a certain segment of government is responsible, they punish those government leaders in charge. When people believe that nature is responsible, they feel better about their government leaders' response. Furthermore, accepting an attribution that makes leaders of one's own party culpable leads to lower evaluations of responsible in-group members. Although predispositions are important to evaluations and for which attributions are accepted and rejected, attributions of responsibility are also directly important and influence performance evaluation.

We also find that there are direct effects of anger for Bush, but not for Blanco or Nagin. This appears to be tied to the fact that the anger variable is linked to a national context and not a state, local, or victim context. Future research needs to expand this line of reasoning with multiple emotion questions that pick up anger and anxiety across levels of government to determine the effects of lower levels actors, such as the governor and the mayor.

Importantly, we saw a strong interaction effect between anger and blaming the national government, consistent with the argument that attributions work in concert with the emotion of anger to punish individuals responsible. This is an important theoretical contribution, given that most studies have relied on direct effects (although see Petersen 2010) and no studies have examined this effect's relationship to evaluation of political leaders.

Overall, the story we see here is a positive one for citizens. Citizens connect specific types of attributions of blame to appropriate leaders. Therefore, we find blaming the evacuees affects Nagin, but not Bush or Blanco, and that blaming the national government affects evaluations of Bush negatively but increases evalutions of Blanco and Nagin. The important conclusion from this is that citizens can discriminate in a complex environment with multiple and often competing messages to determine, based upon their understanding of the situation and their predispositions, who is responsible. Citizens therefore sift through, examine, reject, and accept different attributions of blame, and these attributions inform their evaluations of leaders, allowing citizens to hold their leaders accountable and perform their democratic responsibility.

6

Attributions of Blame, Political Efficacy, and Confidence in Government

During normal times, most government activity goes unnoticed by the average citizen. Government officials sanction and oversee a vast array of activities designed to ensure peaceable commerce along with the health and welfare of citizens. Citizens, at least in stable democracies such as the United States, expect government to serve in this capacity and live their lives accordingly. In fact, the preamble to the U.S. Constitution argues that the purpose of government is to "form a more perfect union, establish justice, ensure domestic tranquility, provide for the common defense, promote the general welfare, and secure the blessings of liberty." However, extraordinary events are, by nature, moments that disrupt tranquility and require rapid government response to return society to a state of normalcy. In these moments, the public is shaken from their daily routines as they are confronted by unusual circumstances and their assumptions about government's role in society are tested. These circumstances provide an opportunity for citizens to examine government and its effectiveness in promoting the general welfare. When government fails, we argue that this has consequences to beliefs in the responsiveness of government and external efficacy, as well as citizen confidence in government's ability to manage other crises.

The collective, emotional nature of extraordinary events imbues them with power to widely influence opinions connected to democratic stability and legitimacy. Dahl (1971) argues that one of five necessary public beliefs for the development and maintenance of democratic societies is confidence in the ability of government to deal with problems effectively. Confidence is a key element to a well-functioning democracy. Widespread feelings of external efficacy, or the belief that government is responsive to citizens, promote regime stability by keeping the public committed to the existing democratic governing structure; its absence can lead to democratic instability and economic insecurity in the wake of citizen discontent (Abramson and Aldrich 1982; Citrin and Green 1986; Erber and Lau 1990; Ginsberg 1982; Pollock 1983). Even if low public confidence in government does not topple the government, it can still have substantial implications for the viability and health of a democratic society, the willingness of citizens to follow their leaders, and the eagerness of citizens to comply with government demands (Barber 1983; Easton 1965; Lawrence 1997; Levi 1998; Scholz and Lubell 1998; Scholz and Pinney 1995; Tyler 1990). Therefore, it is important to understand whether and how extraordinary events shape broader confidence in government.

In this chapter, we examine how affective attributions of blame influence external political efficacy and confidence in government to manage different types of crises. Following Hurricane Katrina, many in the media and the public perceived the national government to have failed in its primary obligation to care for its citizens and keep them safe. At the same time, there was variation in the strength of attributions of blame among individuals, with some excusing government for reasons related to the nature of the catastrophe, the behavior of victims, or the actions of other levels of government. Therefore, Hurricane Katrina is a good test case to see whether attributions of blame that target national government translated into lowered expectations among citizens.

The case of Hurricane Katrina provides an especially favorable environment to connect attributions to broader themes of governance. Simply put, government did not deal with the immediate aftermath of the storm effectively, and the media communicated that message in both subtle and pointed ways. Michael Ignatieff, writing for the *New York Times Magazine* a few short weeks after the storm, highlighted the broken contract between government and citizens:

So it is not – as some commentators claimed – that the catastrophe laid bare the deep inequalities of American society. These inequalities may have been news to some, but they were not news to the displaced people in the convention center and elsewhere. What was bitter news to them was that their claims of citizenship mattered so little to the institutions charged with their protection (Ignatieff 2005: 15).

At the time that the House Select Committee released its investigative report on Hurricane Katrina in 2006, Representative Geoff Davis (R-KY) stated, "Katrina was a national failure, an abdication of the most solemn obligation to provide for the common welfare" (Lipton 2006:1). Similar messages of how government failed to meet its fundamental obligation to citizens were echoed by elected officials, journalists, pundits, and citizen commentators for weeks, months, and even years after the storm.

In general, we argue that citizens who find government is at fault in any crisis are likely to feel less confident in government's ability to manage other crises and more likely to question government's responsiveness to its citizens. We test our general argument through analyzing survey data collected immediately after the storm as well as experimental data collected a year later. The latter test allows us to see whether Hurricane Katrina had discernible longer-term effects on public confidence in government.

PUBLIC CONFIDENCE IN GOVERNMENT

External political efficacy, confidence, or trust in government is foundational to democratic society. Low levels of trust lead to greater support for third parties (Hetherington 1999) and opposition candidates (Aberbach 1969). It also leads to preferences for local decision making over national decision making (Hetherington and Nugent 2001). Trust has important consequences for support for public institutions such as the U.S. Congress (Hetherington 1998). Not surprisingly, low trust is linked to support for public policies such as term limits (Karp 1995) and Proposition 13, the California tax revolt initiative of the 1970s (Lowery and Sigelman 1981; Sears and Citrin 1982). In addition, disaffected citizens are more likely to engage in or support political protests such as riots or sit-ins (Citrin et al. 1975).

In the context of crises, such perspectives are particularly worrisome because government needs cooperation from citizens to ensure their safety and protect their property. Trust in government has been shown to influence the public's willingness to submit to government demands, rules, and laws (Cooper, Knotts, and Brennan 2008; Tyler 1990), particularly the willingness to evacuate (Burton and Silver 2006). Moreover, scholars have shown evidence through experimental tests that cueing subjects to recall a poorly managed catastrophe – specifically Hurricane Katrina – negatively influenced their willingness to comply with government orders to evacuate (Burton and Silver 2006). In contrast, subjects reminded about the successful evacuation for Hurricane Rita were more likely to indicate willingness to evacuate.

Given these findings, it is important to consider how confidence in government and perceptions of government responsiveness are altered by emotionally jarring catastrophic events when government fails to provide needed services. Yet many questions remain about the causes of external efficacy and confidence in government (Cook and Gronke 2004). Is it a type of diffuse support for government that is largely a product of long-term factors such as early socialization, the makeup of government institutions, and long-standing attitudes toward government (Bowler and Donovan 2002; Easton and Dennis 1967; Hero and Tolbert 2004)? Or, is it explained by short-term forces such as political events, election outcomes, the performance of the sitting incumbent, or policy choices made by government (Atkeson and Carrillo 2007; Banducci and Karp 2003; Citrin 1974; Citrin and Green 1986; Craig et al. 2006; Miller, Goldenberg, and Erbring 1979)?

It certainly seems plausible that both short- and long-term factors matter to the evaluation of government, and prior research supports this. For example, one well-accepted finding shows that individuals who supported the "winning side" in an election are better reflected by government and, therefore, feel more efficacious than those who supported the losing side (see Banducci and Karp 2003; Craig et al. 2006). Likewise, those supporting the winners are more trusting of government (Banducci and Karp 2003). However, the results have been weak or mixed in research that attempted to link individual dissatisfaction with specific government policies or performance to feelings of external efficacy or trust in government (Banducci and Karp 2003; Iyengar 1980; Weissberg 1975). Recent work on short-term effects of policy output, measured by views of economic performance, produced inconsistent effects (Banducci and Karp 2003). Instead, results show that one's past efficacy is the strongest predictor of one's current efficacy (Banducci and Karp 2003; Iyengar 1980). From this body of research, we can conclude that efficacy and trust are responsive to high-salience events such as elections, but in the absence of a stimulating environment, these attitudes are relatively stable.

In a world focused on normal politics, we think that this conclusion makes a great deal of sense. Citizens, for the most part, are not well informed about politics (e.g., Delli Carpini and Keeter 1996; Kinder 1998). The day-to-day battles in Congress or the conflicts between the legislative and executive branches of government are, for most, distant, unimportant, and relatively easy to understand and interpret. This state of affairs, however, is not always the case. When crises and events of extraordinary magnitude occur, citizens tune in to take stock and evaluate the situation. Because of this, we believe that epochal events and the attributions that they produce toward government have a greater likelihood of reshaping opinions, particularly those that are typically stable, such as external efficacy or confidence in government. Moreover, anger, the emotion stimulated by assigning blame to government, might magnify the feeling that government is unresponsive to citizens and decrease feelings of confidence in the government's ability to handle future crises.

EFFICACY, CONFIDENCE, AND THE CASE
OF HURRICANE KATRINA

The aftermath of Hurricane Katrina was a direct test of the government's responsiveness to its citizens' needs. However, as evidenced in previous chapters, government culpability was not the only explanation. To determine whether government culpability matters to opinions about government responsiveness and its ability to manage another crisis, we compare the different causal attributions of blame examined previously. We examine the effects of the "blame-national-government," "societal breakdown," "nature-of-the-storm," and "state failure" attribution to see which, if any, affected efficacy and confidence. When government is viewed as the culprit for human suffering and economic loss, the assignment of blame has ramifications for citizens' belief in the government's ability to perform its most vital function of protecting citizens. However, government can be deemed

responsible only if its agents failed to do their job. If they could not fulfill their obligations because of circumstance – in the case of Katrina,
because of the overwhelming nature of the storm – then government
may not be held responsible nor should we expect to see a direct effect
on efficacy or confidence.

Given our theoretical framework, we hypothesize that those who
blame the national government will be less externally efficacious and
have less confidence in the government's ability to manage other crises
than those who do not. This is directly caused by the poor performance of the national government during Katrina and is picked up
with our measure of national government blame. The societal breakdown frames of crime and non-evacuation frames are unlikely to influence external efficacy or confidence in government because neither is
focused on national government response but on local factors related
to individual decisions. As these frames lack concrete connections
to government, we would not predict that they would lead to either
increased or decreased support.

Because the confidence measures that we outline in the next section
explicitly refer to the "U.S. national government," we do not expect
the state-level attribution measure to influence them, even though the
measure represents a specific link to poor governmental performance.
However, external efficacy, unlike confidence, is a more global measure
that does not cue actors at a specific level of government. Therefore,
it is conceivable that attributions of blame to state-level actors could
have a negative effect on efficacy. However, it is more likely that it will
have little or no effect. National government is seen as holding the
greatest authority and power, so we argue that this measure, like measures of trust, largely reflect feelings toward national-level government
(Citrin and Luks 2001).

The attribution to the overwhelming nature of the storm, however, explicitly excuses government and offers a specific alternative
for understanding the scope of the storm and the damage it caused.
Indeed, the wording of our measure of the nature-of-the-storm attribution explicitly denies government's responsibility for the outcome of
the crisis because "the damage was so unexpected and overwhelming
that no government could have adequately responded to it." In this
light, government response is excusable in the face of overwhelming

circumstances and, most importantly, was not the primary reason behind the crisis. Indeed, this is precisely the argument that President Bush and his surrogates made in several major speeches. If the public accepts that the government was not directly responsible because the nature of the storm was so overwhelming and by extension that the government was likely helpful in reducing the magnitude of the crisis, then their confidence in government might be enhanced. We saw a similar type of process in evaluations where blame directed toward nature resulted in improved evaluations for political leaders at all levels of government. In the case of external efficacy and confidence in government, we expect a similar result. The more a citizen agrees with the blame nature frame, the more likely she is to be more confident in government's ability to manage crises and protect citizens under normal conditions of crisis.

We also test the role of emotion by including both anger and anxiety as direct effects in the model and the interaction of anger with attribution of blame to national government. Our theory would expect no significant effect for anxiety, but anger and its interaction with attribution should show negative effects, such that they both lead to lower evaluations of responsiveness and confidence in government. Therefore, we hypothesize the same series of relationships for both external efficacy and confidence in government's ability to manage other crises:

I. Individuals who agreed more strongly that national government was to blame will feel *less* externally efficacious and less confident than those who disagreed.
   a. This effect will be strongest among those who feel the most angry
II. Individuals who felt that state government was to blame for not calling for enough help will feel *less* externally efficacious and less confident than those who did not.
III. Individuals who more strongly agreed that nature was to blame will feel *more* externally efficacious and more confident in government than those who disagreed.
IV. Individuals who more strongly agreed that societal breakdown was to blame should feel *no more or less* externally efficacious and *no more or less* confident than those who disagreed.

Empirical Analysis of External Efficacy

The first models use the most common measure of external efficacy to assess attitudes toward government responsiveness (see Morrell 2003): "Public officials don't care much what people like me think." The scale is seven points and the distribution across categories is as follows: strongly agree (16 percent), agree (31 percent), somewhat agree (13 percent), neither agree nor disagree (6 percent), somewhat disagree (6 percent), disagree (22 percent), and strongly disagree (6 percent). Disagreement with the statement indicates greater external efficacy, thus a higher score implies someone who is more externally efficacious. The median falls in the category of "somewhat agree," indicating that more people than not felt that government is unresponsive.

The dependent variable is ordered and categorical, so we ran an ordered-probit model to test the hypotheses outlined in the previous section. In addition, we control for a number of alternative individual-level influences that might be correlated with both the attributions and external efficacy, such as party identification, ideology, gender, race, age, economic status, and connections to the storm. These controls ensure that our attribution results are not spurious.

Education has nearly always been found to be an important factor of external efficacy; as education increases, so does external efficacy (Atkeson and Carrillo 2007; Finkel 1985; Hayes and Bean 1993; Hougland and Christenson 1983; Soss 1999; Stenner-Day and Fischle 1992). We have also included the standard variables of gender, race, and age, although the gender and race variables are only sometimes found to be important to regime support, and age may be positive, negative, or curvilinear (Abramson 1983; Atkeson and Carrillo 2007; Hayes and Bean 1993; Soss 1999).[1] We capture economic status through two dummy variables. The first captures those respondents who own a home and the second captures those respondents making under $25,000 in income per year.

Partisanship and a lack of partisanship are also important. Partisanship controls for possible differences between those who are politically aligned with the government and those who are not. Holding an affiliation with the same party that controls government

---

[1] Analysis did not indicate a curvilinear relationship, and therefore we relied on the categorical measure that we used in all of our other chapters.

suggests that individuals share many policy opinions with leaders and are more likely to be in a "winning" position politically. Those who affiliate with the out-party are in a losing position politically and therefore may be less externally efficacious. Strong partisans of the out-party feel the greatest gap between their own preferences and government outcomes, while strong partisans of the in-party feel the greatest congruency between their own preferences and government outcomes. This seems especially likely when one party controls the executive and legislative branches of government, as was the case during Hurricane Katrina. Independents, however, are less connected to the political system than partisans. Although weak and strong Democrats may differ in how responsive they believe government is when there is a Republican majority, they still have minority representation in the Congress. Independents, however, do not have even minority representation in Congress and therefore are more likely to feel less efficacious. Because we expect a linear effect from partisans, with strong Republicans the most efficacious and strong Democrats the least efficacious, we include a seven-point partisan identification scale. To control for the fact that independent, nonpartisan identifiers are the least connected to the political system, we use a dummy variable that scores a 1 for independents and 0 for everyone else. We expect partisanship to be positive and significant and the independent dummy to be negative and significant.

Results of the Empirical Analysis

We present the results of our ordered-probit models in Table 6.1. The table shows two models, one with and one without the interaction of angry and blame national government. Greater agreement with blame toward national government predicts lower external efficacy. Attributions of blame to state government and to victims had no effect on external efficacy, as expected. Although we hypothesized that those who thought that government was overwhelmed by the nature of the storm might feel sympathy toward the government's efforts to respond, the results in these models do not bear that out, but importantly, such thoughts did not hurt feelings of external efficacy.

We also considered the effects of emotion, with the expectation that anger might enhance the effects of blaming national government.

TABLE 6.1. *Ordered-Probit Models of External Efficacy*

Frame	B	SE	sig	B	SE	sig
Blame nature	−0.002	0.023		−0.002	0.023	
Blame national government	−0.058	0.031	*	−0.055	0.026	**
Blame non-evacuees	−0.032	0.024		−0.032	0.024	
Blame criminal actions	−0.015	0.022		−0.015	0.022	
State failed to call for help	−0.006	0.042		−0.007	0.042	
Angry	−0.096	0.094		−0.082	0.039	**
Anxious	0.002	0.056		0.002	0.056	
Angry × blame national government	0.003	0.017				
Black	−0.234	0.134	*	−0.234	0.134	*
N	671			671		

***p < .01; **p < .05; *p < .10, two-tailed tests.

Notes: The dependent variable is a seven-point scale, with high values indicating greater external efficacy. Full results with all control variables can be found in Table F.1 in Appendix F.

However, Model 1 in Table 6.1 shows no evidence of such an effect. The coefficient for the interaction between blaming national government and anger is positive, thus oppositely signed, but it is very near zero and the standard error is quite large. Of course, the coefficient significance test for an interaction term applies only for the marginal effect at the mean values of the model, but an investigation into the standard errors around the marginal effects of attribution for different conditioning levels of anger reveals that this effect is insignificant at other values as well (analysis is not shown). When the interaction is included in the model, the statistical significance of the direct effect of anger is greatly reduced. However, Model 2 shows that anger, independent of attributions, serves to lower efficacy. Given that we found that anger is most closely associated with blaming national government following Katrina (see Chapter 4), the direct relationship is expected and not surprising.

It is interesting to contrast this finding with the effects of anxiety, a variable that does not result from attributions of blame. Although anger directly affects efficacy, anxiety does not, and we did not expect that it would. Anxiety alerted people to seek information about events, but had no bearing on beliefs independent of attributions. With attributions and anger controlled for in the model, anxiety offers no additional predictive power. In other specifications, we examined whether anxiety moderated the influence of other variables, such as party identification, but found no evidence in support of this hypothesis. We are left to conclude two things: First, these models provide additional evidence that anger and anxiety function differently in shaping broad political attitudes; and second, anxiety offers little in the way of directional prediction on its own.

To get a better feel for the degree of influence of attributing blame to national government, we examine predicted probabilities that an individual would feel a sense of efficacy. Using the coefficients from Model 2 (Table 6.1), we generated the probabilities by setting all variables at their median value and varying the level of agreement with the "blame national government" attribution from the minimum to the maximum. The "median person" is a white, politically independent, ideologically moderate, middle-aged female with some college education who felt slightly angry at what happened in New Orleans. To simplify the presentation, we have grouped the top three categories and the bottom three categories of efficacy when making predications. This means that the probability that we report for the category "not efficacious" is the combined probability that an individual would report "somewhat agree," "agree," or "strongly agree." We did the same for the category of "efficacious," combining "somewhat disagree," "disagree," and "strongly disagree."

Our model predicts that, for the median person, when agreement with the national government blame frame was set to its lowest level, the predicted probability of agreeing with the external efficacy statement (meaning that she feels unefficacious) was .45 (see Figure 6.1). The predicted probability increases substantially to .58 when the level of agreement with the national blame attribution was at its highest value. Holding constant a wide variety of factors, the model predicts that blaming national government for poor preparation and response following Katrina substantially altered the feeling that government is responsive to the respondent's interests.

A more realistic portrayal, however, allows other variables in the model to vary in ways that are consistent with findings in prior chapters. For example, we know that blaming the national government

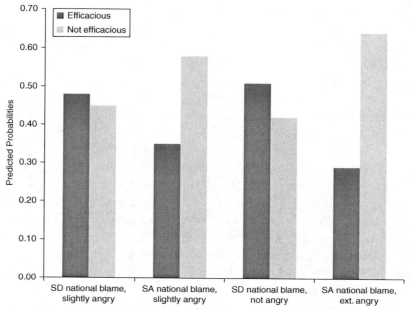

FIGURE 6.1. Predicted Probabilities of Feeling Efficacious by Levels of Blame Attribution and Anger.

was an important predictor of anger. In fact, the modal category of anger for those who strongly disagreed that government was to blame was "not angry," whereas the modal category for those who strongly agreed with the attribution was "extremely angry." When we simultaneously set the attribution level and anger to correspond to these joint conditions, we find an even larger effect. One who strongly disagrees and is not angry was only .42 likely to feel unefficacious, whereas one who strongly agreed and was extremely angry was .62 likely to feel unefficacious. In other words, a respondent had nearly a two in three chance of feeling that the government was unresponsive when she blamed national government and concurrently felt angry.

It is also important to note that several of the control variables in the model were consistent with expectations, including education, race, and party identification (see Table F.1 in Appendix F). Not surprisingly, Democrats were much less externally efficacious than Republicans. Given that Republicans felt more like they had a friend in the White House and friends in Congress, this finding is consistent with our expectations. How did the effects of party identification stack up against the effects of blaming national government? It appears that both are quite similar in magnitude. Holding constant the agreement with the national-government-blame frame at the minimum value but setting party identification to strong Democrat yields a predicted probability of feeling efficacious at .40 compared to .56 for a strong Republican – a difference of .16. The difference between strong Democrats and strong Republicans is slightly smaller among those who strongly blamed government. Strong Democrats were only .28 likely to feel efficacious, whereas strong Republicans were only .43 likely. Clearly, party identification is substantively influential. However, the effect of attributions, independent of party identification, is nearly as strong. Holding constant party identification, strong Democrats who did not blame government had a probability of .40 compared to those who maximally blamed government, who had a probability of .28. We see a similar difference for Republicans. These comparisons suggest that attribution rivals the effect of a strong predisposition in shaping attitudes. In this light, extraordinary events create a substantial pull on opinions.

EMPIRICAL RESULTS, CONFIDENCE IN GOVERNMENT

The second set of dependent variables stems from questions that tap into the inferences people made, based upon their observations of the government's performance during Katrina and Hurricane Rita, about government's ability to respond to other types of crises. These variables are a close kin to the concept of efficacy because they are indicators of confidence in a particular type of government responsiveness – responsiveness to epochal events. As such, understanding what drives variation in citizens' confidence in government for similar types of events offers us a very clear picture of how perceived government failures drive more general feelings toward government. In other words, we expect those who blame government to generalize their experience to a range of alternative crises.

We asked the following question:

Based upon what you've seen after the recent hurricanes, are you more, about the same, or less confident in the US national government's ability to respond to future crises such as: (a) other hurricanes (b) a major flu epidemic, (c) earthquakes, (d) a biological terrorist attack, such as smallpox, and (e) a nuclear terrorist attack?

We also assessed the overall level of confidence change by creating a variable that counted every time that an individual indicated "less confident" on each of the five individual measures. The count variable ranges from 0 to 5, with about two in five respondents (39.2 percent) indicating that it did not make them feel less confident on any of these crises, and just over one in five (21 percent) indicating that they were less confident on all five measures.[2]

The individual measures show that the modal response, with the exception of other hurricanes and earthquakes, was that Katrina made citizens less confident in the government's ability to perform adequately during other crises (see Table 6.2). Nearly half of respondents felt less confident in government's ability to handle a flu epidemic (46 percent), a biological attack (49 percent), or a nuclear attack (48 percent). Expectations of government fared best in the context of future earthquakes (37 percent less confident), and hurricanes (31 percent less confident). Although the modal response of "more confident" for the future hurricanes seems odd at first glance, it makes sense in light of the improvements in performance during Hurricane Rita, which formed only seventeen days after Katrina. The government's response to Rita was generally rated much more highly than its response to Katrina, so it is seems likely that the public felt that the government learned from Katrina and that this development boded well for future storms.[3]

In running the multivariate analysis, we generally include the same controls as for our models of efficacy, but with slight differences. For

[2] The full distribution of the percentage of respondents who felt less confident about different disasters is as follows: less confident about none, 39.2 percent; less confident about 1, 11.6 percent; less confident about 2, 9.8 percent; less confident about 3, 10.0 percent; less confident about 4, 8.3 percent; and less confident about 5, 21 percent.

[3] Our survey data show that Bush's performance during Rita was rated much better, with more than a majority (56 percent) rating him either "excellent" (14.6 percent) or "good" (41.5 percent), compared to his performance during Katrina, when only slightly more than a quarter (26.8 percent) rated him "excellent" (6.8 percent) or "good" (20 percent). A paired difference of means test indicates that people thought significantly more highly of Bush's performance during Rita than during Katrina (two-tail test, $p < .001$, mean Rita = 2.55, mean Katrina = 1.92). These differences attest to the dynamic nature of opinion in response to events and government actions.

TABLE 6.2. *Individual-Level Confidence in Government to Handle Future Catastrophes, in Percentages*

	Hurricanes	Flu	Earthquakes	Biological Attack	Nuclear Attack
Less confidence	31	46	37	49	48
About the same	33	36	42	33	35
More confidence	36	18	20	18	17
N	953	929	920	922	926

Notes: Data are weighted by population proportions for age and sex.

confidence in government to manage crises, we have no reason to believe that independents are less connected to the government for crisis situations. Because we expect partisanship to be the main context from which to view crisis confidence and hypothesize a linear relationship, with strong Democrats the least likely to be confident and strong Republicans the most likely, we do not include a separate dummy variable to allow for additional effect for independents. We also included the respondent's level of attentiveness to Rita. The national government demonstrated greater competence and responsiveness during Hurricane Rita. Its improvement in performance and management likely affected citizen confidence in government to manage alternative crises, especially other hurricanes. Consequently, we expect those who were most attentive to Hurricane Rita coverage to be more confident in government to handle other crises.

Empirical Results for Confidence in the Government's Ability to Handle Future Catastrophes

Table 6.3 shows select coefficients from ordered-probit models of the five confidence variables. In each case, the dependent variable was coded so that higher values indicate greater confidence in government's ability to manage a future crisis. Negative coefficients indicate that the variable *reduced* confidence in government. A full table of results with all control variables and standard errors can be found in Table F.3 of Appendix F.

Consistently, across all five models, it is clear that those who more strongly agreed that the national government was to blame for the aftermath of Katrina were likely to feel less confident in government's

TABLE 6.3. *Select Ordered-Probit Coefficients from Models of Confidence in Government to Handle Future Crises*

	Biological Attack	Earthquakes	Nuclear Attack	Flu Epidemic	Hurricane
Blame nature	0.05**	0.06**	0.06**	0.08***	0.08***
Blame national government	−0.17***	−0.09***	−0.12***	−0.09**	−0.09**
Blame non-evacuees	0.01	0.01	−0.01	−0.01	−0.02
Blame crime	0.00	0.00	0.00	0.02	0.02
Blame state failure	0.05	0.07	0.02	0.01	0.00
Angry	0.04	0.02	0.09	0.03	0.07
Anxious	0.07	0.05	0.09	−0.04	−0.01
Angry × blame national gvt	−0.01	−0.04**	−0.03*	−0.02	−0.02
N	624	622	632	631	645

***$p < .01$; **$p < .05$; *$p < .10$, two-tailed tests.

Notes: The dependent variable in each model is a three-point scale, with the high value indicating that the respondent was "more confident" in government to handle this type of crisis in the future. See report of full model results with all controls, standard errors, and cutpoints in Table F.2 in Appendix F.

ability to deal with other types of crises. We also see that blaming the overwhelming nature of the storm also worked in the hypothesized positive direction. The more that a respondent blamed the overwhelming nature of the storm, the more confident he or she was in the national government's ability to manage future crises. This seems to suggest that when people viewed the storm as overwhelming, their confidence was boosted by their perception that the government did its best under extraordinary circumstances. We also expected that the societal breakdown attributions would not influence confidence, and this expectation is supported by the model. Also, because this series of questions asks about national government, we did not expect that the state government's failure to call for enough help to influence confidence in national-level crisis management, and it did not. The latter finding provides discriminant validity for the attribution item. The state failure blame attribution works in cases we expect it to, such as influencing evaluations of state leaders, but not in cases we do not.

We hypothesized that anxiety would have no effect on confidence measures, but that anger might work to augment attributions of blame. The results for anxiety are consistent across all models, but the anger interaction with blaming national government is not consistently significant. In each case, the interaction term coefficient is signed correctly, but it is statistically significant for only two of the five models. Only the models explaining confidence during a nuclear attack and earthquake show anger augmenting the effects of attribution. In both cases, the negative coefficient for the interaction term indicates that the effect of blaming the national government is *more strongly negative* for individuals who feel greater anger. This enhanced effect is most apparent when considering the predicted probability that the respondent would fall in the category of "less confident."

Table 6.4 shows, for each type of crisis, the difference in the predicted probability between someone who strongly disagreed with the national blame attribution and someone who strongly agreed. To obtain the predicted probabilities, we set all other variables at their median values, then varied the values of the three variables: anger, national government blame attribution, and the multiplicative interaction between anger and blame. We focus specifically on two cases, individuals who were not angry (anger set to 0) and those who were extremely angry (anger set to 3). The first column shows those who were not angry and strongly disagreed with the national blame attribution. As we expect, those who do not blame the national government and were not angry had a very low probability of feeling less confident across all five types of crisis. Of course, this predicted probability increases considerably for those who strongly agreed with the blame attribution. In three of the five types of crises (biological attack, nuclear attack, and flu epidemic), respondents were more likely than not to feel less confident in government's abilities. The third column provides the difference in predicted probabilities for the first two columns. Columns four, five, and six in the table present the same comparisons, but for respondents who were extremely angry. This shows that the predicted probability was affected not only by the direct effect of blaming national government, but also the multiplicative interaction between anger and blame. The value used in the interaction term when producing the estimates in the fourth column of Table 6.4 was three because it is the product of the value of strong disagreement with the national blame frame (1) and very angry (3). In the fifth, it scores 21 because national blame is set to 7, representing

TABLE 6.4. *Predicted Probabilities of Feeling Less Confident, by Attribution Agreement and Level of Anger*

	Not Angry			Extremely Angry		
	SD Blame national gvt.	SA Blame national gvt.	Difference	SD Blame national gvt.	SA Blame national gvt.	Difference
Biological attack	0.25	0.64	0.39	0.25	0.69	0.44
Earthquakes	0.17	0.35	0.18	0.19	0.65	0.46**
Nuclear attack	0.31	0.59	0.28	0.25	0.74	0.49**
Flu epidemic	0.30	0.50	0.20	0.30	0.64	0.34
Hurricane	0.20	0.37	0.17	0.16	0.49	0.33

** Difference of differences between not angry and angry sig at p < .05.

Notes: The predicted probabilities were generated using Clarify 2.1 (Tomz, Wittenberg, and King 2003) and the full models in Table F.2 with all other values set at their median or mode. Party ID comparisons were made by setting the seven-point party ID variable to 1 for strong Democrat and 7 for strong Republican. Attributions of blame to nature and to national government were set to their minimum and maximum values.

strong agreement, while anger is set at 3. The table shows that in all five cases, anger serves to augment the effects of blaming the national government. The difference in predicted probabilities between someone who strongly agrees and strongly disagrees with the national blame frame is substantially greater when the respondent is also extremely angry. However, the standard errors around the interactions for all but two of the five models were large, leaving only two that differ statistically.

Generalized Lowered Confidence

If our argument is correct, one thing we should see is a generalized lower confidence level among those who viewed the national government as culpable. In other words, if extraordinary moments in which government is at fault serve to create a general sense of lowered confidence, we should see that respondents feel less confident in the full range of possible future crises, not just one or two. We think it important to consider the cumulative confidence in government to handle other crises because loss of confidence for many different types of catastrophes signifies a greater problem than loss of confidence for one or two crises. To examine this, we created an index to count the number of times that a respondent indicated that she or he was less confident in the government's ability to manage another type of catastrophe. The distribution of this variable is *U* shaped, with 50 percent of respondents feeling less confident in zero or one crisis. Thirty percent, however, felt less confident in at least four of the five types of crises. The distribution has a mean of two, and a median of one.

The dependent variable is a count and likely overdispersed, meaning that there may be an inherent correlation among responses of "lower confidence" apart from the causal processes that we posit. We ran a negative binomial model to account for this, and the results are reported in Table 6.5 (see Appendix F for the full results with control variables).

The table shows that the blame-government coefficient is positive, as we expected. Higher values of the dependent variable indicate more generalized loss of confidence. Strongly agreeing that national government was to blame increased the likelihood that respondents inferred broadly from this attribution that government is likely to be inept in a range of situations.

If we consider the impact factor of these variables, we see that for every unit increase in the blame-government scale, there is nearly a 16 percent increase in the number of catastrophes in which the respondent is less confident in the government. On the other hand, each unit increase in attributing the problems in the wake of the storm to nature and the storm itself results in a 7 percent decline in the number of catastrophes in which the respondent is less confident in the government. As we hypothesized, none of the other attributions of blame influenced generalized confidence in government's ability to handle future crises.

We also tested the emotion link. Anxiety was insignificant, as we expected, but so was anger and the interaction between anger and blaming national government. Although we saw weak and somewhat mixed evidence for the conditional effects of anger in the individual crisis models, the same result is not apparent in the general count model. These results lead us to believe that although anger plays some role in reducing confidence for particular types of crises, it does not rise to the level of substantive or statistical significance in driving more generalized attitudes. We interpret this to mean that anger works best in situations where attributions and targets are most closely aligned, such as evaluations (see Chapter 5) and policy opinions (see Chapter 7).

TABLE 6.5. *Select Coefficients from a Negative Binomial Model of Lowered Confidence in Crisis Response*

	B	sig	% change, 1 unit	% change 1 SD	SD of X
Blame nature	−0.072	***	−7.000	−14.000	2.082
Blame national government	0.144	***	15.500	35.200	2.092
Blame non-evacuees	−0.008		−0.800	−1.600	1.897
Blame criminal actions	−0.018		−1.800	−3.500	1.996
State failed to call for help	−0.020		−2.000	−2.000	1.029
Angry	−.027		2.800	3.400	1.244
Anxious	0.047		4.800	4.200	0.874
Angry × Blame national government	0.005		0.500	4.200	7.619
Party ID (strong. Rep. highest)	−0.095	***	−9.100	−18.900	2.205
N	653				

***p < .01; **p < .05; *p < .10, two-tailed tests.

Notes: The dependent variable is a count of each response indicating that the respondent was "less confident" in each type of crisis (hurricane, flu epidemic, earthquakes, nuclear attack, or biological attack). The variable ranges from 0 to 5, with the highest value indicating the broadest lack of confidence. See report of full model results with all controls in Table F.3 in Appendix F.

Finally, we compare the effects of partisan predispositions and attributions. We have contended that epochal events enhance collective cohesion by bringing opinions of opposition partisans closer together. Here we see that the effects of attributions of blame are substantially greater than the effects of partisanship. Being a member of the out-party (the Democrats) led to 9 percent greater lack of confidence in a greater range of crises, consistent with what we saw with external efficacy, just more than 6 percent below the effect of negative attributions of blame. Recall that in Chapter 4 we found that even strong Republicans who were emotionally engaged by the storm coverage were likely to agree or strongly agree with the attribution of blame, thus the offsetting effects of attributions and partisans are great among at least a subset of Republicans. When collectively shared attributions of blame serve to counteract normal partisan differences, the stage is set for political entrepreneurs to promote policies that gain broad support, a topic we will turn to more fully in the next chapter.

EXAMINING LONGER-TERM EFFECTS OF KATRINA
WITH A CUING EXPERIMENT

Thus far in this chapter, we have shown that attributions of blame shape broader opinions about the government's responsiveness and ability to manage other future crises. But was the reduction in confidence persistent over time? In 2006, we were able to ask and answer this question using an experimental design applied to a national sample of registered voters (see Appendix B, which covers design and sampling details). The experiment was administered during two waves of a panel survey: one during October prior to the 2006 elections; and the other in November, just following the election. We examined levels of citizens' confidence in government's ability to *assist victims* after a catastrophe and their confidence in government's ability to *maintain order*, depending on whether the survey respondents were given a cue to recall Hurricane Katrina or 9/11. In the first wave, we asked the following questions with no cue for either catastrophe: "The U.S. National government has many responsibilities. How confident are you about the U.S. National Government's ability to: (1) provide assistance to victims of a major crisis and (2) maintain order during a major crisis?" There were five categories of response, including "extremely confident," "very confident," "somewhat confident," "not too confident," and "not confident at all." The same two questions were asked again in the second wave, but in the second wave we added a randomly assigned cue to the end of each question to trigger recall of 9/11 and Hurricane Katrina. Each subject received one of the two added clauses: "like Hurricane Katrina" or "like 9/11." The answer scale was coded so that higher values indicate greater confidence.

Table 6.6 shows the means for each variable in the various cue conditions. Although the means are all very low, indicating that most people are not too confident, it is important to note that the Katrina cue mean scored lower than both the 9/11 cue and the "no cue" condition and that the 9/11 cue condition mean score is the greatest. Cuing Hurricane Katrina lowered confidence in government, whereas cuing 9/11 raised confidence. The difference reflects the long-term power of epochal events as frames for understanding governance in society. One

TABLE 6.6. *Experimental Effects of Crisis Prompts on Level of Confidence in Government*

Prompts	Mean	95% Confidence Interval		N
Assist Victims				
No cue (preelection)	1.41	1.33	1.49	990
Katrina cue	1.28	1.17	1.41	401
9/11 cue	1.49	1.38	1.60	415
Maintain Order				
No cue (preelection)	1.57	1.49	1.66	990
Katrina cue	1.29	1.17	1.40	400
9/11 cue	1.66	1.55	1.78	417

Notes: The dependent variables are responses to the question about how confident the respondent feels about the government's ability to maintain order or assist victims after a crisis with the additional prompt of either "like Hurricane Katrina" or "like 9/11." The question had four response categories, with higher values indicating greater confidence.

year after Hurricane Katrina and five years after 9/11, evoking the catastrophes still alters opinions.

Having multiple responses across time offers us the opportunity to examine how attitudes changed in response to the prompt while controlling for the respondents' prior opinion in a "no cue" condition. This control is an important part of our test because prior research indicates the attitudes such as trust and confidence tend to be stable and strongly related to prior opinions. This provides a very strong control to test our hypothesis that cuing a disaster shapes confidence, because previous attitudes toward government confidence should be a strong predictor of the same attitude only a few weeks to a month later (see Converse 1964). If the cue has an effect above and beyond prior opinions, it testifies to the longer-term importance of high-salience events as symbolic touchstones. We also control for key demographic factors (that is, education, age, gender, and race), partisanship, ideology, knowing or being a victim, recall on attentiveness to Katrina news, and, most importantly, attitudes tapped without any cue in the preelection wave.

The results, presented in Table 6.7 and Figure 6.2, bear out our expectations that even with the strong control of the prior wave opinions, prompting recall of a past catastrophe is influential. Both of these

TABLE 6.7. *Selected Coefficients, Ordered-Probit Models of Confidence in Government*

	Assist Victims		Maintain Order	
	B	sig	B	sig
Katrina prompt (vs 9/11)	−0.219	***	−0.418	***
Attention to Katrina coverage	−0.237	***	−0.097	*
Victim of Katrina	−0.239		−0.356	*
Preelection opinion (no prompt)	0.771	***	0.733	***
N	797		798	

***p < .01; **p < .05; *p < .10, two-tailed tests.

Notes: The dependent variables for the models are responses to the question about how confident the respondent feels about the government's ability to maintain order or assist victims after a crisis with the additional prompt of either "like Hurricane Katrina" or "like 9/11." The question had four response categories, with higher values indicating greater confidence. See the table with a full list of controls in Table F.4 in Appendix F.

national crises continue to haunt the American psyche; extraordinary events provide long-standing cues that prompt recall of attitudes associated with those events. Figure 6.2 presents stacked predicted probabilities where the total probability of falling in any response category is 1, but the subdivisions for each bar represent the probability that the median respondent would fall into one of three categories: low confidence (scoring 1 or 2 on the five-point scale), some confidence (scoring 3 on the five-point scale), or high confidence (scoring 4 or 5 on the five-point scale). For example, Figure 6.2 shows that the Katrina prompt increased the probability of feeling little confidence by .07 compared to respondents receiving the 9/11 prompt. This effect is even stronger for the question pertaining to government's ability to maintain order, where the difference in low confidence is .15.

To see how these events compared across different levels of government, we asked identical questions but substituted the words "local government" for "federal government." When we run the same analysis in the local condition, we find no difference in attitudes regardless of whether respondents were given the 9/11 or Katrina prompt (analysis is not shown). It appears that the long-term effects of Katrina on the American psyche were particularly targeted at the U.S. national government, supporting our earlier contention that anger was targeted

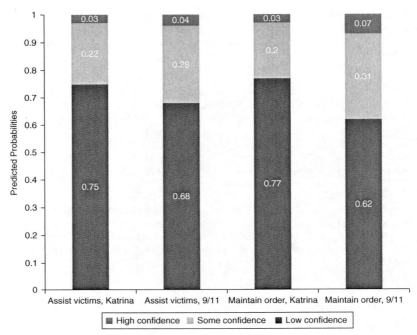

FIGURE 6.2. Predicted Probabilities of Confidence in Government, by Experimental Prompt.

there as well. Memories of the national government's failure to handle the aftermath of the storm adequately led to a decline in confidence in the federal government's ability to handle crises, a key expectation in a democratic society.

SUMMARY AND CONCLUSIONS

In this chapter, we identified additional ways in which epochal events matter – they influence external efficacy and confidence in government's ability to manage crises. We found evidence of both short- and long-term consequences to a federal government failure – it reduced citizens' belief in the responsiveness of government and confidence in future government actions. In extraordinary situations, citizens search for information and pay attention in ways that they do not during periods of normal politics. As a result, attitudes toward government's ability to fulfill its primary mission of protecting the safety and general welfare of its citizens can change in response to those events.

These results are troubling because a reduction in satisfaction with government may lead to fewer citizens complying with government orders in a crisis (Burton and Silver 2006). In the context of catastrophes such as Hurricane Katrina or other natural or man-made disasters, for example, dissatisfaction with government might lead more citizens to ignore evacuation orders. Citizens being distrustful and choosing not to comply has dire consequences for their health and well-being and complicates the government's efforts to work effectively to respond to the disaster. We believe that such consequences are problematic for government because it requires far-reaching powers and citizen compliance to maintain order and promote the general welfare. Ultimately a society will fail without the tacit public support of legal and political authorities. For these reasons, actions by government that reduce satisfaction with government and its leaders are highly problematic and likely have direct effects on public policy preferences.

7

Attributions, Emotions, and Policy Consequences

In the last two chapters, we have seen the effects of attributions of blame on evaluations of government leaders and on confidence in government to manage other catastrophes. How do attributions of blame influence attitudes about policy? Prior research, particularly lab experiments, shows that media framing can encourage particular attributions of blame that, in turn, shape a wide variety of social, foreign, and economic policy opinions (Iyengar 1989, 1991). As we have shown, extraordinary events stimulate a need for journalists and the public to form attributions to make sense of the unexpected. These attributions, however, imply particular avenues for political response and therefore should have direct effects on preferences for policies related to the catastrophe. In fact, catastrophes are well known to be focusing events in the policy world because they allow political entrepreneurs to connect issues related to disasters to policy solutions and move them to the center of the public agenda (Baumgartner and Jones 2009; Birkland 2006 ; Kingdon 2002). The challenge, for policy researchers, is to specify the micro-level pathways that create political opportunities from unexpected circumstances (Wood and Vedlitz 2007).

We have argued throughout the book that the combination of the unique news environment that surrounds catastrophes and the increased likelihood that individual information processing strategies in this environment are more accuracy-based limits the influence of predispositions while enhancing the connections between contemporaneous information and opinions. This process increases the likelihood of shared opinions across the public that can be harnessed by political entrepreneurs. To establish that this is the case, however, we need to demonstrate the connection between attributions of blame and policy opinions and consider whether the emotional context of the storm alters those connections.

Examining public attitudes about policies related to Hurricane Katrina allows us to consider how attributions of blame operate to influence preferences as well as how discrete emotions help to shape policy opinions. The question of how attributions are linked to policy opinions is also closely tied to the themes we developed in the last chapter. We know that attributions of blame influence confidence in government and that one consequence of low satisfaction with government is decreased support for government policies, laws, and rules (Cooper, Knotts, and Brennan 2008; Tyler 1990). Confidence – or, rather, reduced confidence – in the government's ability to respond to crises as needed may result in a direct desire to change government policies in the hopes that such measures will improve future government response.

In addition, we can also tease out important distinctions theoretically and empirically with how anxiety and anger operate differently in the process of forming attitudes. Anxiety plays the key role in making individuals receptive to new information, whereas anger plays the key role in stimulating action to do something, especially when it involves punishing those responsible. Our theory argues that blame cognition leads to anger when the failure is seen as avoidable or unjust. Therefore, we should find that citizens who feel greater anger toward the events after Katrina should also support policies more punitive toward those they deemed responsible. We saw hints of this type of an outcome in Chapter 5, where angry individuals were more likely to punish leaders through harsh evaluations. Anxiety, on the other hand, stimulates a desire to investigate and reduce uncertainty. As a result, those made most anxious by an extraordinary event should seek investigative policies and policies that reduce the probability of similarly unexpected events in the future.

INFORMATIONAL AND PUNITIVE POLICY PROPOSALS
FOLLOWING HURRICANE KATRINA

The dependent variables in this chapter are drawn from several questions about support for various policies that were discussed by elites

TABLE 7.1. *Public Opinions about Post-Katrina Policies, in Percentages*

	Congress should pass a law to limit the type of people whom presidents can appoint to key positions, such as emergency preparedness agencies	Congress should appoint an independent commission to investigate how government handled the response to Hurricane Katrina	The government should create penalties for people who fail to follow mandatory evacuations
Strongly agree	17	23	12
Agree	35	35	26
Somewhat agree	8	8	9
Neither agree nor disagree	7	4	6
Somewhat disagree	2	1	4
Disagree	25	23	35
Strongly disagree	6	5	7
Total	100	100	100
N	959	960	952
Mean	4.01	4.86	4.57

Notes: Data are weighted by population proportions for age and sex.

soon after the storm. Each focuses attention on different targets of policy action – two dependent variables target government while the remaining one targets victims. Of the two policies that we examine that target government actions, one is informational and the other is punitive. The variance in and across policy issues allows us to test how attributions increase or decrease support for specific policy proposals, how discrete emotions operate independently and interactively with attributions and predispositions, and how low confidence reduces the scope of government discretion.

The three questions we examine and their frequencies are shown in Table 7.1. Each question used a Likert response format ranging from strongly disagree (1) to strongly agree (7), with a neither agree nor disagree response in the center (4). The first question asked whether presidential appointment authority should be limited by Congress.

Laws prior to Hurricane Katrina placed no explicit limits on the qualifications for presidential appointments to FEMA. After the dismal response to Hurricane Katrina, considerable media and political discourse focused on the political nature of Bush's appointment of Michael Brown, a man with no prior experience in disaster management, to direct FEMA. Politicos and members of Congress argued that statutory qualifications needed to be enacted to ensure that future appointees have the experience to handle major catastrophes (ABC News 2005a, 2005b). A version of this policy was passed into law by Congress in October 2006 (Savage 2006). Nearly three-fifths (59 percent) of respondents supported this policy.

The second question we analyze pertains to information gathering through an independent commission to investigate the response to Hurricane Katrina. This, too, was often cited in the media by journalists and elite guests as a necessary step for uncovering the reasons for the poor response and forming a plan to prevent similar outcomes in future catastrophes. An important nuance to note in this policy proposal is that journalists and elites called for an *independent* commission to investigate the response so that the Bush administration, which had been judged to have failed, could not manipulate or sequester the fact-finding process. About two-thirds (67 percent) of respondents supported this policy.

The third question we use targets policies that would punish future victims who fail to comply with government evacuation orders. This policy received less attention in the press than the policies that target government, but it is an important one to look at to determine whether attributions are sensibly connected to policy preferences. The news media focus on victims willfully staying behind despite mandatory evacuation orders, and the subsequent lawless behavior of those remaining in the disaster area produced powerful images. The policy calls for increased penalties stemmed both from a desire to keep citizens out of harm's way in future catastrophes, but also to punish those deemed at least partially responsible for the outcome in New Orleans. Just under half (47 percent) of respondents supported this policy.

In the next three sections, we outline the specific expectations for how attributions, confidence in government, and emotions influence the level of agreement with each policy. One benefit from testing these three policies is that they offer "negative controls" in the sense that we have clear expectations about how certain attributions and emotions should and should not influence specific policy opinions.

Limiting the President

The policy proposal to limit presidential authority serves two purposes: It reduces uncertainty surrounding future outcomes by ensuring that the person appointed is qualified to handle catastrophic situations, and it punishes the administrative branch by restricting its discretionary authority. Because the question focuses on limiting the national government, we expect attributions pertaining to national government to matter. In the news media, the post-Katrina crisis was defined and understood as a result of government inaction and, in particular, the inability of FEMA to respond promptly to the crisis. One highly cited reason for government's failure was the incompetence and inexperience of the Bush-appointed head of FEMA, Michael Brown (ABC News 2005a, 2005b; CNN 2005a; *USA Today* 2005). Therefore, blaming national government should relate to a desire to restrict the type of government discretion that was perceived to have led to the negative outcome. In the context of Katrina, we expect that those who agree more strongly that the national government is to blame should support limiting presidential authority in the selection of agency leaders. The societal breakdown and nature attributions target causes external to government and consequently should be unrelated to a desire to limit presidential authority. However, attributions of blame that center on state government should lead to *lower* support for this measure, because making changes in policies and procedures at the federal level would not solve a problem that occurs at the state level. Therefore, we hypothesize that:

    I. Individuals who agree more strongly that national government was to blame are more likely to support limiting presidential appointment authority.

    II. Agreement with the societal breakdown attributions will make no difference to preferences limiting presidential appointment authority.

    III. Individuals who attribute blame to the state government's failure to call for help will be less likely to support limiting presidential appointment authority.

We also expect the level of confidence in government's ability to manage future crises to influence preferences to exercise oversight and/or restrict the discretion of government. We test this explicitly by including the count of the number of times that respondents indicated they had lower confidence in the government's ability to handle other crises given recent experiences with Katrina and Rita, including other hurricanes, earthquakes, a flu epidemic, a nuclear terrorist attack, and a biological terrorist attack. The variables ranges from 0 to 5, with 39 percent of respondents scoring a 0, meaning they did not feel less confident across any of these dimensions, and 21 percent indicating 5, meaning they were less confident across all five dimensions. We expect a negative relationship between this variable and support for limiting presidential authority.

> IV. Those who lack confidence in government's ability to manage future catastrophes across more dimensions will agree more strongly that presidential appointment authority should be limited.

We also expect the anger and anxiety measures to have direct effects on limiting presidential authority and leave until later in the chapter a discussion of potential conditional effects. Evidence that anxiety and anger produce different policy preferences is apparent in previous research on a major epochal event, as we discussed previously. In the case of anxiety, which leads to more thoughtful considerations of the problem at hand, we expect that those who are more anxious to be more likely to support limiting presidential authority. This relationship is based on the notion that anxious people are more risk-averse and therefore want policies that will reduce future risk. This policy purports to do that by insisting that agency executives are qualified and experienced. Thus, we should see a positive effect from anxiety. Those more anxious should be more supportive of increasing competency in disaster management and support limiting presidential authority. This leads to the following hypothesis:

> V. Individuals who felt more anxious will be more supportive of limiting presidential authority than those who felt less anxious.

We also expect a direct effect of anger because it has been shown to spur preferences for punitive policies (Johnson 2009; Lerner, Goldberg, and Tetlock 1998). Limiting government authority is a means of punishing government for its irresponsible behavior. Thus, we expect those with a more emotionally angry response to the storm to feel more intensely about policies that limit the scope of government appointments. This leads to the following hypothesis:

> VI. Individuals who felt angrier will be more supportive of limiting presidential authority than those who did not feel angry.

Appointing an Independent Commission

Our second policy question focused on the need for an independent commission to investigate the underlying causes for the problems after the storm. As with limiting presidential authority, we expect that attributing blame to the national government to be positively related to support for an independent commission. When government is identified as the cause of a crisis, journalists, political elites, and the public generally clamor to learn the reasons why in order to resolve the problem to prevent similar occurrences in the future. Similarly, we might expect state failure to call for help to lead to the desire for an independent commission; however, this question centers on Congress, not the states, which likely draws attention to the national government as opposed to the state government. Therefore, we expect no effect of state failure attribution. We also do not expect to see an effect of other attributions of blame, such as those that ascribe blame to non-evacuees or criminal behavior. Blaming the crime after the storm or blaming victims for not evacuating largely focuses on actors outside of government and therefore does not connect straightforwardly with the desire to investigate how "government handled the response." Blaming the nature of the storm may lead to less support for limiting presidential authority, but only because it offers a justification for the post-storm performance that is not the fault of government. In this case, however, the direct link is less clear, so we do not expect it to be a significant factor.

> VII. Individuals who agree more strongly that the national government was to blame are more likely to agree that Congress should appoint an independent investigative commission than those who disagree that the national government was to blame.

VIII. Attributions of blame to societal breakdown, nature, and state government should have no effect on agreement that Congress should appoint an independent investigative commission.

Lower confidence in government should lead to the desire for more information and hence support for an independent commission. Because the respondent had reduced confidence in government's ability to manage crises, he or she should be more willing to engage in activities that can lead to actions that promote government doing a better job. An independent commission is designed to provide such information and prompt government to make appropriate policy changes. Indeed, this is precisely the role that the commission eventually played as it detailed the causes of the poor response. Thus, we expect a positive relationship between this variable and support for an independent commission.

IX. Individuals who lack confidence across more dimensions in government's ability to manage future catastrophes will agree more strongly that Congress should appoint an independent investigative commission.

With regard to the emotion variables, we see theoretical linkages between anxiety and anger with the desire for an independent commission, but the reasons for the linkages are different, which results in slightly different expectations in the magnitude of the effects. Anxiety creates an inherent need for explanatory information to update causal understandings and identify ways to reduce threats in the environment. An independent commission satisfies this need by supplying additional, independent information that is likely to be credible. It is obvious that anxiety should be an important factor in understanding support for this policy. Anger, however, is a punitive, action-oriented emotion. An independent commission appointed by Congress with a focus on understanding administrative failures is perhaps somewhat punitive, but more importantly it is very action-oriented. Because angry people want to do something, they are also more likely to want an independent commission. However, we argue that the direct theoretical linkage between anxiety and the desire for information should lead to anxiety having a larger effect on this policy than anger.

X. Individuals who felt more anxious will be more likely to agree that Congress should appoint an independent investigative commission than those less anxious.

XI. Individuals who felt angrier will be more likely to agree that Congress should appoint an independent investigative commission than those less angry, but the effect of anger should be weaker than the effect of anxiety.

Penalties for Non-Evacuees

This variable focuses on creating stiffer penalties for victims of crises who do not follow government orders. The target here is an actor completely different from government, so we expect rather different results for the attribution, confidence, and emotion variables. In essence, this variable represents a negative control where we should not see many of the effects that we anticipate with policies that focus on the government dimension of the problem. Not seeing those same effects here bolsters confidence in our theoretical perspective.

For example, the blame-government attributions, both state and national, should not influence the level of agreement with this policy. Neither government attribution excuses victims, so we do not expect a negative effect. Neither one directs attention to victims, so we do not expect a positive effect. However, we do expect to see that other attributions related to societal breakdown influence preferences for this policy. Both the societal breakdown attributions fault the victims for their behavior and are, therefore, more directly connected to this policy consideration. This is especially true for the non-evacuee attribution for failure to evacuate before the storm hit. If victims' wilful behavior was perceived to have prevented first responders from responding, then perhaps legislating penalties against them for not following orders would limit the impact of any future crisis. Thus we expect both of these attributions to be positively related to support for victim penalties.

XII. Individuals who attribute blame more strongly to non-evacuees will be more supportive of the policy proposal to create penalties for victims who ignore evacuation orders.

XIII. Individuals who attribute blame to criminal behavior of victims will be more supportive of the policy proposal to create penalties for victims who ignore evacuation orders.

XIV. We expect government blame (national or state) attributions to have no effect on support for imposing penalties on victims who ignore evacuation orders.

We also do not expect confidence in government's ability to manage crises to matter. Because penalties are focused on victims and not government, there is no reason for lower confidence in government's ability to manage crises to increase or decrease support for victim penalties. We also do not expect to see a direct effect of anger on support for penalties. Because our measure of anger is targeted at government and not victims, we do not expect anger to play a punitive role in penalties.[1] However, anxiety likely has a direct effect, for the same reason it did in limiting presidential authority. Because anxiousness leads to a desire to reduce risk and to more careful consideration of information to determine risk, any policy that limits the impact of future crises should be supported. Therefore, a policy that incentivizes people to leave dangerous areas when told should be supported.

XV. Confidence in government should have no effect on support for imposing penalties on victims who ignore evacuation orders.

XVI. Level of anger should have no effect on support for imposing penalties on victims who ignore evacuation orders.

XVII. Individuals who were more anxious should be more supportive of imposing penalties on victims who ignore evacuation orders.

Other Controls Included in All Three Models

As is the case in all of our models, we control for education, gender, age, income, partisanship, direct connections to victims, political knowledge, race, and ideology. Partisanship may play a role in the

---

[1] If we had a measure that targeted anger at the victims, theoretically it would have a positive effect on supporting victim penalties.

two policies that target government, particularly the Republican Bush administration. We control for ideology (a seven-point scale, from extremely liberal to extremely conservative) because we believe that it is likely that conservatives who favor less government and less spending would be less inclined to support new policies and new oversight. Because blacks may personally identify with many of the victims, we expect an independent effect, especially for the policies related to government: limiting presidential authority and establishing an independent commission. However, the penalty question identifies an area where blacks may disengage and not identify with the victim group. In this policy area, blacks recognize that the victims should have evacuated and consequently do not link victim penalties with their social identity. Because of the negative connotation surrounding victims' choices, blacks reject the social identity cue and consequently are more likely to have attitudes similar to those of whites (White 2009). We saw similar effects when we examined the causal properties for the blame attributions. Therefore, we saw significant effects for the social identity hypothesis for blacks among those who blamed government and nature, but not for those who blamed crime or non-evacuees. Thus we anticipate the same type of relationship here.

RESULTS OF ORDERED-PROBIT MODELS OF AGREEMENT WITH PROPOSED POLICIES

The ordered-probit results for each model are reported in Table 7.2; the full model can be found in Appendix G. Because the dependent variables are scaled identically for all three models, we can make comparisons across models of the effects of key independent variables. Most of the hypotheses we outlined earlier are supported by the results. We see that blaming the national government had the expected effect in all three models. It had a positive and significant relationship in the model of limiting presidential authority and in the model of supporting an independent commission, but, importantly, no such relationship is evident in the model of supporting victim penalties. Those people who blamed the national government for the crisis were more likely to want to make changes in government, both to determine what went wrong and to put in place measures that would help prevent a similar crisis in the future. Their level of blame toward national government

TABLE 7.2. *Select Coefficients from Ordered-Probit Models of Public Policy Preferences*

	Limit Presidential Authority	Independent Commission	Non-evacuee Penalties
Blame national government	.120***	.117***	−.028
Blame state government	−.130***	−.006	.030
Blame non-evacuees	.044*	.039	.110***
Blame criminal behavior	.010	.027	.041*
Blame nature	−.012	−.035	.004
Low confidence	.096***	.066***	−.001
Anger	.054	.066	−.032
Anxiety	.184***	.274***	.201***
Black	.273*	.597***	.034
Party identification	−.053**	−.010	.035
N	646	671	666

***p < .01; **p < .05; *p < .10; two-tailed tests.

Notes: The dependent variables are the level of agreement with each policy proposal on a seven-point scale, with higher-valued categories reflecting greater agreement. See Table G.1 in Appendix G for full model results.

had no influence on policies targeting victims, which is consistent with their causal understanding. Table 7.2 also shows the effects of blaming state government on the other two policy opinions. As we predicted, we saw no effect on the preference for an independent commission or on preferences for penalizing noncompliant victims. Neither policy is focused on factors related to future performance of the state, so state blame is not a factor in shaping support for them.

Of course, we also expected no effect from the societal breakdown attributions of blame on preferences for limiting presidential authority or for establishing an independent commission, but we did expect that blaming the victims would lead to increased support for victim penalties, and this is what we see in Table 7.2. Thus, attributing blame to the victims directly relates to a desire to hold victims more accountable for their behavior in future crises. This is especially true for those who blamed the non-evacuees, as we would expect, as this attribution is most clearly linked to the policy targeting future victims.

We also found a strong effect of confidence in government on agreement with the policy to limit presidential authority and the policy to implement an investigative independent commission. This makes a great deal of sense because both policies serve as ways to address factors that reduce confidence in government's ability to handle future crises. However, as we expected, it was not a significant predictor of support for imposing penalties on victims.

Finally, we note that anger and anxiety work mostly as expected. Anxiety created a general preference for policies that might reduce future risk. This is consistent with anxiety's more general role of alerting people of potential danger and helping them to avoid it. Anger was correctly signed in the two models where we predicted it would influence opinions, but the coefficients were not statistically significant by conventional standards. Our expectation about the direct effect of anger was met in only one of the three models. Recall that in Chapter 4 we demonstrated that anger was most closely related to blaming government but it was not related to blaming non-evacuees. Therefore, we did not expect anger to matter to support for policies imposing victim penalties. That is precisely what we see in Table 7.2. However, because anger springs from beliefs about government failure, we thought it might produce an additional emotional influence on limiting presidential authority and creating an independent commission. The sign of the effect is appropriate for both models, but because the standard error relative to the coefficient is quite large, the coefficient for anger in the model of limiting appointments is significant only at $p = .188$ (two-tailed). For the independent commission model, it is significant at $p = .107$ (two-tailed). Notably, if we drop the government blame attributions from the models, the effect of anger on policy preferences becomes much larger and statistically significant. This suggests that anger has little direct effect once we have accounted for attribution patterns.

Sign and significance tests are useful in providing support for the hypotheses outlined earlier, but they tell us little about the substantive effects of each variable on the outcomes of policy support. To get a sense of the magnitude of effects, we present predicted probabilities that a respondent would at least "somewhat agree" in Table 7.3 or that he or she would at least "somewhat disagree." By this, we mean that we predict whether a respondent would fall in the response category of 5 or greater on the dependent variable (agreement with the policy) or in the category 3 or lower (disagreement with the policy). We

TABLE 7.3. *Predicted Probability of Agreement and Disagreement with Policy When the Independent Variable Is at Its Minimum and Maximum*

	Minimum Value Agree	Minimum Value Disagree	Maximum Value Agree	Maximum Value Disagree
Limiting Presidential Authority				
Blame national government	.41	.51	.69	.25
Blame state government	.69	.25	.54	.38
Confidence	.52	.40	.70	.24
Anxiety	.49	.44	.70	.24
Non-black/black	.59	.34	.70	.24
Independent Commission				
Blame national government	.45	.50	.72	.24
Confidence	.58	.37	.70	.26
Anxiety	.46	.48	.77	.19
Anger	.61	.35	.68	.27
Non-black/black	.63	.32	.82	.15
Non-evacuee Penalties				
Blame non-evacuees	.31	.63	.57	.37
Blame criminal behavior	.42	.52	.52	.42

Notes: The predicted probabilities were generated using Clarify 2.1 (Tomz, Wittenberg, and King 2003) using the models in Table G.1 with all other values in the model set at their median or mode.

used the full models presented in Appendix G to generate the predicted probabilities and held all variables constant at their median or mode except the variable of interest, which we varied from its minimum to maximum values. Probabilities over .5 indicate that the respondent is more likely than not to fall into the predicted outcome category, and probabilities near 1.0 mean the respondent was almost certain to fall into the predicted outcome category.

It is clear from Table 7.3 that the effect of blaming national government is quite strong for policies related to government. When the value of the attribution question blaming the national government was low (1), the probability of at least somewhat agreeing with limiting presidential authority (falling in category 5 or higher) is .41, but when the attribution is at its high value (7), the probability jumps to .69. In other words, those who do not blame national government are likely to be unsupportive of policies limiting presidential appointments while those who assign strong blame are likely to be supportive.

We see a similarly strong effect for the independent commission policy. When attributing blame to national government is at its lowest value, the probability of at least somewhat agreeing that Congress should appoint an independent commission is .45, but when it is high, the probability increases to .72. In both cases, attribution of blame matters to policies, independent of party identification and sociodemographics. This suggests that the news media effects associated with messages of blame in a catastrophic event provide support for policies that might otherwise be at odds with partisan leanings.

We also noted that diffusion of blame to other state sources should reduce the desire to punish national-level leaders. We see this in the substantive effect of blaming state government. This attribution had a nearly equal but opposite effect on limiting presidential authority, potentially offsetting the effect of national blame. Holding constant the level of national blame, those who strongly blamed state government were much less likely to support limiting presidential appointment authority. The predicted probability of at least somewhat agreeing with the policy proposal declined by .15, dropping from a high of .69 when state government blame was at its lowest value to a low of .54 when it was at its highest value. Blaming state government shifts the focus away from the culpability of the president and FEMA leader Michael Brown, so respondents seem to see limiting appointment authority as unnecessary.

One interesting aspect of the joint distribution of attributions of blame is that there is not a clear trade-off in blaming national and state government. Forty-eight percent assigned at least some blame to both state and national government, so the offsetting effect that we have described applies to a large swath of our sample. Twenty-nine percent assign blame primarily to state government and only 14 percent assigned blame to national government but not state government. These results suggest that the strategy employed by the Bush administration of diffusing blame toward Louisiana state government ultimately served the role of buffering the full effect of attributions on policy opinions.

Attribution of blame had a large effect on support for punitive policies toward future victims; however, it is attributions to victims, not
to government, that matter here. We see a rather strong change in
probabilities (Table 7.3) where the probability of at least somewhat
agreeing with this punitive policy increases by .26 from .31 when the
non-evacuee blame attribution is at its lowest value to .57 when it is
at its highest. The effect of blaming criminal behavior is a bit smaller,
with only a .10 probability change, such that when this attribution is
at its lowest, the likelihood of supporting victim penalties is .42 compared to .52 when it is at its highest.

As expected, confidence in government had an effect on the two
government-oriented policies, and the size of the effect was similar in
magnitude to the attributions. Table 7.3 shows the predicted probabilities that the results are similar for both limiting presidential authority
and creating an independent commission. When the scale is at its low
point (representing 39 percent of the cases), the probability of agreeing
at any level with limiting presidential authority is .52, but it increases
.18 to .70 when it is high (representing about 21 percent of the cases).
Support for an independent commission changes about .12, from .58
when it is low to .70 when it is high. The sizable effects are notable,
particularly in light of what we know from Chapter 6: Confidence is
related to attributions of blame toward national government. Thus,
the results that we show here understate the full effects of attributions
because the level of confidence is correlated with blaming government.
We turn now to the direct effects of the emotions of anxiety and anger.
The substantive effect of anxiety is quite large. Table 7.3 shows that
for limiting presidential authority, the probability of support changes
from .49 when anxiety is low (0) to .70 when it is high (3), a total
increase of .21. This actually exceeds the increase associated with attributions and demonstrates the importance of the emotional context of
catastrophes for shaping policy opinions. For an independent commission, the probability of support changes .31 from .46, when anxiety is
low, to .77 when it is high. Anger influences support for the independent commission, but only slightly. If we are willing to accept that the
effect is different from 0 (recall that p = .107, two-tailed test), we see
that the difference in support for an independent commission changes
by about .07, from .61 when anger is low to .68 when it is high. There
is no substantively discernible effect of anger on limiting presidential

authority, a result that is somewhat surprising. In the next section of the chapter, however, we show that anger is better conceived of and modeled as a conditioning variable.

Last, we turn to a few of the more interesting results from control variables. For example, we find that blacks are more likely than non-blacks to agree that presidential powers should be limited and that an independent commission should be established to review government failures, but it is not negative or significant for victim penalties as hypothesized. Therefore, blacks were more likely to want policy change at the national level, but were no different in their attitudes toward victims than whites or other minorities. Table 7.3 shows the effects for whites and blacks, holding all other variables in the model constant at their median, for establishing an independent commission and for limiting presidential authority. The results for the independent commission are slightly more dramatic. Both whites and blacks supported both policies, but the degree of support is substantially different. For establishing an independent commission, the probability of a non-black supporting the policy is .63, but for blacks it is .82, a difference of .19. For limiting presidential authority, the probability is .59 for whites and .70 for blacks, a difference of .11. It is important to note that nearly half of blacks (45 percent) strongly agreed with the blame-government attribution frame, so if we place all other variables at their median and model black attitudes with blame government at its maximum, we find that the probability of agreeing to limit presidential appointment power increases an additional .09 to .79. For the independent commission policy, this increases .06 to .88. In addition, we find that other minorities were also more likely to support limiting presidential authority, but this support had no influence on the other two dependent variables that we examined.

Interestingly, party identification is important for limiting presidential authority, but does not influence attitudes toward an independent commission or victim penalties. This makes sense for limiting presidential power because Republicans are less likely to seek limits on a co-partisan. The partisan implications of an independent commission are less clear because the cue is not directly related to the president or his party. Therefore, the partisan lens is less influential. This same argument holds for victim penalties. With no clear partisan cues, both partisan groups equally support the policy.

In terms of other variables in our model, we find that those who are more educated and those who own homes are significantly more likely to want to limit presidential authority and that those who are more politically knowledgeable are less supportive. The only other control that significantly affected support for an independent commission was ideology, which indicated that people who are more conservative were less likely to support an independent commission, all else being equal. Politically knowledgeable people and those who knew a victim were also less likely to support victim penalties.

A CLOSER LOOK AT LIMITING PRESIDENTIAL AUTHORITY AND UNDERSTANDING THE INFLUENCE OF EMOTION

We found that anxiety had direct effects on limiting presidential authority whereas anger had weak and insignificant effects. However, it is likely that a simple direct effect is not capturing the proper theoretical connection between the emotion and anger and the blame-government attribution. As we pointed out in Chapter 5, scholars have examined whether each type of emotion has direct effects (i.e., Huddy, Feldman, and Cassese 2007; MacKuen et al. 2010), but some scholars (see Petersen 2010) argue that emotions operate to condition other variables. Settling this argument requires an interaction term in the model. In Chapter 2, we argued, theoretically, that anger is a punitive and moral emotion that, when activated, increases the desire for punishment. This hypothesis suggests that emotion should *strengthen* the effect of an attribution on punitive policy preferences. In other words, those who blame the national government *and* are angry as a result of the blame are especially likely to support punitive policy remedies. In the case of the government-related policy variables that we examine, limiting presidential authority has the most obvious punitive quality. It creates a rule limiting presidential authority to appoint people, decreasing presidential discretion. Therefore, we expect to see that, all else being equal, the *effect* of blaming the national government on agreement with this policy option should be stronger among those who felt angry than among those who did not. As in earlier chapters, anger should serve as a catalyst for transforming attributions into support for punitive actions.

> XV. The effect of attributing blame toward national government on support for limiting presidential authority is greater among those who are angry than among those who are not angry.

The theoretical expectations regarding anxiety also suggest both direct and interactive effects on policy. Anxiety activates a search for information and a suspension of current habits to survey and evaluate the situation. In the political world, this reduces the importance of party identification and its powerful lens, thereby creating an environment where new opinions can more easily be formed in response to the new and more balanced information retrieved in the search. The partisan context of Hurricane Katrina created psychological pressures for Republicans to support the president, reject blame toward national government, and limit punitive actions toward the Republican Bush administration. However, emotions should attenuate these pressures so that Republicans who exhibit more anxiety are more likely to support policies that reduce future risk even if they limit co-partisan officials. Part of the path through which this occurs is through the greater likelihood of attributing blame to national government, which in turn influences policy preferences. However, this path also works through dampening the effects of partisanship so that the net effect of attributions on support is greater. Accordingly, we expect the policy preferences of anxiety-laden Democrats and anxiety-laden Republicans to look more similar to one another than those of unanxious Democrats and unanxious Republicans. This hypothesis can be tested only in the limiting presidential authority model because it is the only model where partisanship played a key role in understanding attitudes.

XVI. The effect of party identification on support for limiting presidential appointments is weaker among those who are anxious compared to those who are not anxious.

To test these more nuanced hypotheses regarding the differing roles of the emotions of anxiety and anger, we ran a model that included the direct effects of each emotion and the multiplicative interaction terms to tap conditional effects along with the same set of controls used in the prior models. We added a variable that multiplied anger by "blame national government" and anxiety by strength of partisanship.[2] The results showed that the blaming government and blaming non-evacuees remained positive and significant whereas blaming the

---

[2] We also tried a fully interactive model, where anger was multiplied by all of the attributions. The coefficients and model parameters were largely the same, but the standard errors were increasingly problematic due to multicollinearity.

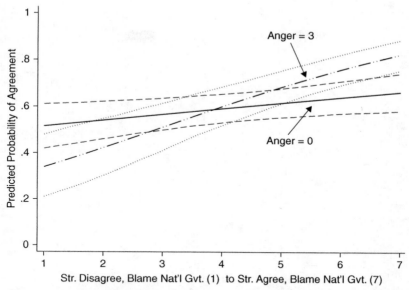

FIGURE 7.1. The Effect of Blaming National Government on Agreement with Limiting Presidential Authority, Conditioned by Level of Anger.

state's failure to call for help remained negative and significant. Thus the primary hypotheses and results presented earlier in the chapters were not affected by the changes in our model specification.

Figure 7.1 shows the effect of the interaction of anger and blaming national government on the predicted probability of any level of agreement with limiting presidential authority (a score of 5, 6, or 7 on the policy agreement scale). We held all variables other than the interaction and its constituent terms at their median, then compared the effects of varying the national government blame attribution from its low value of one to its high value of 7 for those who were "not at all angry" to those who were "extremely angry." The large-dashed line represents those who are very angry, while the black solid line represents those who are not angry. The small-dashed and dotted lines represent the confidence interval around each line. When the lines overlap, there are no significant differences between the two, but when they do not overlap, they are statistically different, showing that anger conditions the effect of blame attribution. Notice that the slope for those who were not angry is flatter compared to the slope for those who were very angry. The increase in the likelihood of at least somewhat agreeing with the

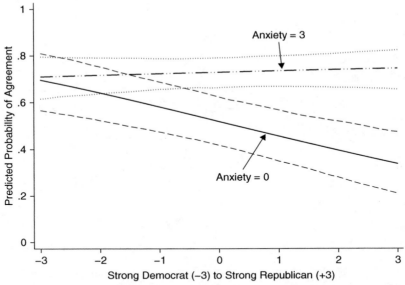

FIGURE 7.2. The Effect of Party Identification on Agreement with Limiting Presidential Authority, Conditioned by Level of Anxiety.

policy statement due to blame attribution is greater among the angry. Furthermore, we see that at the high end of values for blaming government, the predicted probability of angry and non-angry individuals is statistically different, even though their attributions of blame are identical. Angry attributors are much more likely to support the policy to limit presidents than are non-angry attributors, by a considerable margin. In fact, the model predicts that those who felt extremely angry were more likely than not to at least somewhat agree with the policy. However, the threshold of .50 of supporting the policy was not crossed until attribution of blame was in the range of agreement. Those who were not angry and those who did not agree that government was to blame were predicted to be unsupportive of the punitive policy.

Figure 7.2 represents the total effect from the interaction of anxiety with partisanship. Once again, the solid black line represents those who are not anxious, whereas the large-dashed line represents the predicted probabilities of those very anxious. The dotted and small-dashed lines again represent the confidence interval. First, emotional Democrats are not much different from emotional Republicans, with both predicting a probability of agreement with limiting presidential authority just above .7. Second, anxious Democrats are not really different from unanxious Democrats. This is as we would expect, because unanxious Democrats' partisanship drives them automatically toward reducing Republican presidential authority. However, and most importantly, Republicans who are anxious versus Republicans who are not anxious are significantly different from one another. Unanxious Republicans see the world through their partisan lens and thus are much less supportive, with only a 0.3 predicted probability for the strongest Republicans of taking power away from a Republican president. But anxious Republicans are less influenced by partisanship, as our hypothesis predicted, and support limiting presidential authority by a probability of more than .7. Anxiety attenuates the effects of partisanship, whereas anger accentuates the effects of blaming national government.

Given the relatively small size of our model N (646), we believe these results are highly suggestive and support continued theoretical and empirical investigations into how the emotions of anxiety and anger differ and when and how they independently alter both attitudes and behavior. Previous studies have mostly focused on anger's direct effect without considering whether it serves as a catalyst for other variables to influence opinions more strongly. These studies may be underestimating the effects of anger because of a misspecification of how anger operates to stimulate a desire to punish those thought to be culpable for negative outcomes.

SUMMARY AND CONCLUSIONS

To summarize, we see that attributions, emotions, and confidence in government have important effects on preferences for policies that influence both the structure of government and the oversight of government. They also influence policies directed toward citizens. The attribution–policy connection is vital to establishing our claim that catastrophes are consequential politically. The story, thus far, shows that the emotional context surrounding highly visible catastrophes creates an environment fertile for attributing blame, which, in turn, generates anger and dampens confidence in government. Our results support the notion that anger and anxiety are very different emotions and that they operate in very distinct fashion. Anger leads to a greater desire to punish those responsible, whereas anxiety reduces the importance of partisanship. Anger is connected to attributions of blame and comes after the crisis is assessed and blame is laid, while anxiety likely comes first and reduces the importance of predispositions. But, importantly, anger increases the strength of the tie between attributions and political responses.

Emotions, along with confidence in government and attributions of blame, powerfully prompt citizens to support policies that they might not otherwise prefer. Catastrophes create moments in which the public is ready for and responsive to entrepreneurial policy makers who can connect their policy solutions to the attributions of blame that resonate with the public.

These results and those in the previous chapter point to potential longer-term policy consequences as well. Jennings (1999: 3) argues that epochal events are unique in the political world because they "facilitate reference" to those events in policy debates that follow. Evidence presented in the last chapter supports this argument, as the power of cues from extraordinary events persisted over time. In this chapter, we see that attributions of blame and emotions connect in clear ways to policy preferences. These findings are important because even today, Hurricane Katrina and 9/11 are used as cues by leaders and activists in framing policy debates. Hurricane Katrina crops up as a symbolic reference in policy areas far removed from disaster management. For example, a *Washington Post* article pertaining to the government's economic stimulus plan quoted the president of the Professional Services Council as saying, "We cannot repeat the Federal Government's response to Hurricane Katrina," as a frame for his remarks on the problems of understaffing and general mismanagement of funds for stimulus projects (Davidson 2009). This type of symbolic appropriation encourages the recall and application of attitudes about Hurricane Katrina to a new policy area, and our results suggest that such cues are likely to be very effective.

8

Extraordinary Events and Public Opinion

Some Broader Perspectives

Hurricane Katrina, like many extraordinary events, still lurks in the minds of the news media and the public and, therefore, in the minds of politicians. Years later, it still stands as a journalistic benchmark for judging leadership in subsequent disasters faced by presidents Bush and Obama. The political fallout from the storm was considerable for those directly involved, particularly President Bush. The positive political capital that he accrued following 9/11 eroded even further after the national government's seemingly inexcusable neglect of victims in New Orleans. The media firestorm that erupted after the catastrophe was considered a turning point in Bush's presidency (Murphy and Purdum 2009), and the negative evaluations dogged the remainder of his term. Lawmakers in the aftermath of Hurricane Katrina were quick to commission studies and hold hearings that resulted in numerous policy proposals to prevent similar failures of this magnitude in the future, including placing new limits on executive appointment authority. Most importantly, however, the aftermath of Katrina left persistent questions about government's capability and willingness to aid those in need, particularly America's poor and minority communities. The catastrophe shook the confidence of the public long after the event itself and provided a comparative baseline for evaluating government performance in subsequent catastrophes.

There can be no doubt that Hurricane Katrina is an important event in its own right, and many have studied its political consequences at both the national and local levels (Birkland 2006; Birkland

and Waterman 2008; Haider-Markel, Delehanty and Beverlin 2007; Huddy and Feldman 2006a; Maestas et al. 2008; Malhotra and Kuo 2009; Schneider 2005, 2008; Sinclair, Hall, and Alvarez 2011). We add to those voices by analyzing the media message environment following the catastrophe and tracing its influence on attributions of blame and public opinions. However, we also leverage Hurricane Katrina as a context for testing more general theories about how extraordinary events affect national public opinion.

Extraordinary events such as Hurricane Katrina are part of a general class of events that inform both the politically interested and uninterested about the functioning of government at critical moments in history. In these moments, the resources and capabilities of private citizens are overwhelmed. Government aid is both necessary and expected. When government responds as expected, its leaders are touted as strong, empathetic, and worthy of trust – the public feels calmed, stimulating a renewed sense of confidence in government (Bucy 2003; Merolla and Zechmeister 2009). When public expectations are violated, journalists aggressively seek answers for why government failed to render aid in times of crisis. Leaders face harsh criticism and penetrating questions, and public confidence declines.

In either case, human nature compels individuals to tune in to coverage of catastrophic events. When they do, they receive a hefty side dish of political information along with information about the disaster. The high-salience, emotion-provoking context embedded with political information can become an engine that shapes society's views of government, its leaders, and public policy. Extraordinary moments differ from normal politics because the object of interest – the catastrophe – falls outside the realm of ordinary politics, so the political information embedded in the coverage is also processed in less political ways. Instead, the public processes information with an eye toward accurately understanding the nature and threat of the catastrophe rather than with a goal of bolstering existing political positions.

The general process of opinion formation, which links emotions, attributions, and broader political opinions, applies whenever individuals face anxiety-provoking events. A national catastrophe is not a necessary condition to motivate one to switch from routine, predisposition-driven processing to anxiety-driven, accuracy-based processing, but for many it is sufficient. The unique feature of catastrophic moments is the breadth to which this model applies in the public. When disasters strike, conditions are ripe for a large proportion of the population – perhaps even the majority – to shift their information gathering and assessment strategies. They tune in to common sources of news and absorb similar messages. It is the collective nature of catastrophes that gives them a special power and place in public life. As we conclude the book, we step back to review not only the individual-level evidence from the prior chapters but to also consider their aggregate-level implications.

A REVIEW OF INDIVIDUAL-LEVEL FINDINGS

Throughout the book, but especially in Chapter 2, we have drawn together research and ideas from several bodies of research – including communications, media and politics, cognitive and political psychology, neuroscience, and public opinion – to create a framework from which to view the information environment and determine how it affects the way that citizens process information about novel, anxiety-provoking events. Specifically, we highlighted three key mechanisms at work in shaping opinions during catastrophic moments: media-driven emotional triggers, emotional engagement of the public, and attributions of blame. As we theorized in Chapter 2, each plays a role in shaping broader opinions about government, and as we showed in Chapters 5, 6, and 7, this has ramifications for how the public views government institutions and public policy.

Table 8.1 summarizes the general individual-level hypotheses that stem from the theoretical arguments we made in Chapter 2 and the results from testing each in the context of Hurricane Katrina. At the core of our story is the process through which individuals form attributions of blame following extraordinary events – a process driven by the combination of the media message environment and individual-level, emotion-driven processing of dominant causal stories offered in the media. Prior research has recognized the importance of attributions of blame in assigning political responsibility and holding leaders accountable, but no studies have explicitly considered how catastrophes naturally generate conditions that encourage attributions of credit and blame. On the whole, our hypotheses received strong and consistent results, with a few notable exceptions that we discuss in

TABLE 8.1. *Summary of Main Hypotheses and Supportive Evidence*

Expectation	Evidence
Emotion and Attention	
• Attentiveness to media and emotional engagement (shock and anxiety) are positively related.	Supported, Table 3.1
Affective Attributions of Blame	
• Shock and anxiety increase the likelihood of accepting dominant media attributions, independent of partisan predispositions.	Strongly supported for government attributions, weakly supported in other attributions, Table 4.4, Figures 4.1–4.5
• Shock and anxiety reduce the effects of predispositions on attributions of blame.	Supported for 4 of 5 attributions, with very strong support for government attributions, Table 4.4, Figures 4.1–4.5
• Attribution of blame to actors who could have controlled outcomes stimulate the emotion of anger.	Supported for attributions of blame to government but not other attributions, Table 4.6
Attributions, Emotions, and Evaluations of Leaders	
• Attributions of blame to government negatively affect evaluations of government leaders, independent of partisan predispositions.	Supported for evaluations of Bush and Blanco, Table 5.4
• Diffusion of attribution of blame to actors or events outside of government positively influences evaluations of government officials.	Supported for evaluations of Bush and Blanco, partially supported for Nagin, Table 5.4
• Anger magnifies the negative effect of attributions of blame on evaluations.	Supported for evaluations of Bush, Table 5.7, Figure 5.1
Attributions, Emotions, and Confidence in Government	
• Attributions of blame to government decrease external efficacy.	Supported, Table 6.1, Figure 6.1
• Attributions of blame to government decrease confidence in government's ability to handle future catastrophes.	Strongly supported in Tables 6.3–6.5 and Figure 6.2
• Anger magnifies the negative effect of attributions of blame to government on confidence.	Supported in two of five models in Table 6.3

Expectation	Evidence
Attributions, Emotions and Public Policy	
• Attributions of blame increases support for punitive policy directed at target.	Supported in punitive policy models, Table 7.2
• Anger directly increases support for punitive policies.	Not supported in Table 7.2
• Anger magnifies the effects of attribution of blame on support for punitive policies.	Supported, Table G.2, Figure 7.1
• Anxiety decreases the effect of party identification on punitive policy.	Supported, Table G.2, Figure 7.2
• Anxiety, independent of attribution, increases the desire for policy response.	Supported in all three policy models, Table 7.2

more detail in this chapter. Taken together, this book offers a complete picture of how a critical moment in American politics permeates individual public opinions.

One important contribution of our study is that it extends political scientists' understanding of the importance of emotions in politics. Many previous studies have largely focused on the role that cognition, reason, and deliberation play in the formation of opinions, but have often ignored the role of discrete emotions to lubricate deliberation and create the appropriate environment for opinion change. Our theory of affective attributions weds research on emotion-based information processing to research on the causes and consequences of attributions of blame. In doing so, our theoretical and empirical story extends both literatures. The emotion of anxiety is key because it primes attentiveness and receptiveness. Anxiety, created by a shocking story with perceived implications for the broader economy, engaged the public at very high levels. Those who were attentive to coverage gave consideration to the many frames in the media, and anxiety encourages greater deliberation and consideration of conflicting messages. Although we see some evidence of normal partisan responses to frames – meaning larger numbers of Democrats blamed the national government, controlled by Republicans, while larger numbers of Republicans blamed Louisiana state and local government, controlled by Democrats – we also see that anxiety helped to reduce the partisan gap, especially among those who felt the strongest emotional impact from the coverage. Anxiety-charged Republicans were much more likely to accept the "blame national government" frame, lower their evaluations of President Bush and, more broadly, seek to punish the government for its inaction. Even though there were alternative frames that were more consistent with Republican perspectives, emotionally engaged partisans also accepted the dominant causal stories that ran counter to their predispositions. Consistent with our story, we also saw emotionally engaged Democrats accept causal frames that pinned blame on co-partisan Governor Blanco, lowering their evaluations of her performance (see Chapter 5).

We also find a distinct role for the emotions of anxiety and anger. For example, in Chapter 7, we found that anxiety increased support for information-seeking policies, namely, an independent investigative commission. Because anxiety leads individuals to investigate the causes of the anxiety-inducing event to understand potential threats, it is not surprising that anxiety also leads to a desire for policies that fulfill this need at the collective level. Indeed, investigative policies are designed to soothe the anxiety that surrounds extraordinary events by reassuring the public that steps are in progress to prevent similar negative events in the future.

We also find a distinct role for anger in how it operates independently and in conjunction with attribution, but we recognize its limits. We found mixed evidence for direct effects of anger on policy opinions, but we found clear evidence of conditional effects that helped link attributions to other attitudes. Anger conditioned the effects of attributions of blame to produce more extreme negative evaluations of Bush and to produce stronger preferences for policies that limit presidential authority. These results are very important because they help to distinguish how different emotions operate in translating the events of an extraordinary moment into more lasting and consequential political change. Anxiety is a primary emotion formed in response to unexpected events that stimulates a search and appraisal of information (see Chapter 3) while reducing the influence of predispositions in forming opinions (see Chapters 4 and 7). Anger, on the other hand, is a secondary emotion triggered by the *outcome* of attributions, and thus comes later in the cognitive process by directing punitive energy toward the target of responsibility (see Chapters 5 and 7). Whereas anxiety prompts deliberation, anger serves as a catalyst for both short- and long-term accountability in government by translating the results of deliberation into motivation for action through changes in policy or changes at the ballot box.

However, we also found that anger's effect on opinion was bounded by its target of blame, meaning that anger is most effective at spurring targeted punitive evaluations or policies rather than global evaluations. We argue that because anger is a focusing emotion, it does not operate easily out of the bounds of the actors and specific politics related to the event. We did not see any direct relationship between anger and attitudes toward efficacy or confidence in government to handle crises, and the evidence for a conditional relationship was either weak or absent. Given the broad nature of the institutions and crises considered, the findings suggest an important limit to the role of anger in influencing opinion. Overall, however, our argument asserts that emotional responses happen at different points in the opinion formation process and for different reasons. Therefore, it is important to recognize the discrete qualities of anger and anxiety both theoretically and empirically.

The collection of results summarized in Table 8.1 offers compelling evidence for our theoretical framework that we outlined in Chapter 2 and should be observable in other extraordinary events that provoke similar emotional responses among the public. To be sure, Hurricane Katrina was an epochal event – one that exhibited the most extreme qualities of disasters and catastrophic events. The high level of mortality, the shocking violations of expectations for government response, and the deeply emotional coverage that dominated every source of media made this an event that stands out even among catastrophes. Importantly for this research, the context provided a multimessage environment and involved multiple actors across parties and levels of government, allowing us to test general theories in a complex setting.

COLLECTIVE TRAUMA, SHARED HISTORY, AND THE POLITICAL IMPLICATIONS OF DISASTERS

The evidence from the individual-level models is compelling, but it is the implications at the aggregate level that make disasters an important engine of political awareness, learning, and ultimately political change. Catastrophes create new demands for policy solutions from the public, which create opportunities for political entrepreneurs to build coalitions around policy proposals (Baumgartner and Jones 2009; Birkland 1997, 2006; Kingdon 2002). As part of this, disasters create an opportunity for citizens to learn collectively about government, its leaders, and its policies (Birkland 2006). But disasters and the policy problems that result from them are socially constructed, meaning that the media, the public, and political leaders must reach a shared understanding about the definition of a problem and the bounds of acceptable solutions (Birkland 2006; Stone 1989). Prior research delves little into the factors that encourage consensus among the public. Our work shows that extraordinary events that stimulate widespread shock and anxiety increase the likelihood of producing the conditions conducive to political learning as well as opinion and policy change. At the individual level, anxiety promotes attentiveness and reduces the effects of partisan or other predisposition filters when evaluating new information. Writ large, an anxious population exposed to relatively homogeneous information about unfolding events is likely to become more accepting of the dominant stories and therefore become more homogeneous in their attributions of blame and subsequent political attitudes. This collective homogenization of opinion that occurs in the wake of major events, especially when it involves the role of government, affords political entrepreneurs a fertile ground, particularly if collective attributions of blame target countries, groups, individuals, or institutions that can be punished for causing a negative outcome.

The general theory and results that we have presented help to identify specific contextual and individual-level microfoundations that increase the probability of punctuated political change. One of the challenges facing scholars in the policy community is identifying the circumstances in which policy is likely to remain stable, and the circumstances in which it is likely to change quickly or abruptly (Wood and Doan 2003; Wood and Vedlitz 2007). Although extraordinary events are seen as one type of crises that spurs punctuated policy changes, the microfoundations that give rise to such changes have been poorly understood (Wood and Vedlitz 2007). It appears likely that a "tipping point" or threshold of public agreement must be exceeded before a negative social condition becomes defined as a policy problem, and extraordinary events provide the type of catalyst necessary to tip the balance (Wood and Doan 2003:645).

However, not all extraordinary events are equally effective at spawning political change. Birkland (2006) finds that the variation in policy response to disasters depends partly upon the nature of the policy community surrounding issues raised by it, but also partly upon public salience and media attention. When media messages are both loud and credible and when an extraordinary event stimulates broad emotional engagement in the public, a greater proportion of the population is likely to accept the dominant attributions of blame.

We suggest that the important factors that scholars should consider when evaluating the potential impact of extraordinary events include their emotional intensity and their breadth of personal relevance. Both factors are likely to drive the duration of coverage and the strength of the emotional primes embedded in the coverage because broadcasters, under pressure for ratings, make strategic choices about which stories stay in the headlines persistently and which cycle out quickly. Emotional intensity of the disaster reflects the degree to which a catastrophe possesses the raw material that is necessary for the press to construct emotional primes that engage the public. This material is defined by four characteristics: abruptness of the event, human suffering or death, violations of public expectations for social or government conduct, and breadth of relevance to the public. Only those seen as broadly relevant and anxiety provoking are likely to reach a sufficient tipping point to spawn the desire for collective policy changes to prevent or mitigate future catastrophes.

Scholars must also consider the heterogeneity of the media message environment in shaping broader political outcomes. The number and clarity of causal attributions are likely key components of persuasiveness. In the case of Katrina, there were multiple stories for why aid failed to arrive in New Orleans, but the dominant story that persisted over time was one of the national government's failure to manage the crisis. The convergence on the national government blame frame opened the door to policy changes pertaining to the scope and authority of the national government and FEMA, as well as the appointment powers of presidents. What about other disasters? Does the winnowing of causal stories differ for drawn-out or ongoing events, such as the recent Gulf oil spill or slow-moving economic crises, compared to extraordinary events that begin and end abruptly, such as 9/11, Katrina, or the Oklahoma City bombing? These questions are unanswered at this point, but they are important to examine because they are likely to shape the power of events as agenda setters. The many permutations of disasters provide opportunities for understanding how variation in the context of media coverage influences public emotion, attribution, and ultimately collective political attitudes.

Catastrophes and Partisan Realignment?

Because extraordinary events encourage deliberation, attributions, and evaluations that transcend typical party boundaries, might they become a mechanism for widespread shifts in partisanship? Could they generate a partisan realignment? Perhaps, but only under rare conditions. Realignment involves mass transition of allegiance away from one party and toward another – something not easily achieved in normal political times when partisanship serves to filter most information that attentive individuals encounter. An epochal moment where people set aside partisanship when examining government performance seems ripe for realignments. However, we see two factors likely to limit the ability of an epochal event to realign the electorate more generally. First, the types of policies that are raised in the wake of disasters fall outside the usual partisan lines of debate. Policies pertaining to disaster preparedness, agency organization and budgets, building codes, disaster insurance, lines of authority for disaster response, and the like rarely generate strong partisan divisions. The public can easily unite around these nonpartisan, safety-related issues, as we saw in Chapter 7 in regard to policies related to victim penalties and the preference for an independent commission. Even contentious issues may transcend party in extraordinary moments. Policy responses to 9/11 raised fundamental and thorny political issues pertaining to privacy and civil liberties. Yet the proposed policies generated little partisan strife at the elite or mass level. The public desire to see government restore a sense of order and safety appeared to transcend normal political lines (Davis and Silver 2004).

The second is that the media and the public seem to see catastrophe response the responsibility of *leaders* rather than parties. In times of catastrophes, the public fixates on the competency of individuals – presidents, agency heads, governors, local officials, and the like (see Bucy 2003; Merolla and Zeichmeister 2009). Disaster leadership is placed squarely in the executive branch of government, with most executives appointing agency leaders directly responsible for organizing and overseeing both preparedness and response. The legislative branch serves only as an oversight to executive authority in this matter. When disaster strikes and the executive branch fails, the legislative branch is typically quick to step in to identify problems and offer new legislative solutions. Electoral reward or punishment, then, is most likely targeted toward executives, with legislators facing minimal or only coattail effects. Thus the dynamic following an epochal event encourages accountability for individual leaders rather than collective parties.

This is not to say that epochal events never spawn realignments. Over eight decades ago, an extraordinary event, Black Friday, rippled throughout the country, a tragedy that marked the beginning of an extended period of economic contraction with long-term consequences for the vibrancy of American life. During this time, banks closed, unemployment rose to 25 percent, and many people lost their homes, property, and livelihood. As a result, the election of 1932 was a realigning election, with the public overwhelmingly supporting a new Democratic president, Congress, and political agenda. There is no doubt that the Great Depression was an extraordinary event that led to extraordinary political outcomes, including the beginnings of a social welfare state in the United States. However, an important distinction between this extraordinary event and many of those today is that consequences of economic failure directly touched nearly every community and family across the nation. For government leaders to heed calls to rescue the "victims" of the economic catastrophe, they had to make sweeping changes in the role of government in society. The anxiety felt by the public during the economic catastrophe created an opportunity for political entrepreneurs to map out a new political course for the public, and the public, seeking security, took it. We have seen similar types of sweeping changes in response to recent catastrophes – namely after 9/11, when we saw the widespread willingness of citizens to trade privacy for greater security (Davis 2007; Davis and Silver 2004; Huddy, Khatib, and Capelos 2002; Huddy et al. 2005; Merolla and Zechmeister 2009). Unlike during the Great Depression, however, the policy debates following 9/11 did not create new partisan cleavages because both parties were united in supporting the shift in policy.

At the time of this writing, it is still unclear whether the economic crises that began in 2008 could lead to realignment in the 2012 or 2014 elections, but it is possible. During the time period of 2008 to 2011, there were several major crises that brought to light deep partisan divisions in the management of the economy, such as the sudden and unexpected stock market declines in 2008 and 2009, the near-collapse of banks in 2008, and the partisan stalemate surrounding the debt ceiling in 2011. As in the Great Depression, citizens and communities across the nation were directly touched by the anxiety associated with the deep recession, sparked by declining home values, stock values, and job opportunities. And, as in the Great Depression, there were clear partisan divisions in attributions of blame and, thus, problem definition. Therefore, the probability is greater that these and any additional related economic catastrophes could create deep and meaningful shifts in public partisan allegiances.

This discussion points to an important difference in the types of catastrophes that the public encounters. Economic crises, unlike natural disasters, have long been a critical issue in understanding political swings in the United States and internationally. Bad times in particular seem to hurt the incumbent party because the standard pattern of causal attribution is to blame the executive and party in power. Unlike most disasters that are experienced vicariously and through emotional empathy, an economic catastrophe is a doorstep issue, one that individuals encounter every day in their personal lives and one that is discussed regularly in political debates. Citizens see strains in the economy when they encounter higher food or gas prices, they notice when factories close nearby and unemployment rises, and they notice when they cannot sell their home or when they see foreclosures in their neighborhood. Even without the media, which provide additional aggregate evidence and confirm individual perspectives on the collective nature of the problem (Mutz 1994), economic outcomes are powerful and easy cues about the nature of the times and the success of the current administration. Economic crises naturally raise fundamental issues related to taxing, spending, and regulation for which both parties have well-established and distinct partisan positions. When individuals seek solutions to a crisis by embracing a fundamentally different approach to the economy, they are most likely also embracing the approach of a different party. As a result, economic calamity is much more likely to produce partisan realignment than other types of catastrophes, especially if parties take clearly different stands on how to proceed.

Regardless, whether natural, economic, or man-made, a catastrophe matters to politics and policy because extraordinary events create a *collective* environment conducive to opinion change. In turn, greater collective agreement about the root cause and potential solutions to unexpected problems increases the odds of policy change. Media coverage following disasters helps to circumvent normal political processing of information and encourage deliberation that transcends normal partisan filters. Events that are abrupt, shocking, and unexpected and that generate emotional anxiety and empathy are those most ripe for creating a collective environment that reaches the tipping point for problem definition. When a large portion of the public feels personally connected to a catastrophic event and worries over personal ramifications, they respond by seeking to learn who or what is at fault and how best to resolve the crisis. This provides ample fuel for entrepreneurs to build political coalitions around newly shared understandings of the world.

Do Extraordinary Events Matter More in Today's Media Environment?

Although any particular type of extraordinary event does not happen frequently, extraordinary events, broadly speaking, happen with great regularly and journalists increasingly pay attention to the public's response. One indicator of this media attention is the increase in the number of poll questions about disasters over the last twenty-five years (see Figure 8.1). The top line in this figure indicates all poll questions classified in the category of "disaster" by Roper's IPOLL databank search. The bottom line reflects the number of disaster questions fielded by Gallup, *USA Today*, and the *New York Times*. Frequent polling is especially evident during the epochal crises of 9/11 and Hurricane Katrina, with more than 500 total questions asked about the latter and more than 1,500 asked about the former. In part, this increase is due to changes in the media that have increased the number of polls generally. The increased interest in catastrophes is also due, in part, to the substantially smaller world that we live in as technology brings remote places and events to our doorstep and, more importantly, to our consciousness.

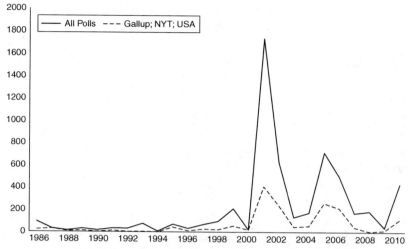

FIGURE 8.1. Frequency of Disaster Polling Questions, 1986–2010.

What does it mean for the public to be constantly bombarded by catastrophes? Does it make them seem more routine and therefore less important? Perhaps for some types of events, this is the case, but for others, it is likely to magnify their significance. In the nationalized media climate of today, localized events within and beyond the boundaries of the United States are brought to the forefront of a national audience with greater frequency, but they also dissipate more quickly in the fast news-cycle environment unless the media identify dimensions that warrant continued national attention. An important task of future research is to identify which characteristics of catastrophes increase the odds that they become meaningful collective moments. Our theoretical framework suggests that this may hinge heavily on whether coverage reveals a gap between what the public expects to happen during and after a disaster and how it actually plays out, particularly with regard to government performance. So, for example, the earthquakes in Japan in 2011 had a strong impact on national and international policy discussions because, unexpectedly, the nuclear power reactors damaged by the tsunami could not be cooled down. In this case, an "ordinary" disaster was transformed into an extraordinary nuclear crisis because the reactors proved unexpectedly vulnerable to this particular disaster. This expectations gap commanded increased public attention and raised the salience of nuclear energy debates worldwide. Germany, in response to Japan's catastrophe, designed an aggressive plan to abandon nuclear power over the next eleven years (Baetz 2011). The nationalization and even internationalization of catastrophe coverage point to why we should care about extraordinary events and their influence on public opinions. They are sources of energy for political leadership and for policy change. But variation in the context of catastrophes raises important questions about the conditions necessary to catapult ordinary disasters to extended national prominence in the media.

It is also important to note that the postwar media environment, enhanced over the last twenty-five years with easy access to 24/7 Internet and cable news, has had a profound influence on both the creation of collective moments and the nationalization of policy. Local disasters that might once have only created demands for local policy solutions are now viewed broadly by a national audience, opening opportunities for national-level political entrepreneurs to tie policy solutions to disasters. A century ago, disasters such as factory fires, crime sprees, and even hurricanes or earthquakes were felt most keenly at the local level. With only limited technological resources for nationalizing news stories, the bulk of the public shock and emotional response occurred within these localized communities. As a result, calls for policy solutions were targeted toward local or state officials – those closest to the disaster. For example, the Triangle Shirtwaist Factory fire in 1911 in New York City, where 146 women perished when trapped by a locked door in the upper stories of the factory, generated a massive public outcry for changes to safety codes in the workplace. Hundreds of thousands of people turned out for the funeral and many protested the working conditions that lead to their deaths (Hoenig 2005). However, in 1911, news was localized rather than nationalized, so the shock and horror touched deeply those in New York and change was sought in primarily the halls of state government (Hoenig 2005; Von Drehle 2003). That same disaster, if played out today, would command the national media stage, and calls for policy reform would likely be targeted not only at local and state governments, but also at national government. Thus, one key difference between then and now is the public expectation that *national government* is responsible for preventing and responding to extraordinary events at all levels of society.

Extraordinary events of today also tug at emotions more frequently and potentially in different directions, creating greater volatility in opinions about leaders, parties, or policies. For example, 9/11 brought Americans together around a single president and a national cause, yet just a few years later Hurricane Katrina pulled evaluations of President Bush in the opposite direction. Interestingly, nearly a decade prior, his father, President George H. W. Bush, faced almost identical opposing tugs for much the same reason. The Gulf War rallied opinions in his direction, but the slow federal response to Hurricane Andrew reduced his popularity. Thus, one additional reason that we may see limited realignment in response to regular extraordinary events is that events that stimulate credit and blame for political leaders cycle rapidly, reducing the chance of sustained electoral effects.

In summary, the dominance of an instantaneous, rich, extensive, visual, and rather low-cost media environment has the power to draw in hundreds of millions of viewers and engage them emotionally. The frequency with which such engagement happens in today's world is greater, and therefore it is important to understand how extraordinary events become politicized and nationalized. Clearly, they create unique moments of mass collective attentiveness that can nudge mass opinion formation to greater consensus and create a political environment ripe for policy entrepreneurship. But much remains to be done to understand fully how the nature of extraordinary events and their coverage shape the media message environment that influences collective public opinion.

SOME FINAL NORMATIVE THOUGHTS

V. O. Key (1966) argued long ago that voters are no fools and can and do hold leaders accountable. But to do so, citizens must engage the political world independently and thoughtfully so that they are leading the democratic process, not being manipulated by it (Bartels 2003; Entman 1993; Zaller 1992). Our results support the belief that citizens are capable of rendering opinions and judgments that are consistent with a deliberative and attentive public and thus provide a positive picture of citizens fulfilling the demands of democratic responsibility. Citizens link their attributions of blame to leaders appropriately, regardless of their political predispositions. This is a critical point because political science sometimes paints a picture of a knee-jerk citizenry who have little interest in thoughtful evaluation of leaders and government. Our results show that extraordinary moments yield opinions that are more consistent with evaluations of government in action and a logical understanding of cause and effect. When evaluating leaders and determining preferences for public policies, citizens rely not only on their prior understanding of the world, but also their attributions of blame. Furthermore, our story is an optimistic one about the press. In normal political times, the press serves simply to index elite debate and their independent power to shine a critical light on government is limited. However, in moments of crisis, the press holds an upper hand as it investigates and interprets unfolding crises.

Our study brings good news, at least in a particular setting, to the connection between deliberation and democracy. Theorists note that multiple perspectives are important to a healthy democracy because they increase political engagement and tolerance (Mendelberg 2002; Mill 1859). It also leads, theoretically, to higher-quality opinions that are based upon reason and rationality (Dryzek 2000; Fishkin 1999; Mill 1859). It appears that people accept and reject explanations above and beyond those to which they are predisposed, and once a frame is accepted, it leads to more consistent opinion across a host of political domains. This finding suggests that the public can be responsive to the events around them and use the information to make informed judgments about political actors. In this way, fundamental values inherent in a democratic society, including representation and accountability, are enhanced.

Appendix A

Survey Data and Methodology

Data for much of the analysis in this book were collected through the study funded by the National Science Foundation entitled "Who's to Blame? Public Perceptions of the Aftermath of Hurricane Katrina" (SGER SES-0320585). Survey results are based on telephone interviews conducted under the direction of the Earl Survey Research Laboratory at Texas Tech University in Lubbock Texas from September 21 through November 13, 2005. The sample was purchased from Marketing Systems Group. The random digit dialing (RDD) sample of 1,019 adults had a cooperation rate of 27.7 percent and a response rate of 16.0 percent. The telephone interview averaged 20 minutes in length. For results based upon the entire sample, this survey has a margin of error of +/– 3.07 percent, with a confidence interval of 95 percent. The survey instrument was updated on September 27 to include revised and additional questions pertaining to Hurricane Rita. Therefore, the results presented in this book are based upon 981 interviews completed after the implementation of the revised instrument on September 27. Univariate and bivariate statistics reported in each chapter are weighted to reflect the age and sex composition of the underlying population. A full frequency report can be found at http://polisci.fsu.edu/katrina/.

Appendix B

Data and Methodology for Survey Experiment

Data for the survey experiment in Chapter 6 were collected through an online survey. The questions were designed and fielded as part of the Florida State University team module survey in conjunction with the 2006 Cooperative Congressional Elections Study (CCES). The data were collected by YouGov–Polimetrix via Internet using respondents from an opt-in panel designed to reflect the characteristics of a nationally drawn stratified sample. In all, the full CCES study had a total of 36,500 adult respondents, and team modules were given a random sample of 1,000 of the 36,500. The full sample was stratified into sixteen strata based on voter registration status, state size, and competitiveness of the congressional district. The selection of panelists into the study was based on the degree to which they matched a set of enumerated characteristics of a target national sample reflecting this stratification. Specific details about the matching procedures used to draw the full sample can be found in Ansolabehere (2010). The quality of this technique was assessed by comparing the CCES survey results to actual election outcomes and to other phone-based surveys taken during the same time period. Validation results based on gubernatorial votes, senate votes, and statewide proposition votes show that the survey had high accuracy and low bias. Additional information about the study and data can be found at the CCES Dataverse at http://projects. iq.harvard.edu/cces/data?dvn_subpage=/faces/study/StudyPage.xhtml? globalId=hdl:1902.1/14002.

The survey was collected in two waves, and we utilize data from both. The first wave was fielded in October of 2006 prior to the November general election. The second wave was fielded immediately after the election. Due to panel attrition, the number of respondents to the second wave was lower than the first, so our total number of cases available for the survey experiment was 817. In the first wave, we asked about respondents' confidence in government. In the second wave, respondents were given the same set of confidence questions, but a randomized treatment cuing 9/11 or Hurricane Katrina was added to the question to determine the effect of cuing recall of the disasters. We draw conclusions about causal relationships based on the randomized application of treatments and do not purport to draw inferences from the results to a national population. The panel design allows for strong within-subject controls, and the randomization in the second stage provides leverage for cross-treatment comparisons.

Appendix C

Coding of News Transcripts and Video Data

The analysis of media content presented throughout the manuscript is based on two datasets compiled by coding transcripts and video of televised news broadcasts during the weeks following the storm. The data collection was funded by the National Science Foundation (NSF SES-055304).

METHODOLOGY FOR VIDEO CODING OF FNC AND CNN BROADCASTS

Coders examined video broadcasts of cable news coverage during the period of August 27, 2005, to September 14, 2005, for two shows: the *Fox Report with Shepard Smith* on FNC and *News Night with Aaron Brown* on CNN. We selected these networks for analysis because they were the networks most frequently watched by survey respondents in our study. Thirty-three percent of our respondents reported following coverage on CNN, while 19 percent reported following the storm coverage on FNC. Copies of each of the shows were obtained from Vanderbilt News Archives.

The primary purpose of this coding was to record the emotional and substantive content that a typical viewer would receive through exposure to the combination of visual and verbal content. Two student coders were assigned to code either odd or even days of coverage. Coding the broadcasts entailed filling out structured code sheets to record the instances of video images and verbal cues as well as noting general impressions about the tone of coverage. The unit of analysis, for coding purposes, is the show-segment. Coders identified a total of 761 segments on the two stations. Of these, 257 segments were short introduction or closing segments with little substantive content. In these instances, coders recorded the general tone and visual images, but did not complete the full code sheet because most of the items were inapplicable. For the remainder, coders filled out an extensive structured code sheet to record the visual and verbal content of each segment. In general, segments for FNC were much shorter and therefore more numerous compared to CNN. Data reported in this manuscript are from the 504 substantive segments, 308 were from FNC, and 196 were from CNN. Code sheets for the televised transcripts are available from the authors upon request.

Each coder watched the full broadcast to identify the beginning and end points of segments, then watched each segment a minimum of two times. During the first review, the coder recorded the time length of the segment, the nature of the segment (i.e., elite interview, victim interview, reporter summary, etc.), the overall tone of the verbal content of the segment, and the overall tone of the visuals of the segment. During the second review, coders identified and counted specific visual images and verbal and visual content related to a defined list of actors or attributions. In many cases, the coder watched segments more than twice to ensure accurate coding. Code sheets, data, and replication files for the analysis are available upon request from the authors.

METHODOLOGY FOR TRANSCRIPT CODING FOR ABC, CBS, NBC, CNN, AND FNC BROADCASTS

News transcripts from five major regularly scheduled news networks were coded for tone and attribution content. The broadcast network programs were each one half-hour in length, while the cable news network programs were one hour in length.[1] The news programs included in the analysis were *ABC World News Tonight*, *NBC Nightly News*, *The CBS Evening News*, *The CNN Special Report with Aaron Brown*, and *The FOX News Hour*. Transcripts were coded for the

---

[1] To maintain consistency across networks, when networks offered extended coverage of the storm, we coded only the coverage occurring during the normal broadcast time.

selected news programs for every day between August 27, 2005, and October 1, 2005. There were 1,170 segments coded for this time period, 139 for ABC (11.8 percent), 187 for CBS (15.9 percent), 241 for NBC (20.6 percent), 343 for CNN (29.3 percent), and 260 for FNC (22.2 percent). Because of the time differences involved, cable news network segments are significantly longer than broadcast news programs. The average word counts for the news segments were 501 (ABC), 348 (CBS), 377 (NBC), 693 (CNN), and 596 (FOX).

To collect attribution information, coders read each segment a minimum of two times, once to attain an overall feeling for the article, followed by a second reading to assess direct speaker attributions. In many cases, the transcript was read additional times to ensure proper coding. Following the first read, the coder would complete the general information section of a segment-level code sheet that included information such as the station name; segment name; anchor and reporter information; word count; the type of segment (news/informational, editorial, human interest, etc.); the overall tone of the segment (optimistic, pessimistic, or neutral); and the portion of the segment that focused on nature, government, victims, preparation failure, and response failure, among other things. Additionally, coders noted whether or not there were any implied or explicit positive or negative attributions that were identified on a predefined list. Coders also had the option of identifying "other" attributions not listed on the predefined list.

An attribution was coded as implied if an anchor, reporter, or guest on a show created the impression of causality. This often occurred through leading questions or through comments that suggested a cause of the situation in New Orleans without explicitly laying blame. For example, on August 27, 2005, *NBC Nightly News* reported, "This is now a category 3 storm with winds of up to 115 miles per hour. Authorities have already started to advise residents along the coast to begin evacuations. The latest information from the National Hurricane Center puts Katrina on a path headed for New Orleans, where it could be a category 5 storm when it makes landfall sometime Monday." This was coded in the data as an implied negative attribution toward "Nature/Size of the Storm." The information being presented does not specifically attribute the storm with the need for evacuations or preparation, but it implies that the size of the storm requires evacuation of residents; therefore, this would be coded as an implied negative attribution toward nature or the size of the storm.

After coding general information and implied attributions, coders reread the article, noting explicit attributions of credit or blame. Direct attributions place blame for the positive or negative situation surrounding the hurricane and aftermath explicitly. When an attribution occurred in the broadcast transcript, it was coded for the following characteristics: the speaker making the attribution; the target of the attribution; whether the attribution was positive, negative, or neutral; the time frame to which the attribution was referring, such as a preparation failure or a response failure; and the reason that the attribution was made. On August 31, 2005, *The CBS Evening News* opened with the statement, "The federal government is taking over relief efforts as many in the devastated area are asking 'What took so long?'" This was coded as a direct negative attribution, during the response period, toward the federal government for slow response time with assistance and supplies. The speaker was listed as Bob Schieffer, who was the anchor on *The CBS Evening News* at that time. Anchors and reporters were responsible for 68.7 percent (1,301) of the direct attributions. Government or elected officials (13.1 percent) and residents (7.1 percent) were responsible for the majority of the remaining direct attributions.

Appendix D

Multivariate Model Results for Chapter 4

Tables D.1 and D.2 provide full results from ordered-probit models. All models in the book were run in Stata 11.0. Replication data and files for models in all chapters are available from authors upon request.

TABLE D.1. *Ordered-Probit Models of Attributions of Blame*

	National Government		Nature of Storm		Criminal Behavior	
	B	SE	B	SE	B	SE
Party ID (strong Dem to strong Rep)	-0.309	0.039***	0.165	0.037***	0.125	0.038***
Anxiety	0.309	0.045***	-0.111	0.044**	0.063	0.044
Anxiety x Party ID	0.057	0.019***	-0.024	0.019	-0.035	0.019*
Attention to coverage	0.070	0.056	-0.022	0.056	-0.073	0.056
Political knowledge	0.007	0.052	-0.164	0.051***	-0.083	0.052
Harmed/knew someone harmed by hurricane	-0.001	0.031	-0.006	0.030	0.007	0.030
Black	0.475	0.119***	-0.127	0.113	-0.129	0.114
Other minority	0.245	0.134*	0.257	0.133*	0.046	0.133
Race unknown	0.724	0.257***	-0.489	0.245**	0.074	0.238
Female	0.088	0.075	-0.074	0.074	-0.026	0.074
Age	0.002	0.025	0.041	0.025*	-0.007	0.025
Education	-0.003	0.036	-0.056	0.035	-0.089	0.035**
Homeowner	-0.277	0.101***	0.040	0.097	0.164	0.097*
Low income (<25K)	0.025	0.110	0.102	0.106	0.233	0.108**
μ_1	-1.168	0.233	-1.737	0.229	-1.946	0.232
μ_2	-0.036	0.228	-0.709	0.224	-0.840	0.225
μ_3	0.166	0.227	-0.555	0.224	-0.684	0.224
μ_4	0.291	0.228	-0.486	0.224	-0.516	0.224
μ_5	0.704	0.228	-0.084	0.223	-0.153	0.223
μ_6	1.623	0.232	0.825	0.227	0.778	0.225
N	919		922		902	
χ^2	346.74	***	97.31	***	42.73	***
LnL	-1437.20		-1553.39		-1562.79	

*** $p < .01$; ** $p < .05$; * $p < .10$; two-tailed tests.

TABLE D.1. *(cont.)*

	Non-evacuation		State Failure	
	B	SE	B	SE
Party ID (strong Dem to strong Rep)	0.151	0.037***	0.210	0.045***
Anxiety	0.036	0.044	0.101	0.053*
Anxiety × Party ID	-0.027	0.019	-0.071	0.022***
Attention to coverage	-0.012	0.055	0.222	0.066***
Political knowledge	-0.150	0.051***	-0.066	0.061
Harmed/knew someone harmed by hurricane	0.007	0.030	-0.062	0.036*
Black	-0.051	0.113	0.272	0.133**
Other minority	-0.140	0.130	-0.160	0.150
Race unknown	0.095	0.234	-0.384	0.268
Female	-0.188	0.074**	-0.185	0.088**
Age	-0.012	0.025	0.035	0.029
Education	-0.158	0.035***	0.037	0.042
Homeowner	0.055	0.097	0.016	0.113
Low income (<25K)	0.175	0.107	0.064	0.127
μ_1	-2.579	0.237	-0.403	0.264
μ_2	-1.578	0.226	0.037	0.262
μ_3	-1.399	0.225	0.856	0.264
μ_4	-1.253	0.225		
μ_5	-0.716	0.222		
μ_6	0.195	0.223		
N	922		763	
χ^2	87.48	***	57.48	***
LnL	-1560.23		-890.79	

*** p < .01; ** p < .05; * p < .10; two-tailed tests.

TABLE D.2. *Ordered-Probit Model of Anger about New Orleans*

	B	SE
Blame nature	−0.119	0.026***
Blame national government	0.074	0.029**
Blame non-evacuees	−0.074	0.027***
Blame crime	−0.017	0.026
Blame state	0.124	0.050**
Anxiety	0.488	0.065***
Attention to Katrina	0.138	0.088
Political knowledge	0.062	0.072
Knew victim	0.075	0.040*
Party ID (Republican highest)	−0.038	0.029
Political ideology (Conservative highest)	−0.079	0.038**
Education	0.035	0.049
Black	−0.213	0.150
Other minority	0.044	0.176
Race unknown	−0.051	0.346
Female	0.204	0.100**
Age	−0.026	0.034
Attention to Rita	0.033	0.064
Homeowner	−0.227	0.132*
Low income (<$25,000)	−0.063	0.151
$\mu 1$	0.628	0.435
$\mu 2$	0.824	0.435
$\mu 3$	1.754	0.438
N	653	
Ln likelihood	−662.98	
χ^2	250.15	***

***p < .01; **p < .05; *p < .10; two-tailed tests.

Appendix E

Multivariate Model Results for Chapter 5

TABLE E.1. *Ordered-Probit Models of Evaluations of Leaders*

	Bush Evaluation		Blanco Evaluation		Nagin Evaluation	
	B	SE	B	SE	B	SE
Nature of storm	0.119	0.026 ***	0.130	0.027 ***	0.084	0.026 ***
National government	−0.212	0.029 ***	0.154	0.030 ***	0.118	0.029 ***
Non-evacuation	0.012	0.028	−0.022	0.027	−0.062	0.027 **
Crime	0.050	0.026 *	0.031	0.025	0.006	0.025
State failure	−0.085	0.049 *	−0.366	0.048 ***	−0.278	0.047 ***
National Guard (state)	0.055	0.123	−0.249	0.116 **	−0.259	0.113 **
National Guard (don't know)	0.214	0.155	−0.038	0.148	−0.120	0.147
Anxiety	−0.081	0.067	0.049	0.066	0.096	0.065
Angry	−0.168	0.046 ***	−0.043	0.045	−0.037	0.044
Political knowledge	−0.160	0.075 **	−0.105	0.071	−0.070	0.070
Knew Katrina victim	−0.001	0.042	−0.056	0.041	0.020	0.039
Party ID	0.157	0.029 ***	−0.056	0.029 **	−0.034	0.028
Ideology	0.069	0.039 *	−0.016	0.038	−0.053	0.037
Education	−0.116	0.050 **	0.050	0.048	−0.060	0.048
Black	−0.474	0.175 ***	−0.003	0.147	0.183	0.144
Other minority	−0.108	0.181	0.058	0.173	−0.142	0.171
Minority (don't know)	0.095	0.340	0.237	0.305	−0.228	0.326
Female	−0.020	0.103	0.242	0.101 **	0.365	0.100 ***
Age (categorical)	0.014	0.034	−0.070	0.033 **	−0.096	0.033 ***
Homeowner	0.017	0.137	0.009	0.132	−0.004	0.131
Low income (<$25,000)	−0.003	0.153	0.500	0.149 ***	0.045	0.149
Attention to Rita	0.147	0.058 **	−0.033	0.059	−0.012	0.057
μ_1	−0.914	0.434	−0.186	0.439	−0.953	0.425
μ_2	0.374	0.434	1.037	0.439	−0.012	0.424
μ_3	1.634	0.439	2.277	0.450	1.067	0.427
N	637		606		609	
χ^2	409.19	***	189.82	***	164.05	***
LnL	−575.75		−614.20		−671.84	

***$p < .01$; **$p < .05$; *$p < .10$; two-tailed tests.

TABLE E.2. *Ordered-Probit Models of Evaluations of Leaders with Anger Interaction*

	Bush Evaluation		Blanco Evaluation		Nagin Evaluation	
	B	SE	B	SE	B	SE
Nature of storm	0.119	0.026***	0.130	0.027***	0.083	0.026***
National government	-0.171	0.035***	0.164	0.036***	0.148	0.036***
Non-evacuation	0.008	0.028	-0.023	0.027	-0.064	0.027**
Crime	0.048	0.026*	0.030	0.025	0.003	0.025
State failure	-0.099	0.049**	-0.369	0.048***	-0.289	0.047***
National Guard (state)	0.058	0.123	-0.248	0.116**	-0.256	0.113**
National Guard (don't know)	0.221	0.155	-0.039	0.148	-0.121	0.147
Angry	0.024	0.105	0.013	0.115	0.109	0.111
Anxiety	-0.088	0.067	0.048	0.066	0.093	0.065
Anger × national government	-0.042	0.020**	-0.011	0.021	-0.029	0.020
Political knowledge	-0.163	0.075**	-0.105	0.071	-0.072	0.070
Knew Katrina victim	-0.007	0.042	-0.058	0.041	0.017	0.039
Party ID	0.156	0.029***	-0.057	0.029**	-0.035	0.028
Ideology	0.069	0.039*	-0.016	0.038	-0.053	0.037
Education	-0.114	0.050**	0.050	0.048	-0.059	0.048
Black	-0.480	0.176***	-0.005	0.147	0.181	0.144
Other minority	-0.127	0.183	0.055	0.173	-0.151	0.171
Minority (don't know)	0.078	0.341	0.235	0.305	-0.236	0.325
Female	-0.031	0.103	0.242	0.101**	0.364	0.100***
Age (categorical)	0.014	0.034	-0.070	0.033**	-0.097	0.033***
Homeowner	0.021	0.138	0.011	0.132	0.001	0.131
Low income (<$25,000)	0.009	0.154	0.502	0.149***	0.050	0.149
Attention to Rita	0.152	0.059***	-0.032	0.059	-0.008	0.057
μ_1	-0.814	0.438	-0.154	0.443	-0.861	0.430
μ_2	0.477	0.438	1.069	0.443	0.081	0.429
μ_3	1.732	0.443	2.310	0.455	1.163	0.432
N	637		606		609	
χ^2	413.41	***	190.10	***	166.08	
LnL	-573.65		-614.06		-670.82	

***$p < .01$; **$p < .05$; *$p < .10$; two-tailed tests.

Appendix F

Multivariate Model Results for Chapter 6

TABLE F.1. *Ordered-Probit Model of External Efficacy*

	Model 1			Model 2		
	B	**SE**	**sig**	**B**	**SE**	**sig**
Blame nature	−0.002	0.023		−0.002	0.023	
Blame national government	−0.058	0.031	*	−0.055	0.026	**
Blame non-evacuees	−0.032	0.024		−0.032	0.024	
Blame criminal actions	−0.015	0.022		−0.015	0.022	
State failed to call for help	−0.006	0.042		−0.007	0.042	
Angry	−0.096	0.094		−0.082	0.039	**
Anxious	0.002	0.056		0.002	0.056	
Angry × blame national government	0.003	0.017				
Knew victim of storm	−0.073	0.035	**	−0.074	0.035	**
Party ID (str. Dem to str. Rep)	0.065	0.025	***	0.065	0.025	***
Independent	−0.144	0.098		−0.145	0.098	
Political ideology (conservative)	0.024	0.033		0.024	0.033	
Education	0.214	0.041	***	0.214	0.041	**
Black	−0.234	0.134	*	−0.234	0.134	*
Other minority	0.106	0.152		0.105	0.152	
Race unknown	−0.223	0.285		−0.224	0.285	
Female	0.074	0.086		0.073	0.086	
Age (categorical)	−0.026	0.028		−0.026	0.028	
Homeowner	0.141	0.117		0.141	0.116	
Low income (<$25,000)	0.074	0.132		0.074	0.132	
μ_1	−0.996	0.352		−0.989	0.349	
μ_2	−0.035	0.351		−0.027	0.348	
μ_3	0.324	0.351		0.332	0.348	
μ_4	0.498	0.351		0.505	0.348	
μ_5	0.684	0.351		0.692	0.348	
μ_6	1.811	0.356		1.819	0.354	
N	671			671		
LnL	−1134			−1134		
χ^2	109.69			109.66		

***p < .01; **p < .05; *p < .10; two-tailed tests.

TABLE F.2. *Ordered-Probit Models of Confidence in National Government to Handle Future Catastrophes*

	Biological Attack		Earthquakes		Nuclear Attack		Flu Epidemic		Hurricane	
Blame nature	0.05	0.03**	0.06	0.03**	0.06	0.03**	0.08	0.03***	0.08	0.03***
Blame nat'l gvt.	-0.17	0.04***	-0.09	0.04***	-0.12	0.04***	-0.09	0.04**	-0.09	0.03**
Blame non-evacuees	0.01	0.03	0.01	0.03	-0.01	0.03	-0.01	0.03	-0.02	0.03
Blame crime	0.00	0.03	0.00	0.03	0.00	0.03	0.02	0.03	0.02	0.02
Blame state failure	0.05	0.05	0.07	0.05	0.02	0.05	0.01	0.05	0.00	0.05
Angry	0.04	0.10	0.02	0.11	0.09	0.11	0.03	0.10	0.07	0.11
Anxious	0.07	0.07	0.05	0.07	0.09	0.07	-0.04	0.06	-0.01	0.06
Angry × blame national gvt.	-0.01	0.02	-0.04	0.02**	-0.03	0.02*	-0.02	0.02	-0.02	0.02
Knew victim	-0.02	0.04	-0.04	0.04	0.00	0.04	-0.01	0.04	0.05	0.04
Party ID (Dem to Rep)	0.09	0.03***	0.08	0.03***	0.11	0.03***	0.11	0.03***	0.06	0.03**
Ideology (lib to cons)	0.03	0.04	0.02	0.04	0.03	0.04	0.03	0.04	0.06	0.04
Education	-0.05	0.05	0.03	0.05	-0.07	0.05	-0.04	0.05	-0.05	0.05
Black	0.32	0.16**	0.24	0.15	0.36	0.16**	0.47	0.15***	0.13	0.15
Other minority	0.09	0.19	-0.22	0.19	0.19	0.19	-0.06	0.18	0.06	0.18
Race unknown	0.35	0.33	0.48	0.32	0.72	0.32**	-0.06	0.34	0.47	0.33
Female	-0.01	0.10	0.01	0.10	0.02	0.10	0.07	0.10	-0.03	0.10
Age (categorical)	-0.03	0.03	-0.02	0.03	-0.05	0.03	0.04	0.03	-0.03	0.03
Attention to Rita	0.03	0.06	0.03	0.06	0.09	0.06	0.00	0.06	0.07	0.06
Homeowner	-0.15	0.13	-0.05	0.13	0.05	0.13	-0.07	0.13	-0.10	0.13
Low income (<$25,000)	-0.23	0.16	-0.11	0.15	-0.02	0.15	0.06	0.15	-0.26	0.15*
μ₁	-0.54	0.42	-0.45	0.41	-0.17	0.42	-0.19	0.41	-0.63	0.40
μ₂	0.54	0.42	0.90	0.41	1.03	0.42	0.91	0.41	0.33	0.40
N	624		622		632		631		645	
LnL	-572		-575		-563		-594.9		-648	
χ²	131.9		161		141.2		129.5		120	

***p < .01; **p < .05; *p < .10; two-tailed tests.

TABLE F.3. *Negative Binomial Model of "Less Confident" Count*

	B	SE	sig
Blame nature	−0.072	0.021	***
Blame national government	0.144	0.031	***
Blame non-evacuees	−0.008	0.021	
Blame criminal actions	−0.018	0.020	
State failed to call for help	−0.020	0.038	
Angry	0.027	0.101	
Anxious	0.047	0.052	
Angry × blame national government	0.005	0.017	
Knew victim of storm	0.003	0.033	
Party ID (st. Rep, high value)	−0.095	0.023	***
Political ideology (ext. conservative is high value)	−0.040	0.029	
Education	−0.006	0.038	
Black	−0.135	0.112	
Other minority	0.143	0.132	
Race unknown	−0.359	0.275	
Female	−0.049	0.080	
Age (categorical)	0.005	0.027	
Homeowner	0.138	0.107	
Low income (<$25,000)	0.136	0.116	
Attention to Rita	−0.061	0.046	
Constant	0.430	0.339	
Alpha (LR test of alpha, 57.03 p < .001)	0.340	0.066	***
N	653		
LnL	−116.78		
χ^2	195.11		

***p < .01; **p < .05; *p < .10; two-tailed tests.

TABLE F.4. *Ordered-Probit Model of Confidence in Government to Assist Victims and Maintain Order*

	Assist Victims		Maintain Order	
	B	SE	B	SE
Katrina prompt	−0.219	0.080***	−0.418	0.080***
Attention to Katrina coverage	−0.237	0.055***	−0.097	0.055*
Harmed by Katrina	−0.239	0.166	−0.356	0.167*
Preelection opinion	0.771	0.043***	0.733	0.041***
Age	−0.002	0.003	−0.005	0.003*
Education	−0.081	0.029***	−0.070	0.029**
Female	−0.053	0.082	−0.096	0.082
Black	0.172	0.239	0.019	0.234
Other minority	−0.031	0.117	−0.192	0.117
Democrat	0.066	0.103	0.164	0.102
Republican	0.269	0.106**	0.362	0.105***
Other party ID	0.030	0.179	0.115	0.178
μ_1	−0.964	0.253	−0.687	0.247
μ_2	0.052	0.252	0.226	0.247
μ_3	1.295	0.256	1.435	0.252
μ_4	2.435	0.268	2.571	0.263
N	797		798	
Log likelihood	−886.92		−923.64	
χ^2	565.43		537.64	

***$p < .01$; **$p < .05$; *$p < .10$; two-tailed tests.

Appendix G

Multivariate Model Results for Chapter 7

TABLE G.1. *Ordered-Probit Models of Policy Preferences*

	Limit Presidential Authority		Independent Commission		Non-evacuee Penalties	
	B	SE	B	SE	B	SE
Nature of storm	−0.012	0.024	−0.035	0.023	0.004	0.023
National government	0.120	0.028 ***	0.117	0.027***	−0.028	0.027
Non-evacuation	0.044	0.025 *	0.039	0.025	0.110	0.024***
Crime	0.010	0.023	0.027	0.023	0.041	0.022*
State failure	−0.130	0.043 ***	−0.006	0.043	0.030	0.042
Less confident	0.096	0.025 ***	0.066	0.025***	−0.001	0.025
Angry	0.054	0.041	0.066	0.041	−0.032	0.040
Anxiety	0.184	0.058 ***	0.274	0.059***	0.201	0.057***
Political knowledge	−0.098	0.064	−0.009	0.064	−0.122	0.063**
Knew Katrina victim	−0.044	0.037	0.006	0.036	−0.108	0.036***
Party ID	−0.053	0.026 **	−0.010	0.026	0.035	0.025
Ideology	0.016	0.034	−0.092	0.034***	−0.049	0.033
Education	−0.094	0.044 **	0.020	0.044	−0.002	0.043
Black	0.273	0.141 *	0.597	0.143***	0.034	0.134
Other minority	0.157	0.159	−0.023	0.156	0.412	0.154***
Minority (don't know)	−0.148	0.291	0.481	0.307	0.374	0.289
Female	0.001	0.090	−0.079	0.089	0.016	0.087
Age (categorical)	−0.016	0.029	0.038	0.029	0.003	0.029
Homeowner	0.228	0.122 *	−0.114	0.120	0.082	0.118
Income (<$25,000)	0.110	0.139	0.124	0.138	0.187	0.134
μ_1	−1.042	0.378	−0.767	0.372	−0.932	0.365
μ_2	0.290	0.373	0.489	0.369	0.401	0.363
μ_3	0.392	0.373	0.527	0.369	0.518	0.363
μ_4	0.578	0.373	0.649	0.369	0.679	0.364
μ_5	0.842	0.374	0.914	0.370	0.948	0.364
μ_6	1.992	0.378	2.029	0.374	1.899	0.368
N	646		671		666	
χ^2	218.90	***	244.17	***	90.34	***
LnL	−964.59		−937.33		−1081.04	

***p < .01; **p < .05; *p < .10; two-tailed tests.

TABLE G.2. *Ordered-Probit Models of Policy Preferences, with Emotion Interactions*

	Limit Presidential Authority		Independent Commission		Non-evacuee Penalties	
	B	SE	B	SE	B	SE
Nature of storm	−0.008	0.024	−0.035	0.023	0.005	0.023
National government	0.065	0.033*	0.126	0.033***	−0.020	0.032
Non-evacuation	0.046	0.025*	0.038	0.025	0.109	0.024***
Crime	0.016	0.023	0.026	0.023	0.039	0.022*
State failure	−0.105	0.044**	−0.007	0.044	0.031	0.043
Less confident	0.095	0.026***	0.068	0.025***	0.002	0.025
Angry	−0.205	0.102**	0.118	0.097	0.025	0.098
Anxiety	0.191	0.059***	0.273	0.059***	0.201	0.057***
Anger × national gvt.	0.054	0.019***	−0.011	0.018	−0.011	0.018
Anxiety × party	0.059	0.024**	0.013	0.023	0.020	0.023
Political knowledge	−0.090	0.064	−0.009	0.064	−0.122	0.063*
Knew Katrina victim	−0.036	0.037	0.006	0.036	−0.107	0.036***
Party ID (str. Rep.)	−0.160	0.051***	−0.034	0.050	−0.002	0.049
Ideology (ext. cons)	0.025	0.035	−0.090	0.034***	−0.047	0.033
Education	−0.102	0.044**	0.021	0.044	−0.002	0.043
Black	0.295	0.142**	0.597	0.143***	0.036	0.134
Other minority	0.190	0.160	−0.023	0.156	0.416	0.154***
Minority (don't know)	−0.132	0.291	0.479	0.307	0.372	0.289
Female	−0.001	0.090	−0.083	0.089	0.010	0.088
Age (categorical)	−0.016	0.029	0.039	0.029	0.005	0.029
Homeowner	0.210	0.123*	−0.117	0.121	0.077	0.118
Income (<$25,000)	0.103	0.140	0.124	0.138	0.189	0.134
μ_1	−1.171	0.381	−0.740	0.375	−0.905	0.369
μ_2	0.176	0.377	0.520	0.373	0.431	0.367
μ_3	0.279	0.377	0.558	0.373	0.548	0.367
μ_4	0.466	0.377	0.681	0.373	0.709	0.367
μ_5	0.732	0.377	0.946	0.373	0.978	0.368
μ_6	1.895	0.381	2.060	0.377	1.929	0.371
N	646		671		666	
χ^2	230.77	***	244.97	***	91.72	***
LnL	−958.66		−936.93		−1080.35	

***p < .01; **p < .05; *p < .10; two-tailed tests.

References

ABC News. 2005a. "FEMA Director Removed from Katrina Duty." September 9. Available at http://abcnews.go.com/Politics/HurricaneKatrina/story?id=1111074andpage=1, accessed August 3, 2010.

  2005b. "Who's to Blame for Delayed Response to Katrina?" September 6. Available at http://abcnews.go.com/print?id=1102467, accessed February 17, 2010.

Aberbach, Joel D. 1969. "Alienation and Political Behavior." *American Political Science Review* 63(1): 36–99.

Abramowitz, Alan I., David J. Lanoue, and Subha Ramesh. 1988. "Economic Conditions, Causal Attributions, and Political Evaluations in the 1984 Presidential Election." *Journal of Politics* 50:848–63.

Abramson, Paul R. 1983. *Political Attitudes in America*. San Francisco: Freeman.

Abramson, Paul R. and John H. Aldrich. 1982. "The Decline of Electoral Participation in America." *American Political Science Review* 76:502–21.

Althaus, Scott. 2002. "American News Consumption during Times of National Crisis." *PS: Political Science and Politics* 35: 517–21.

Althaus, Scott and Young Mie Kim. 2006. "Priming Effects in Complex Information Environments: Reassessing the Impact of News Discourse on Presidential Approval." *Journal of Politics*. 68 (November):960–76.

Alvarez, R. Michael. 1999. *Information and Elections*. Michigan Studies in Political Analysis. Ann Arbor: University of Michigan Press.

Anderson, Christopher. 1995. *Blaming the Government: Citizens and the Economy in Five European Democracies*. Armonk, NY: M.E. Sharpe.

  2000. "Economic Voting and Political Context: A Comparative Perspective." *Electoral Studies* 19:151–70.

Ansolabehere, Stephen. 2010. "Guide to the 2006 Cooperative Congressional Election Survey." Available at http://projects.iq.harvard.edu/cces/data?dvn_subpage=/faces/study/StudyPage.xhtml?globalId=hdl:1902.1/14002, accessed January 9, 2012.

Arceneaux, Kevin. 2005. "Does Federalism Weaken Democratic Representation in the United States?" *Publius:The Journal of Federalism* 35:297–312.

Arceneaux, Kevin, and Robert M. Stein. 2006. "Who Is Held Responsible When Disaster Strikes? The Attribution of Responsibility for a Natural Disaster in an Urban Election." *Journal of Urban Affairs* 28:43–53.

Atkeson, Lonna Rae and Nancy Carrillo. 2007. "More Is Better: The Impact of Female Representation on Citizen Attitudes toward Government Responsiveness." *Gender and Politics* 3:79–101.

Atkeson, Lonna Rae and Randall Partin. 1995. "Economic and Referendum Voting: A Comparison of Gubernatorial and Senatorial Elections." *American Political Science Review* 89:634–7.

1998. "Economic and Referendum Voting and the Problem of Data Choice: A Reply." *American Journal of Political Science* 42:1003–7.

2001. "Candidate Advertisements, Media Coverage, and Citizen Attitudes: The Agendas and Roles of Senators and Governors in a Federal System." *Political Research Quarterly* 54:795–813.

Averill, James R. 1983. "Studies on Anger and Aggression." *American Psychologist* 38:1145–60.

Baetz, Uergen. 2011. "Germany Set to Abandon Nuclear Power for Good." Available at http://abundanthope.net/pages/Political_Information_43/Germany-set-to-abandon-nuclear-power-for-good_printer.shtml, accessed September 23, 2011.

Ball-Rokeach, S. J. and M. l. Defleur. 1976. "A Dependency Model of Mass-Media Effects." *Communication Research* 3:3–21.

Bamberger, Robert L. and Lawrence Kumins. 2005. *Oil and Gas: Supply Issues after Katrina and Rita.* Washington, DC: Congressional Research Service, October 3.

Banducci, Susan A. and Jeffrey A. Karp. 2003. "How Elections Change the Way Citizens View the Political System: Campaigns, Media Effects and Electoral Outcomes in Comparative Perspective." *British Journal of Political Science* 33:443–67.

Barber, Bernard. 1983. *The Logic and Limits of Trust.* New Brunswick, NJ: Rutgers University Press.

Barnes, Michael D., Carl L Hanson, Len M. Novilla, Aaron T. Meacham, Emily McIntyre, and Brittany C. Erickson. 2008. "Analysis of Media Agenda Setting during and after Hurricane Katrina: Implications for Emergency Preparedness, Disaster Response, and Disaster Policy." *American Journal of Public Health* 98(4):604–10.

Bartels, Larry M. 2002. "Beyond the Running Tally: Partisan Bias in Political Perceptions." *Political Behavior* 24(2):117–50.

2003. "Democracy with Attitudes." In *Electoral Democracy*, eds. M. B. MacKuen and G. Rabinowitz. Ann Arbor: University of Michigan Press, 48–82.

2006. "Is the Water Rising? Reflections on Inequality and American Democracy." *PS: Political Science and Politics* 39:39–42.

Baumgartner, Frank R. and Bryan D. Jones. 2009. *Agendas and Instability in American Politics*. 2nd ed. Chicago: University of Chicago Press.

Beaudoin, Christopher. 2007. "Media Effects on Public Safety Following a Natural Disaster." *Journalism and Mass Communication Quarterly* 84:695–712.

Beer, Samuel H. 1978. "Federalism, Nationalism, and Democracy in America." *American Political Science Review* 72(March):9–21.

Bellantoni, Christina. 2009. "Obama Taps N.O. for U.S. Blueprint: Some Neighborhoods Still Wait for Government to Clear Red Tape." *Washington Times*, March 9. Available at http://www.washingtontimes.com/news/2009/mar/09/obama-taps-big-easy-for-us-blueprint/?page=all, accessed February 6, 2012.

Benjamin, Scott. 2005. "In Katrina's Wake: The Blame Game." CBS News, September 7. Available at http://www.cbsnews.com/stories/2005/09/07/katrina/main821705.shtml, accessed July 27, 2010.

Bennett, W. Lance, Regina G. Lawrence, and Steven Livingston. 2007. *When the Press Fails: Political Power and the News Media from Iraq to Katrina*. Chicago: University of Chicago Press.

Berelson B. R., P. F. Lazarsfeld, and W. N. McPhee. 1954. *Voting: A Study of Opinion Formation in a Presidential Campaign*. Chicago: University of Chicago Press.

Betancourt, Hector and Irene Blair. 1992. "A Cognition (Attribution)-Emotion Model of Violence in Conflict Situations." *Personality and Social Psychology Bulletin* 18:343–50.

Birkland, Thomas A. 1997. *After Disaster. Agenda Setting, Public Policy, and Focusing Events*. Washington, DC: Georgetown University Press.

1998. "Focusing Events, Mobilization, and Agenda Setting." *Journal of Public Policy* 18(1):53–74.

2006. *Lessons of Disaster: Policy Change after Catastrophic Events*. Washington, DC: Georgetown University Press.

Birkland, Thomas and Sarah Waterman. 2008. "Is Federalism the Reason for Failure in Hurricane Katrina?" *Publius: The Journal of Federalism* 38(4):692–714.

Bobo, Lawrence D. 2006. "Katrina: Unmasking Race, Poverty, and Politics in the 21st Century." *Du Bois Review* 3:1–6.

Bodenhausen, Galen, Lori A. Sheppard, and Geoffrey P. Kramer. 1994. "Negative Affect and Social Judgment: The Differential Impact of Anger and Sadness." *European Journal of Social Psychology* 24:45–62.

Bohannon, John Neil, III. 1988. "Flashbulb Memories of the Space Shuttle Disaster: A Tale of Two Theories." *Cognition* 29:179–96.

Bohannon, John Neil, III, Sami Gratz, and Victoria Symons Cross. 2007. "The Effects of Affect and Input Source on Flashbulb Memories." *Applied Cognitive Psychology* 21:1023–36.

Bowler, Shaun and Todd Donovan. 2002. "Democracy, Institutions, and Attitudes about Citizen Influence on Government." *British Journal of Political Science* 32:371–90.

Brader, Ted. 2005. "Striking a Responsive Chord: How Political Ads Motivate and Persuade Voters by Appealing to Emotions." *American Journal of Political Science* 49:388–405.

2006. *Campaigning for Hearts and Minds: How Emotional Appeals in Political Ads Work.* Chicago: University of Chicago Press.

Brambor, Thomas, William Clark, and Matt Golder. 2006. "Understanding Interaction Models: Improving Empirical Analyses." *Political Analysis* 14:63–82.

Bucy, Erik P. 2003. "Emotion, Presidential Communication, and Traumatic News: Processing the World Trade Center Attacks." *Harvard International Journal of Press/Politics* 8:76–96.

Burton, Paul W. and Brian D. Silver. 2006. "The Credibility of Disaster Evacuation Warnings: The Effects of Issue Framing and Trust in Government." Presented at the American Political Science Association, Philadelphia, PA.

Campbell, Angus, Philip E. Converse, Warren E. Miller, and Donald E. Stokes. 1960. *The American Voter.* New York: Wiley.

Carver, Charles S. 2004. "Negative Affects Deriving from the Behavioral Approach System." *Emotion* 4:3–22.

Chanley, Virginia A. 2002. "Trust in Government in the Aftermath of 9/11: Determinants and Consequences." *Political Psychology* 23:469–83.

Chertoff, Michael. 2005. "Briefing Remarks" from Homeland Security Briefing, reported in transcripts of CNN, "The Aftermath of Katrina," September 3. Available at http://transcripts.cnn.com/TRANSCRIPTS/0509/03/cst.04.html, accessed September 24, 2011.

Chong, Dennis 1996. "Creating Common Frames of Reference on Political Issues." In *Political Persuasion and Attitude Change*, eds. Diana C. Mutz, Paul M. Sniderman, and Richard A. Brody. Ann Arbor: University of Michigan Press, pp. 195–224.

Chong, Dennis and James N. Druckman. 2007c. "Framing Public Opinion in Competitive Democracies." *American Political Science Review* 101(4):637–55.

2007b. "Framing Theory." *Annual Review of Political Science* 10:103–26.

2007a. "A Theory of Framing and Opinion Formation in Competitive Elite Environments." *Journal of Communication* 57:99–118.

Chong, Dennis and Reuel Rogers. 2005. "Racial Solidarity and Political Participation." *Political Behavior* 27:347–74.

Chubb, John E. 1988. "Institutions, the Economy, and the Dynamics of State Elections." *American Political Science Review* 82:133–54.

Citrin, Jack. 1974. "Comment: The Political Relevance of Political Trust in Government." *American Political Science Review* 68:979–88.

Citrin, Jack, and Donald P. Green. 1986. "Presidential Leadership and the Resurgence of Trust in Government." *British Journal of Political Science* 16:431–53.

Citrin, Jack and Samantha Luks. 2001. "Comment: Political Trust Revisited: Déjà vu All Over Again?" In *What Is It about Government that Americans Dislike?* eds. John R. Hibbing and Elizabeth Theiss-Morse. New York: Cambridge University Press, 9–27.

Citrin, Jack, Herbert McClosky, John M. Shanks, and Paul Sniderman. 1975. "Personal and Political Sources of Political Alienation." *British Journal of Political Science* 5:1–31.

Clore, G. and D. Centerbar. 2004. "Analyzing Anger: How to Make People Mad." *Emotion* 4:139–44.

CNN. 2005a. "'Can I Quit Now?' FEMA Chief Wrote as Katrina Raged." November 4. Available at http://www.cnn.com/2005/US/11/03/brown. fema.emails/, accessed August 3, 2010.

2005b. "Bush: 'I Take Responsibility' for Federal Failures after Katrina." September 13. Available at http://www.cnn.com/2005/POLITICS/09/13/ katrina.washington/index.html, accessed July 27, 2010.

2005c. *CNN Reports: Hurricane Katrina.* Marietta, GA: Lionheart.

Cohen, Cathy. 1999. *The Boundaries of Blackness: AIDS and the Breakdown of Black Politics.* Chicago: University of Chicago Press.

Cohen, Jeffrey E. and James D. King. 2004. "Relative Unemployment and Gubernatorial Popularity." *Journal of Politics* 66:1267–82.

Conover, Pamela Johnston and Stanley Feldman. 1986. "Emotional Reactions to the Economy: I'm Mad as Hell and I'm Not Going to Take It Anymore." *American Journal of Political Science* 30:50–78.

Conover, Pamela Johnston, Stanley Feldman, and Kathleen Knight. 1987. "The Personal and Political Underpinnings of Economic Forecasts." *American Journal of Political Science* 31:559–83.

Converse, P. E. 1964. "The Nature of Belief Systems in Mass Publics." In *Ideology and Discontent*, ed. D. Apter. New York: Free Press, 206–61.

Cook, Timothy E. and Paul Gronke. 2004. "The Skeptical American: Revisiting the Meanings of Trust in Government and Confidence in Institutions." *Journal of Politics* 67:784–803.

Cooper, Christopher A., H. Gibbs Knotts, and Kathleen Brennan. 2008. "Trust in Government, Citizen Competence, and Public Opinion on Zoning." *Public Administration Review* 68:459–68.

Craig, Stephen C., Michael D. Martinez, Jason Gainous, and James G. Kane. 2006. "Winners, Losers, and Election Context: Voter Responses to the 2000 Presidential Election." *Political Research Quarterly* 59:579–92.

Crittenden, Kathleen S. 1983. "Sociological Aspects of Attribution." *Annual Review of Sociology* 8:425–46.

Dahl, Robert A. 1971. *Polyarchy: Participation and Opposition.* New Haven, CT: Yale University Press.

Davidson, Joe. 2009. "Will Stimulus Package Lead to Another Contracting Fiasco?" *Washington Post*, February 24. Available at http://voices.washingtonpost.com/federal-diary/2009/02/will_stimulus_package_lead_to.html, accessed August 1, 2010.

Davidson, R. J. 1995. "Cerebral Asymmetry, Emotion and Affective Style." In *Brain Asymmetry*, eds. R. J. Davidson and K. Hugdahl. Cambridge, MA: MIT Press, 361–87.

Davidson, Richard J., Darren C. Jackson, and Ned H. Kalin. 2000. "Emotion, Plasticity, Context, and Regulation: Perspectives from Affective Neuroscience." *Psychological Bulletin* 126:890–909.

Davis, Darren W. 2007. *Negative Liberty: Public Opinion and the Terrorist Attacks on America.* New York: Russell Sage Foundation.

Davis, Darren W. and Brian D. Silver. 2004. "Civil Liberties vs. Security: Public Opinion in the Context of the Terrorist Attacks on America." *American Journal of Political Science* 48:28–46.

Delli Carpini, Michael X. and Scott Keeter. 1996. *What Americans Know about Politics and Why It Matters.* New Haven, CT: Yale University Press.

Devroy, Ann. 1995. "Clinton Praised for Responding to Disaster Swiftly and Strongly." *Washington Post*, Final Edition, April 24, p. A10.

DiMaggio, Paul. 1997. "Culture and Cognition." *Annual Review of Sociology* 23:263–87.

Dolan, R. J. 2002. "Emotion, Cognition, and Behavior." *Science* 298(5596):1191–4.

Downs, Anthony. 1957. *An Economic Theory of Democracy.* New York: Harper.

Druckman, James and Rose McDermott. 2008. "Emotion and the Framing of Risky Choice." *Political Behavior* 30:297–321.

Dryzek, J. K. 2000. *Deliberative Democracy and Beyond: Liberals, Critics, Contestation.* Oxford: Oxford University Press.

Easton, David B. 1965. *A Systems Analysis of Political Life.* New York: Wiley.

Easton, David and Jack L. Dennis. 1967. "The Child's Acquisition of Regime Norms: Political Efficacy." *American Political Science Review* 64:389–410.

Edelman, Murray. 1985. *The Symbolic Uses of Politics.* Champaign: University of Illinois Press.

Eisenberg, Nancy, and Richard A. Fabes. 1990. "Empathy: Conceptualization, Measurement, and Relation to Prosocial Behavior." *Motivation and Emotion* 14:131–49.

Eisenberg, Nancy, R. A. Fabes, M. Schaller, P. Miller, G. Carlo, R. Poulin, C. Shea, and R. Shell. 1991. "Personality and Socialization Correlates of Vicarious Emotional Responding." *Journal of Personality and Social Psychology* 61(3):459–70.

Elder, Keith, Sudha Xirasagar, Nancy Miller, Shelly Ann Bowen, Saundra Glover, and Crystal Piper. 2007. "African Americans' Decisions Not to Evacuate New Orleans before Hurricane Katrina: A Qualitative Study." *American Journal of Public Health* 97(S1): S124-S129.

Elliot, Michael. 2002. "They Had a Plan." *Time Magazine*, August 4.

Enticott P. G., P. J. Johnston, S. E. Herring, K. E. Hoy, and P. B. Fitzgerald. 2008. "Mirror Neuron Activation Is Associated with Facial Emotion Processing." *Neuropsychologia.* 46(11):2851–4.

Entman, Robert M. 1993. "Framing: Toward Clarification of a Fractured Paradigm." *Journal of Communication* 43:51–8.

2003. *Projections of Power: Framing News, Public Opinion, and U.S. Foreign Policy.* Chicago: University of Chicago Press.

Erber, Ralph and Richard R. Lau. 1990. "Political Cynicism Revisited: An Information Processing Reconciliation of Policy-Based and Incumbency-Based Interpretations of Changes in Trust in Government." *American Journal of Political Science* 34:236–53.

Federico, Christopher M. and Samantha Luks. 2005. "The Political Psychology of Race." *Political Psychology* 26:661–6.

Fiddick, Laurence. 2004. "Domains of Deontic Reasoning: Resolving the Discrepancy between the Cognitive and Moral Reasoning Literatures." *Quarterly Journal of Experimental Psychology* 57A:447–74.

Finkel, Steven E. 1985. "Reciprocal Effects of Participation and Political Efficacy: A Panel Analysis." *American Journal of Political Science* 29:891–913.

Finn, Kathy. 2009. "In La., FEMA Wants Trailers Vacated Soon: May 30 Deadline Confronts Some Families Who Have Nowhere Else to Go." *Washington Post*, May 24, p. A02.

Fiorina, Morris P. 1978. "Economic Retrospective Voting in American Elections: Micro-analysis." *American Journal of Political Science* 27:426–43.

1981. *Retrospective Voting in American National Elections.* New Haven, CT: Yale University Press.

Fischer, Henry W., III. 1998. *Response to Disaster: Fact versus Fiction and Its Perpetuation: The Sociology of Disaster.* 2nd ed. New York: University Press of America.

Fischoff, Stuart. 2004. "Media Crisis Coverage: To Serve and to Scare." *Journal of Media Psychology* 9:1–16.

Fisher, Marc. 2005. "Essential Again." *American Journalism Review* October/November. Available at http://www.ajr.org/article.asp?id=3962, accessed September 17, 2011.

Fishkin, J. and R. Luskin. 1999. "Bringing Deliberation to the Democratic Dialogue: The NIC and Beyond." In *A Poll with a Human Face: The National Issues Convention Experiment in Political Communication*, eds. M. McCombs and A. Reynolds. New York: Erlbaum 30–8.

Fiske, Susan T. 1980. "Attention and Weight in Person Perception: The Impact of Negative and Extreme Behavior." *Journal of Personality and Social Psychology* 38:889–906.

Forsterling, Friedrich. 2001. *Attributions: An Introduction to Theories, Research and Applications*. Philadelphia, PA: Psychology Press.

Frank, Thomas. 2005. "Katrina Inspires Record Charity." *USA Today*. Available at http://www.usatoday.com/news/nation/2005–11–13-ka-trina-charity_x.htm, accessed August 29. 2010.

Gaines, Brian J., James H. Kuklinski, Paul J. Quirk, Buddy Peyton, and Jay Verkuilen. 2007. "Same Facts, Different Interpretations: Partisan Motivation and Opinion on Iraq." *The Journal of Politics* 69:957–974.

Gallup/CNN /USA Today. 2005. Poll, September. Available at http://www.ropercenter.uconn.edu.proxy.lib.fsu.edu/data_access/ipoll/ipoll.html, accessed February 5, 2012.

Gamson, William A. and Andre Modigliani. 1987. "The Changing Culture of Affirmative Action." *Research in Political Sociology* 3:137–77.

1989. "Media Discourse and Public Opinion on Nuclear Power: A Constructionist Approach." *American Journal of Sociology* 95:1–37.

Gay, Claudine. 2004. "Putting Race into Context: Identifying the Environmental Determinants of Black Racial Attitudes." *American Political Science Review* 98:547–63.

Gelman, Andrew and Gary King. 1993. "Why Are American Presidential Election Campaign Polls So Variable When Voters Are So Predictable?" *British Journal of Political Science* 23(1):409–51.

Genovese, Michael A. 2002. *The Presidential Dilemma: Leadership in the American System*. New York: Longman.

Gilens, Martin. 1999. *Why Americans Hate Welfare*. Chicago: University of Chicago Press.

Gilliam, Franklin D., Jr., and Shanto Iyengar. 2000. "Prime Suspects: The Influence of Local Television News on the Viewing Public." *American Journal of Political Science* 44:560–73.

Ginsberg, Benjamin. 1982. *The Consequences of Consent: Elections, Citizen Control and Popular Acquiescence*. Reading, PA: Addison-Wesley.

Gomez, Brad T. and J. Matthew Wilson. 2001. "Political Sophistication and Economic Voting in the American Electorate: A Theory of Heterogeneous Attribution." *American Journal of Political Science* 45:899–914.

2003. "Causal Attribution and Economic Voting in American Congressional Elections." *Political Research Quarterly*. 56:271–82.

2008. "Political Sophistication and Attributions of Blame in the Wake of Hurricane Katrina." *Publius: The Journal of Federalism* 38:633–50.

Grabe, Maria Elizabeth, Annie Lang, and Xiaoquan Zhao. 2003. "News Content and Form: Implications for Memory and Audience Evaluations." *Communication Research* 30:387–413.

Graber, Doris 2005. *Mass Media in American Politics.* 7th ed. Washington, DC: CQ Press.

Griffin, Stephen M. 2007. "Stop Federalism before It Kills Again: Reflection on Hurricane Katrina." *St. John's Journal of Legal Commentary* 21(2):527–40.

Guarino, Mark. 2009. "New Orleans' 'Katrina Generation' Struggles with Drugs and Depression: Suicides Are Up and Hard Drugs Are More Prevalent – Trends That Are Both Linked to the Hurricane's Legacy, Experts Say." *Christian Science Monitor,* May 13. Available at: http://www.csmonitor.com/USA/Society/2009/0513/p02s04-ussc.html, accessed February 6, 2012.

Gugliotta, Guy and Peter Whoriskey. 2005. "Floods Ravage New Orleans; Two Levees Give Way." *Washington Post,* August 31. Available at http://www.highbeam.com/doc/1P2-60771.html, accessed Sepember 23, 2011.

Guimond, Serge, Guy Begin, and Douglas L. Palmer. 1989. "Education and Causal Attributions: The Development of 'Person Blame' and 'System-blame' Ideology." *Social Psychology Quarterly* 52(2):126–40.

Haider-Markel, Donald P., William Delehanty, and Matthew Beverlin. 2007. "Media Framing and Racial Attitudes in the Aftermath of Katrina." *Policy Studies Journal* 35:587–605.

Haider-Markel, Donald P. and Mark R. Joslyn. 2001. "Gun Policy, Opinion, Tragedy, and Blame Attribution: The Conditional Influence of Issue Frames." *Journal of Politics* 63:520–43.

Haidt, Jonathan. 2003. "The Moral Emotions." In *Handbook of Affective Sciences*, eds. Richard Davidson, Klaus Scherer, and H. Hill Goldsmith. Oxford: Oxford University Press, 852–70.

Hall, Mimi, Rick Jervis, and Alan Levin. 2010. "Is Oil Spill Becoming Obama's Katrina? Majority Polled Say His Response Has Been Poor." *USA Today,* May 27, p. 1A.

Hastie, R., S. D. Penrod, and N. Pennington. 1983. *Inside the Jury.* Cambridge, MA: Harvard University Press.

Hayes, Bernadette C. and Clive S. Bean. 1993. "Political Efficacy: A Comparative Study of the United States, West Germany, Great Britain and Australia." *European Journal of Political Research* 23:261–80.

Heath, Brad. 2009. "$3.9B in Hurricane Aid Still Unspent; Gulf Coast Officials Blame Bureaucracy." *USA Today,* available at http://www.usatoday.com/printedition/news/20090209/1akatrina09_st.art.htm, accessed February 9, 2012.

Hero, Rodney and Caroline Tolbert. 2004. "Minority Voices and Citizen Attitudes about Government Responsiveness in the American States: Do

Social and Institutional Context Matter?" *British Journal of Political Science* 34:109–21.

Hetherington, Marc J. 1998. "The Political Relevance of Political Trust." *American Political Science Review* 92:791–808.

1999. "The Effect of Political Trust on the Presidential Vote, 1968–1996." *American Political Science Review* 93:311–26.

Hetherington, Marc J., and John D. Nugent. 2001. "Explaining Public Support for Devolution: The Role of Political Trust." In *What Is It about Government That Americans Dislike?* eds. John R. Hibbing and Elizabeth Theiss-Morse. New York: Cambridge University Press, 134–51.

Hewstone, Miles. 1989. *Causal Attribution: From Cognitive Processes to Collective Beliefs.* Cambridge, MA: Blackwell.

Hirst, William, Elizabeth Phelps, Randy L. Buckner, Andrew E. Budson, Alexandru Cuc, John D. E. Gabrieli, Marcia K. Johnson, Cindy Lustig, Keith B. Lyle, Mara Mather, Robert Meksin, Karen J. Mitchell, Kevin N. Ochsner, Daniel L. Schacter, Jon S. Simons, and Chandan J. Vaidya. 2009. "Long-Term Memory for the Terrorist Attack of September 11: Flashbulb Memories, Event Memories, and the Factors That Influence Their Retention" *Journal of Experimental Psychology: General* 138(2):161–76.

Hoenig, John M. 2005. "The Triangle Fire of 1911." *History* 7(May):20–3.

Hoffner, Cynthia A., Yuki Fujoka, Jiali Ye, and Amal G. S. Ibrahim. 2009. "Why We Watch: Factors Affecting Exposure to Tragic Television News." *Mass Communication and Society* 12(2):193–216.

Hougland, James G., Jr. and James A. Christenson. 1983. "Religion and Politics: The Relationship of Religious Participation to Political Efficacy and Involvement." *Sociology and Social Research* 67:406–20.

Howard, Judith A. and Kenneth C. Pike. 1986. "Ideological Investment in Cognitive Processing: The Influence of Social Statuses on Attribution." *Social Psychology Quarterly* 49:154–67.

Howell, Susan E. and James M. Vanderleeuw. 1990. "Economic Effects on State Governors." *American Politics Quarterly* 15:471–83.

Huddy, Leonie and Stanley Feldman. 2006a. "The Subtle Political Effects of Race on American Responses to Hurricane Katrina." Presented at the American Political Science Association's Annual Meeting, August 30–September 3, Philadelphia, PA.

2006b. "Worlds Apart: Blacks and Whites React to Hurricane Katrina." *Du Bois Review* 3:97–113.

Huddy, Leonie, Stanley Feldman, and Erin Cassese. 2007. "On the Distinct Political Effects of Anxiety and Anger." In *The Political Dynamics of Feeling and Thinking*, eds. Ann Crigler, Michael MacKuen, George E. Marcus, and W. Russell Neuman. Chicago: University of Chicago Press, 202–30.

Huddy, Leonie, Stanley Feldman, Gallya Lahav, and Charles Taber. 2003. "Fear and Terrorism: Psychological Reactions to 9/11." In *Framing*

Terrorism: The News Media, the Government, and the Public, eds. Pippa Norris, Montague Kern, and Marion Just. New York and London: Routledge, 255–78.

Huddy, Leonie, Stanley Feldman, Charles Taber, and Gallya Lahav. 2005. "Threat, Anxiety and Support of Anti-Terrorism Policies." *American Journal of Political Science* 49:593–608.

Huddy, Leonie, Nadia Khatib, and Theresa Capelos. 2002. "The Polls-Trends: Reactions to the Terrorist Attacks of September 11, 2001." *Public Opinion Quarterly* 66:418–50.

Ignatieff, Michael. 2005. "The Broken Contract." *New York Times*, September 25. Available at http://www.nytimes.com/2005/09/25/magazine/25wwln.html?pagewanted=print, accessed August 1, 2010.

Iyengar, Shanto. 1980. "Subjective Political Efficacy as a Measure of Diffuse Support." *Public Opinion Quarterly* 44:249–56.

1989. "How Citizens Think about National Issues: A Matter of Responsibility." *American Journal of Political Science* 33:878–900.

1991. *Is Anyone Responsible? How Television Frames Political Issues.* Chicago: University of Chicago Press.

Jenkins-Smith, Hank C., Carol Silva, and Richard W. Waterman. 2005. "Micro- and Macrolevel Models of the Presidential Expectations Gap." *Journal of Politics* 67(3):690–715.

Jennings, M. Kent. 1999. "Political Responses to Pain and Loss Presidential Address, American Political Science Association." *American Political Science Review* 93:1–13.

Jerit, Jennifer, Jason Barabas, and Toby Bolsen. 2006. "Citizens, Knowledge and the Information Environment." *American Journal of Political Science* 50:266–83.

Johnson, Devon. 2009. "Anger about Crime and Support for Punitive Criminal Justice Policies." *Punishment and Society* 11:51–66.

Kahn, Kim Fridkin and Patrick J. Kenney. 2002. "The Slant of the News: How Editorial Endorsements Influence Campaign Coverage and Citizen's Views of Candidates." *American Political Science Review* 96(2):381–94.

Karp, Jeffry. 1995. "Explaining Public Support for Legislative Term Limits." *Public Opinion Quarterly* 59:373–91.

Kernell, Samuel 1997. *Going Public: New Strategies of Presidential Leadership.* Washington, DC: CQ Press.

Key, V. O. 1966. *The Responsible Electorate.* New York: Vintage.

Kiewiet, D. Roderick. 1981. "Policy Oriented Voting in Response to Economic Issues." *American Political Science Review* 75:448–59.

Kinder, Donald R. 1998. "Opinion and Action in the Realm of Politics." In *The Handbook of Social Psychology*, eds. Daniel T. Gilbert, Susan T. Fiske, and Gardner Lindzey. Boston: McGraw-Hill, 778–867.

Kinder, Donald R. and D. Roderick Kiewiet. 1978. "Economic Discontent and Political Behavior: The Role of Personal Grievances and Collective

Economic Judgments in Congressional Voting." *American Journal of Political Science* 23:495–527.

1981. "Sociotropic Politics: The American Case." *British Journal of Political Science* 11:125–61.

Kinder, Donald R. and Walter R. Mebane. 1983. "Politics and Economics in Everyday Life." In *The Political Process and Economic Change,* ed. Kristen R. Monroe. New York: Agathon Press, 141–80.

King, Gary, Michael Tomz, and Jason Wittenberg. 2000. "Making the Most of Statistical Analyses: Improving Interpretation and Presentation." *American Journal of Political Science* 44(2):347–61.

Kingdon, John W. 2002. *Agenda, Alternatives and Public Policies.* 2nd ed. New York: Longman.

Kramer, Gerald H. 1971. "Short-Term Fluctuations in U.S. Voting Behavior, 1896–1964." *American Political Science Review* 65:131–43.

Kunda, Ziva. 1987. "Motivated Inference: Self-Serving Generation and Evaluation of Causal Theories." *Journal of Personality and Social Psychology* 53:636–47.

1990. "The Case for Motivated Reasoning." *Psychological Bulletin* 108:480–98.

Kurtz, Howard. 2005. "At Last, Reporters' Feelings Rise to the Surface." *Washington Post,* September 5. Available at http://www.washington-post.com/wp-dyn/content/article/2005/09/04/AR2005090401320.html, accessed September 3, 2011.

Kvavilashvili, Lia, Jennifer Mirani, Simone Schlagman, Kerry Foley, and Diana E. Kornbrot. 2009. "Consistency of Flashbulb Memories of September 11 over Long Delays: Implications for Consolidation and Wrong Time Slice Hypotheses." *Journal of Memory and Language.* 61(4):556–72.

Ladner, Matthew and Christopher Wlezien. 2007. "Partisan Preferences, Electoral Prospects, and Economic Expectations." *Comparative Political Studies* 40(5):571–96.

Lang, A. 2000. "The Limited Capacity Model of Mediated Message Processing." *Journal of Communication* 50:46–70.

Lang, Annie, John Newhagen, and Byron Reeves. 1996. "Negative Video as Structure: Emotion, Attention, Capacity, and Memory." *Journal of Broadcasting and Electronic Media* 40:460–77.

Lang, Annie, Byungho Park, Ashley Sanders-Jackson, Brian D. Wilson, and Zeng Wang. 2007. "Cognition and Emotion in TV Message Processing: How Valence, Arousing Content, Structural Complexity, and Information Density Affect the Availability of Cognitive Resources." *Media Psychology* 10:317–38.

Langer, Gary. 2005. "Poll: Bush Approval Drops." *ABC News,* September 12. Available at http://abcnews.go.com/Politics/PollVault/story?id=1117357, accessed July 29, 2010.

Lau, Richard R. and David P. Redlawsk. 2006. *How Voters Decide: Information Processing in Election Campaigns* Cambridge Studies in Public Opinion and Political Psychology. New York: Cambridge University Press.

Lau, Richard R. and David O. Sears. 1981. "Cognitive Links between Economic Grievances and Political Responses." *Political Behavior* 3:279–302.

Lavine, Howard, Milton Lodge, and Kate Freitas. 2005. "Threat, Authoritarianism, and Selective Exposure to Information." *Political Psychology* 26:219–44.

Lawrence, Robert. 1997. "Is It Really the Economy, Stupid?" In *Why People Don't Trust Government*, eds. Joseph S. Nye, Jr., Philip D. Zelikow, and David C. King. Cambridge, MA: Harvard University Press, 111–32.

Lengell, Sean. 2008. "Jobless Benefits Eyed for Increase; House Pushes 2nd Stimulus." *Washington Times*, April 16, p. A07.

Lerner, Jennifer S. and Dacher Keltner. 2000. "Beyond Valence: Toward a Model of Emotion-specific Influences on Judgment and Choice." *Cognition and Emotion* 14:473–93.

Lerner, Jennifer S., Julie H. Goldberg, and Philip E. Tetlock. 1998. "Sober Second Thought: The Effects of Accountability, Anger and Authoritarianism on Attributions of Responsibility." *Personality and Social Psychology Bulletin* 24:563–74.

Lerner, Jennifer S., Roxana M. Gonzalez, Deborah A. Small, and Baruch Fischhoff. 2003. "Effects of Fear and Anger on Perceived Risks of Terrorism: A National Field Experiment." *Psychological Science* 14:144–50.

Lerner, Jennifer S. and Larissa Z. Tiedens. 2005. "Portrait of the Angry Decision Maker: How Appraisal Tendencies Shape Anger's Influence on Cognition." *Journal of Behavioral Decision Making* 19:115–37.

Levi, Margaret. 1998. "A State of Trust." In *Trust and Governance*, eds. Valerie Braithwaite and Margaret Levi. New York: Russell Sage, 77–101.

Levin, Gary. 2005. "10.5 Viewers Visit 'Prison.'" *USA Today*, September 7. Available at http://www.usatoday.com/life/television/news/2005-09-07-nielsens_x.htm, accessed January 5, 2012.

Lewis, C. W. 2000. "The Terror that Failed: Public Opinion in the Aftermath of the Bombing in Oklahoma City." *Public Administration Review.* 69(3):201–10.

Lewis-Beck, Michael S., William G. Jacoby, Helmut Norpoth, and Herbert F. Weisberg. 2008. *The American Voter Revisited*. Ann Arbor: University of Michigan Press.

Lewis-Beck, Michael S. and Mary Stegmaier. 2007. "Economic Models of the Vote." In *The Oxford Handbook of Political Behavior*, eds. Russell Dalton and Hans-Dieter Klingemann. Oxford: Oxford University Press, 518–37.

Leyden, Kevin M. and Stephen A. Borrelli. 1995. "The Effect of State Economic Conditions on Gubernatorial Elections: Does Unified Government Make a Difference?" *Political Research Quarterly* 48:275–90.

Lipton, Eric. 2006. "Republicans' Report on Katrina Assails Administration Response." *New York Times*, February 13. Available at http://www. nytimes.com/2006/02/13/politics/13katrina.html, accessed August 3, 2010.

Lipton, Eric, Christopher Drew, Scott Shane, and David Rohde. 2005. "Breakdowns Marked Path from Hurricane to Anarchy." *New York Times*, September 11. Available at http://www.highbeam.com/doc/1P2-60771.html, accessed September 23, 2011.

Lodge, Milton and Charles Taber. 2000. "Three Steps toward a Theory of Motivated Political Reasoning." In *Elements of Reason: Cognition, Choice, and the Bounds of Rationality*, eds. Arthur Lupia, Matthew McCubbins, and Samuel Popkin. London: Cambridge University Press, 183–213.

　　2005. "The Automaticity of Affect for Political Leaders, Groups, and Issues: An Experimental Test of the Hot Cognition Hypothesis." *Political Psychology.* 26(3):455–82.

Lowery, David and Lee Sigelman. 1982. "Political Culture and State Public Policy: The Missing Link." *Western Political Quarterly* 35: 376–84.

Lowi, Theodore J. 1985. *The Personal President*. Ithaca, NY: Cornell University Press.

Lowry, Robert C., James E. Alt, and Karen E. Ferree. 1998. "Fiscal Policy Outcomes and Electoral Accountability in the American State." *American Political Science Review* 92:759–74.

MacCash, Doug and James O'Byrne. 2005. "Levee Breech Floods Lakeview, Mid-City, Carrollton, Gentilly, City Park." *New Orleans Times-Picayune*, August 30. Available at http://www.nola.com/newslogs/breakingtp/index.ssf?/mtlogs/ nola_Times-Picayune/archives/2005_08. html, accessed February 6, 2012.

MacKuen, Michael, Jennifer Wolak, Luke Keele, and George E. Marcus. 2010. "Civic Engagements: Resolute Partisanship or Reflective Deliberation." *American Journal of Political Science* 54:440–58.

MacLeod, Colin and Andrew Mathews. 1988. "Anxiety and the Allocation of Attention to Threat." *Quarterly Journal of Experimental Psychology* 38(A):659–70.

Madison, James. 2010. Federalist #10 and #51. Available at http://www. foundingfathers.info/federalistpapers/, accessed July 29, 2010.

Maestas, Cherie, Lonna Atkeson, Thomas Croom, and Lisa Bryant. 2008. "Shifting the Blame: Federalism, Media and Public Assignment of Blame Following Hurricane Katrina." *Publius: The Journal of Federalism* 38:4.

Malhotra, Neil and Alexander G. Kuo. 2009. "Emotions as Moderators of Information Cue Use: Citizen Attitudes toward Hurricane Katrina." *American Politics Research* 37:301–26.

Marcus, George E. 2000. "Emotions in Politics." *Annual Review of Political Science* 3:221–50.

Marcus, George E. and Michael B. MacKuen. 1993. "Anxiety, Enthusiasm, and the Vote: The Emotional Underpinnings of Learning and Involvement during Presidential Campaigns." *American Political Science Review* 87:672–85.

Marcus, George E., Michael MacKuen, Jennifer Wolak, and Luke Keele. 2006. "The Measure and Mismeasure of Emotion." In *Feeling Politics: Emotion in Political Information Processing*, ed. David Redlawsk. New York: Palgrave Macmillan, 31–45.

Marcus, George E., W. Russell Neuman, and Michael MacKuen. 2000. *Affective Intelligence and Political Judgment.* Chicago: University of Chicago Press.

Marsh, Michael and James Tilley. 2009. "The Attribution of Credit and Blame to Governments and Its Impact on Vote Choice." *British Journal of Political Science* 40:115–34.

Mathews, A. and C. MacLeod. 1986. "Discrimination of Threat Cues without Awareness in Anxiety States." *Journal of Abnormal Psychology* 95:131–8.

McAllister, D. W., T. R. Mitchell, and L. R. Beach. 1979. "The Contingency Model for the Selection of Decision Strategies: An Empirical Test of the Effects of Significance, Accountability, and Reversibility." *Organizational Behavior and Human Performance* 24:228–44.

McFadden, Robert and Ralph Blumenthal. 2005. "Bush Sees Long Recovery for New Orleans; 30,000 Troops in Largest U.S. Relief Effort; Higher Toll Seen; Evacuation of Stadium? Police Ordered to Stop Looters." *New York Times*, September 1. Available at http://query.nytimes.com/gst/fullpage.html?res=9906E2DA1731F932A3575AC0A9639C8B63&p agewanted=all, accessed September 23, 2011.

McGraw, Kathleen. 1990. "Avoiding Blame: An Experimental Investigation of Political Excuses and Justifications." *British Journal of Political Science* 20:119–31.

    1991. "Managing Blame: An Experimental Test of the Effects of Political Accounts." *American Political Science Review* 85:1133–57.

Mendelberg, Tali. 1997. "Executing Hortons: Racial Crime in the 1988 Presidential Campaign." *Public Opinion Quarterly* 61:134–57.

    2001. *The Race Card: Campaign Strategy, Implicit Messages, and the Norm of Equality.* Princeton, NJ: Princeton University Press.

    2002. "The Deliberative Citizen: Theory and Evidence." In *Political Decision Making, Deliberation and Participation: Research in Micropolitics*, volume 6, edited by Michael X. Delli Carpini, Leonie Huddy, and Robert Y. Shapiro. Greenwich, CT: JAI Press.

Merolla, Jennifer L. and Elizabeth J. Zechmeister. 2009. *Democracy at Risk: How Terrorist Threats Affect the Public.* Chicago: University of Chicago Press.

Meyer, W. U. 1988 "The Role of Surprise in the Attribution Process" *Psychologische Rundschau* 29:136.

Meyer, W. U., M. Niepel, U. Rudolph, and A. Schutzwohl. 1991. "An Experimental Analysis of Surprise." *Cognition and Emotion* 5:295–31.

Meyer, W. U., Rainer Reisenzein, and Achim Schuzwohl. 1997. "Toward a Process Analysis of Emotions: The Case of Surprise." *Motivation and Emotion* 21(3): 251–74.

Mill, John Stuart. [1859] 1956. *On Liberty*, ed. C. V. Shields. Indianapolis, IN: Bobbs-Merrill.

Miller, Arthur H., Edie N. Goldenberg, and Lutz Erbring. 1979. "Type-Set Politics: Impact of Newspapers on Public Confidence." *American Political Science Review* 73:67–84.

Miller, Jon. 1987. "The Challenger Accident and Public-Opinion: Attitudes towards the Space Program in the USA." *Space Policy* 3(2):122–40.

Mogg, Karin, Andrew Mathews, Carol Bird, and Rosanne Macgregor-Morris. 1990. "Effects of Stress and Anxiety on the Processing of Threat Stimuli." *Journal of Personality and Social Psychology* 59:1230–7.

Molnar-Szakacs, Istavn. 2011. "From Actions to Empathy and Morality: A Neural Perspective." *Journal of Economic Behavior & Organization* 77:76–85.

Mondak, Jeffery J. 2001. "Developing Valid Knowledge Scales." *American Journal of Political Science* 45:224–38.

Morrell, Michael E. 2003. "Survey and Experimental Evidence or a Reliable and Valid Measure of Internal Political Efficacy." *Public Opinion Quarterly* 67:589–602.

Murphy, Cullen and Todd S. Purdum. 2009. "Farewell to All That: An Oral History of the Bush White House." *Vanity Fair*. Available at http://www.vanityfair.com/politics/features/2009/02/bush-oral-history200902, accessed September 17, 2011.

Mutz, Diana C. 1994. "Contextualizing Personal Experience: The Role of Mass Media." *Journal of Politics* 56(3):689–714.

Nelson, Thomas E. 1999. "Group Affect and Attribution in Social Policy Opinion." *Journal of Politics* 61:331–62.

Newhagen, J. E. and B. Reeves. 1992. "This Evening's Bad News: Effects of Compelling Negative Television News Images on Memory." *Journal of Communication* 42(2):25–41.

Nickerson, R. S. 1998. "Confirmation Bias: A Ubiquitous Phenomenon in Many Guises." *Review of General Psychology* 2:175–220.

Niemi, Richard G., Harold W Stanley, and Ronald J. Vogel. 1995. "State Economies and State Taxes: Do Voters Hold Governors Accountable?" *American Journal of Political Science* 39(November):936–57.

Norrander, Barbara. 1986. "Correlates of Vote Choice in the 1980 Presidential Primaries." *Journal of Politics* 48:156–67.

NPR. 2005. "Blanco, Nagin Defend Katrina Response." December 14. Available at http://www.npr.org/templates/story/story.php?storyId=5053831, accessed July 29, 2010.

O'Harrow, Robert, Jr. 2009. "If Spending Is Swift, Oversight May Suffer; Plan's Pace Could Leave Billions Wasted." *Washington Post*, February 9, p. A01.

Orth, Deborah A. 2001. "Accountability in a Federal System: The Governor, the President, and Economic Expectations." *State Politics and Policy Quarterly* 1:412–32.

Ortony, Andrew, Gerald Clore, and Allan Collins. 1988. *The Cognitive Structure of Emotions*. New York: Cambridge University Press.

Page, Benjamin I. and Robert Y. Shapiro. 1992. *The Rational Public Fifty Years of Trends in Americans' Policy Preferences*. Chicago: University of Chicago Press.

Peffley, Mark and John T. Williams. 1985. "Attributing Presidential Responsibility for National Economic Problems." *American Politics Quarterly* 13:393–425.

Pennington, N. and R. Hastie. 1986. "Evidence Evaluation in Complex Decision Making." *Journal of Personality and Social Psychology* 51:242–58.

Petersen, Michael Bang. 2010. "Distinct Emotions, Distinct Domains: Anger, Anxiety and Perceptions of Intentionality." *Journal of Politics* 72:357–65.

Pew Research Center. 2005. "Huge Racial Divide over Katrina and Its Consequences," September 8. Washington, DC: Pew Research Center.

Pew Research Center for the People. 2005. iPOLL Databank, Roper Center for Public Opinion Research, University of Connecticut, September. Available at http://www.ropercenter.uconn.edu.proxy.lib.fsu.edu/data_access/ipoll/ipoll.html, accessed February 5, 2012.

Pew Research Center's Project for Excellence in Journalism. 2005. "Reporting Katrina. What's Getting Covered," September 13. Available at http://www.journalism.org/node/1681, accessed January 5, 2012.

Piotrowski, Chris and Terry R. Armstrong. 1998. "Mass Media Preferences in Disaster: A Study of Hurricane Danny." *Social Behavior and Personality* 26:341–5.

Pollock, Philip H., III. 1983. "The Participatory Consequences of Internal and External Political Efficacy: A Research Note." *Western Political Quarterly* 36:400–9.

Popkin, Samuel L. 1994. *The Reasoning Voter: Communication and Persuasion in Presidential Campaigns*. Chicago: University of Chicago Press.

Potter, Hillary. 2007. *Racing the Storm. Racial Implications and Lessons Learned from Hurricane Katrina*. Lanham, MD: Lexington.

Powell, G. Bingham and Guy D. Whitten. 1993. "A Cross-National Analysis of Economic Voting: Taking Account of the Political Context." *American Journal of Political Science* 37:391–414.

Prior, Markus. 2002. "Political Knowledge after September 11." *PS: Political Science and Politics* 35:523–30.

Revkin, Andrew C. 2005. "Gazing at Breached Levees, Critics See Years of Missed Opportunities." *New York Times*, September 2. Available at: http://www.nytimes.com/2005/09/02/national/nationalspecial/02levee. html?pagewanted=all, accessed February 6, 2012.

Ricchiardi, Sherry. 2010. "The Anti-Anchor." *American Journalism Review* (December/January). Available at http://www.ajr.org/Article. asp?id=4841, accessed July 27, 2010.

Risen, James. 2001. "A Nation Challenged: Intelligence; In Hindsight, C.I.A. Sees Flaws That Hindered Efforts on Terror." *New York Times*, October 7. Available at http://www.nytimes.com/2001/10/07/world/ nation-challenged-intelligence-hindsight-cia-sees-flaws-that-hindered-efforts.html?pagewanted=all, accessed February 6, 2012.

Robertson. Campbell. 2009. "With Mayoral Election on Horizon, New Orleans Wants What It Lacks." *New York Times*, October 29, p. 16.

Robinson, Eugene. 2010. "What's That Smell? Toxic Hypocrisy." *Washington Post*, March 16, p. A-19.

Roig-Franzia, Manuel and Spencer Hsu. 2005. "Many Evacuated but Thousands Still Waiting." *Washington Post*, September 3. Available at http://www.washingtonpost.com/wp-dyn/content/article/2005/09/03/ AR2005090301680.html, accessed July 27, 2010.

Ruddy, Christopher. 2005. "Don't Blame Bush for Katrina." Newsmax. com, September 5. Available at http://archive.newsmax.com/archives/ articles/2005/9/4/151327.shtml, accessed July 27, 2010.

Rudolph, Thomas J. 2003a. "Triangulating Political Responsibility." Paper presented at the American Political Science Association Meetings, Philadelphia, PA, August 28–31.

2003b. "Who's Responsible for the Economy? The Formation and Consequences of Responsibility Attributions." *American Journal of Political Science* 47:698–713.

Rudolph, Thomas J. and J. Tobin Grant. 2002. "An Attributional Model of Economic Voting: Evidence from the 2000 Presidential Election." *Political Research Quarterly* 55:802–23.

Rudolph, Udo, Scott C. Roesch, Tobias Greitemeyer, and Bernard Weiner. 2004. "A Meta-analytic Review of Help Giving and Aggression from an Attributional Analysis." *Cognition and Emotion* 18(6):815–48.

Russell, Gordon. 2005. "Nagin Gets Mixed Reviews: Evacuation Plans, Superdome Use Criticized." *New Orleans Times-Picayune*, October 23. Available at: http://www.freerepublic.com/focus/f-news/1507608/posts, accessed September 23, 2011.

Rutenberg, Jim. 2007. "Bush Tours Tornado-Ravaged Town in Kansas and Promises Governor Help in Rebuilding." *New York Times*, Late Edition, May 10, p. 24.

Sack, Kevin and Timothy Williams. 2011. "Government's Disaster Response Wins Praise from Those Affected." *New York Times*, May 1, Section 1, p. 28.

Savage, Charlie. 2006. "Bush Cites Authority to Bypass FEMA Law Signing Statement Is Employed Again." *Boston Globe*, October 6. Available at http://www.boston.com/news/nation/washington/articles/2006/10/06/bush_cites_authority_to_bypass_fema_law/, accessed June 18, 2010.

Schiffer, Adam. 2009. *Conditional Press Influence in Politics*. Lanham, MD: Lexington.

Schloz, John T. and Mark Lubell. 1998. "Trust and Taxpaying: Test the Heuristic Approach to Collective Action." *American Journal of Political Science* 42:398–417.

Schneider, Saundra K. 2005. "Administrative Breakdowns in the Governmental Response to Hurricane Katrina." 2005. *Public Administration Review* 65(September):515–17.

——— 2008. "Who's to Blame? (Mis) perceptions of the Intergovernmental Response to Disasters." *Publius: The Journal of Federalism* 38:715–38.

Scholz, John and Neal Pinney. 1995. "Duty, Fear and Tax Compliance: The Heuristic Basis of Citizenship Behavior." *American Journal of Political Science* 39:490–512.

Schützwohl, Achim and Kirsten Borgstedt. 2005. "The Processing of Affectively Valenced Stimuli: The Role of Surprise." *Cognition and Emotion* 19:583–600.

Sears, David O. and Jack Citrin.1982. *Tax Revolt: Something for Nothing in California*. Cambridge, MA: Harvard University Press.

Seattle Times. 2005. "Government's Failures Doomed Many." September 11. Available at http://seattletimes.nwsource.com/html/hurricanekatrina/2002486672_katresponse11.html, accessed February 17, 2010.

Shah, D. V., M. D. Watts, D. Domke, and D. P. Fan. 2002. "News Framing and Cueing of Issue Regimes: Explaining Clinton's Public Approval in Spite of Scandal." *Public Opinion Quarterly* 66:339–70.

Shambaugh, George, Richard Matthew, Roxane Cohen Silver, Bryan McDonald, Michael Poulin, and Scott Blum. 2010. "Public Perceptions of Traumatic Events and Policy Preferences during the George W. Bush Administration: A Portrait of America in Turbulent Times." *Studies in Conflict and Terrorism*. 33:55–91.

Shane, Scott and Eric Lipton. 2005. "Government Saw Flood Risk but Not Levee Failure." *New York Times*, September 2. Available at http://www.nytimes.com/2005/09/02/national/nationalspecial/02response.html?pagewanted=all, accessed February 6, 2012.

Sharp, Elaine B. and Mark Joslyn. 2001. "Individual and Contextual Effects on Attributions about Pornography." *Journal of Politics* 63:501–19.

Shaver, P., J. Schwartz, D. Kirson and C. O'Connor 1987. "Emotion Knowledge: Further Exploration of a Prototype Approach." *Journal of Personality and Social Psychology* 52:1061–86.

Shoemaker, Pamela J. 1996. "Hardwired for News: Using Biological and Cultural Evolution to Explain the Surveillance Function." *Journal of Communication* 46(3):32.

Shoemaker, Pamela and Stephen Reese. 1996. *Mediating the Message: Theories of Influence on Mass Media Content.* 2nd ed. New York: Longman.

Sigelman, Lee and Susan Welch. 1993. "The Contact Hypothesis Revisited: Black–White Interaction and Positive Racial Attitudes." *Social Forces* 71:781–95.

1994. *Black Americans' Views of Racial Inequality: The Dream Deferred.* New York: Cambridge University Press.

Simons, Robert F., Benjamin H. Detenber, Jason E. Reiss, and Christopher W. Shults. 2000. "Image Motion and Context: A Between- and Within-Subjects Comparison." *Psychophysiology* 37:706–10.

Simons, Robert F., Benjamin H. Detenber, Thomas M. Roedema, and Jason E. Reiss. 1999. "Emotion Processing in Three Systems: The Medium and the Message." *Psychophysiology* 36:619–27.

Sinclair, Besty, Thad Hall, and R. Michael Alvarez. 2011. "Flooding the Vote: Hurricane Katrina and Voter Participation in New Orleans." *American Politics Research* 39(5):921–57.

Smith, Craig A. and Phoebe C. Ellsworth. 1985. "Patterns of Cognitive Appraisal in Emotion." *Journal of Personality and Social Psychology.* 48:813–38.

Sornette, Didier. 2002. "Predictability of Catastrophic Events: Material Rupture, Earthquakes, Turbulence, Financial Crashes, and Human Birth." *Proceedings of the National Academy of Sciences* 99(1):2522–9.

Soss, Joe. 1999. "Lessons of Welfare: Policy Design, Political Learning and Political Action." *American Political Science Review* 93:363–78.

Spezio, Michael L. and Ralph Adolphs. 2007. "Emotional Processing and Political Judgment: Toward Integrating Political Psychology and Decision Neuroscience." In *The Affect Effect: Dynamics of Emotion in Political Thinking and Behavior,* eds. W. Russell Neuman, George E. Marcus, Michael MacKuen, and Ann N. Crigler. Chicago: University of Chicago Press, 71–96.

Steenbergen, Marco and Christopher Ellis. 2006. "Fear and Loathing in American Elections: Context, Traits, and Negative Candidate Affect." In *Feeling Politics,* ed. David P. Redlawsk. New York: Palgrave Macmillan, 109–33.

Steger, Wayne. 2007. "Who Wins Nominations and Why? An Updated Forecast of the Presidential Primary Vote." *Political Research Quarterly* 60(1):91–9.

Stein, Robert M. 1990. "Economic Voting for Governor and US Senator: The Electoral Consequences of Federalism." *Journal of Politics* 52:29–53.

Stenner-Day, Karen and Mark Fischle. 1992. "The Effects of Political Participation on Political Efficacy: A Simultaneous Equations Model." *Australian Journal of Political Science* 27:282–305.

Stets, Jan E. and Peter J. Burke. 2000. "Identity Theory and Social Identity Theory." *Social Psychology Quarterly* 63:224–37.

Stock, Paul V. 2007. "Katrina and Anarchy: A Content Analysis of a New Disaster Myth." *Sociological Spectrum* 27(6):705–26.

Stolberg, Sheryl Gay. 2007. "A Firestorm, a Deluge and a Sharp Political Dig." *New York Times*, October 27. Available at http://www.nytimes.com/2007/10/27/washington/27bush.html, accessed February 6, 2012.

Stone, Deborah A. 1989. "Causal Stories and the Formation of Policy Agendas." *Political Science Quarterly* 104(2):281–322.

Stone, Walter J., Ronald Rapoport, and Lonna Rae Atkeson. 1995. "A Simulation Model of Presidential Nomination Choice." *American Journal of Political Science* 39:135–61.

Sundquist, James. 1988. "Needed: A Political Theory for the New Era of Coalition Government in the United States." *Political Science Quarterly* 103(4):613–35.

Sweeney, Kathryn A. 2006. "The Blame Game: Racialized Responses to Hurricane Katrina." *Du Bois Review* 3:161–74.

Sylvester, Judith. 2008. *The Media and Hurricanes Katrina and Rita*. New York: Palgrave Macmillan.

Taber, Charles S. and Milton Lodge. 2006. "Motivated Skepticism in the Evaluation of Political Beliefs." *American Journal of Political Science* 50:755–69.

Tate, Katherine. 1993. *From Protest to Politics: The New Black Voters in American Elections*. New York: Russell Sage.

Tetlock, P. E. 1983. "Accountability and the Perseverance of First Impressions." *Social Psychology Quarterly* 46:285–92.

Thomas, Evan. 2005. "Katrina: How Bush Blew It." *Newsweek*. September 19.

Tiedens, Larissa Z. 2001. "The Effect of Anger on the Hostile Inferences of Aggressive and Non-Aggressive People: Specific Emotions, Cognitive Processing, and Chronic Accessibility." *Motivation and Emotion* 25:233–51.

Tiedens, Larissa Z. and Susan Linton. 2001. "Judgment under Emotional Certainty and Uncertainty: The Effects of Specific Emotions on Information Processing." *Journal of Personality and Social Psychology* 81:973–88.

Tierney, Kathleen, Christine Bevc, and Erica Kuligowski. 2006. "Metaphors Matter: Disaster Myths, Media Frames and Their Consequences in Hurricane Katrina." *Annals of the American Academy of Political and Social Science* 604:57–81.

Tomz, Michael, Jason Wittenberg, and Gary King. 2003. CLARIFY: Software for Interpreting and Presenting Statistical Results. Version 2.1 Cambridge, MA: Harvard University, June 1. Available at http://gking.harvard.edu, accessed February 23, 2012.

Treaster, Joseph and N. R. Kleinfield. 2005. "New Orleans Is Inundated as 2 Levees Fail; Much of Gulf Coast Is Crippled; Toll Rises." *New York Times*, August 31. Available at http://query.nytimes.com/gst/fullpage.html?res=940CE4DF1731F932A0575BC0A9639C8B63&pagewanted=all, accessed September 23, 2011.

Tuchman, Gaye. 1978. *Making News. A Study in the Construction of Reality*. New York: Free Press.

Tyler, Tom R. 1982. "Personalization in Attributing Responsibility for National Problems to the President." *Political Behavior* 4:379–99.

1990. *Why People Obey the Law*. New Haven, CT: Yale University Press.

U.S. House. 2006. "A Failure of Initiative: Final Report of the Select Bipartisan Committee to Investigate the Preparation for and Response to Hurricane Katrina." February 15. Available at http://katrina.house.gov/, accessed August 30, 2010.

USA Today. 2005. "Exposed by Katrina, FEMA's Flaws Were Years in Making." September 7. Available at http://www.usatoday.com/news/opinion/editorials/2005–09–07-our-view_x.htm, accessed September 2, 2010.

Valentino, Nicholas A., Vincent L. Hutchings, Antoine J. Banks, and Anne K. Davis. 2008. "Is a Worried Citizen a Good Citizen? Emotions, Political Information Seeking, and Learning via the Internet." *Political Psychology* 29(2): 247–73.

2009. "Selective Exposure in the Internet Age: The Interaction between Anxiety and Information Utility." *Political Psychology* 30(4):591–613.

Van Belle, Douglas A. 2000. "New York Times and Network TV News Coverage of Foreign Disasters: The Significance of the Insignificant Variables." *Journalism and Mass Communications Quarterly* 77:50–70.

Van der Brug, Wouter. 2001. "Perceptions, Opinions, and Party Preferences in the Face of a Real World Event: Chernobyl as a Natural Experiment in Political Psychology." *Journal of Theoretical Politics* 13(1):53–80.

Vettehen, Paul Hendriks, Koos Nuijten, and Allerd Peeters. 2008. "Explaining Effects of Sensationalism on Liking of Television News Stories: The Role of Emotional Arousal." *Communication Research* 35:319–38.

Von Drehle, David. 2003. *Triangle: The Fire That Changed America*. New York: Atlantic Monthly Press.

Wason, P. C. 1968. "Reasoning about a Rule." *Quarterly Journal of Experimental Psychology* 20:273–81.

Waterman, Richard W., Hank C. Jenkins-Smith, and Carol L. Silva. 1999. "The Expectations Gap Thesis: Public Attitudes toward an Incumbent President." *Journal of Politics* 61:944–66.

Weatherford, M. Stephen. 1978. "Economic Conditions and Electoral Outcomes: Class Differences in the Political Response to Recession." *American Journal of Political Science* 22: 917–38.

Weiner, Bernard. 1985. "'Spontaneous' Causal Search." *Psychological Bulletin* 97:74–94.

———. 1995. *Judgments of Responsibility: A Foundation for a Theory of Social Responsibility.* New York: Guilford.

Weiner, Bernard, Valerie S. Folkes, James Amirkhan, and Julie A. Varette. 1987. "An Attributional Analysis of Excuse Giving: Studies of a Naïve Theory of Emotion." *Journal of Personality and Social Psychology* 52:316–24.

Weiner, Bernard, Sandra Graham, and Carla Chandler. 1982. "Pity, Anger and Guilt: An Attributional Analysis." *Personality and Social Psychology Bulletin* 8:226–32.

Weiner, Bernard, Danny Osborne, and Udo Rudolph. 2011. "An Attributional Analysis of Reactions to Poverty: The Political Ideology of the Giver and the Perceived Morality of the Receiver." *Personality and Social Psychology Review* 15(2):199–213.

Weiss, Howard M., Kathleen Suckow, and Russell Cropanzano. 1999. "Effects of Justice Conditions on Discrete Emotion." *Journal of Applied Psychology* 84:786–94.

Weissberg, Robert. 1975. "Political Efficacy and Political Illusion." *Journal of Politics* 37:469–87.

Wenger, Dennis and Barbara Friedman. 1986. "Local and National Media Coverage of Disaster: A Content Analysis of the Print Media's Treatment of Disaster Myths." *International Journal of Mass Emergencies and Disasters* 4(3):27–40.

White, Ismail K. 2009. "When Race Matters and When It Doesn't: Racial Group Differences in Response to Racial Cues." *American Political Science Review* 101(2):339–54.

White, Ismail K., Tasha S. Philpot, Kristin Wylie, and Ernest McGowen. 2007. "Feeling the Pain of My People: Hurricane Katrina, Racial Inequality, and the Psyche of Black America." *Journal of Black Studies* 37:523–38.

Wild, Barbara, Michael Erbs, and Mathias Bartels. 2001. "Are Emotions Contagious? Evoked Emotions While Viewing Emotionally Expressive Faces: Quality, Quantity, Time Course and Gender Differences." *Psychiatry Research* 102:109–24.

Williams, J. Mark, G. Fraser, N. Watts, Colin MacLeod, and Andrew Mathews. 1997. *Cognitive Psychology and Emotional Disorders.* 2nd ed. Chichester, UK: John Wiley and Sons.

Wood, B. Dan and Alesha Doan. 2003. "The Politics of Problem Definition: A Theory and Application to Sexual Harrassment." *American Journal of Political Science* 47: 640–53.

Wood, B. Dan and Arnold Vedlitz. 2007. "Issue Definition, Information Processing, and the Politics of Global Warming." *American Journal of Political Science* 51(3):552–68.

Zaller, John. 1992. *The Nature and Origins of Mass Opinion.* New York: Cambridge University Press.

Zillmann, Dolf, Kay Taylor, and Kelly Lewis. 1998. "News as Nonfiction Theater: How Dispositions toward the Public Cast of Characters Affect Reactions." *Journal of Broadcasting and Electronic Media* 42:153–69.

Index

2000 census, 58

ABC, 14, 47–8, 50, 52, 64, 71, 163–4
Aberbach, Joel D., 137
Abramowitz, Alan I., 110
Abramson, Paul R., 136, 142
Adolphs, Ralph, 42
affective attributions.
    See attributions of blame
affective intelligence, 29, 36, 103
al Qaeda, 31
Aldrich, John H., 136
Alt, James E., 110
Althaus, Scott, 2, 48
Alvarez, R. Michael, 26, 184
American Journalism Review, 63, 71
American National Election Studies
    (ANES), 49
Amirkhan, James, 43
Anderson, Christopher, 110
anger, 17, 98–100
    action-oriented emotion, as, 43, 99, 167
    anxiety, difference from, 42, 44
    anxiety, effect of, 98–104
    attribution, causal link, 43–4
    and attributions. *See* attributions
        of blame

definition of, 43, 98
model of, 100
control variables, 101, 103
results, 84, 102, 185, 189–90, 199
survey measures, 100–3
partisanship, effect of, 103
punitive feelings, cause of, 42–3
theoretical framework, 99–100
secondary emotion, as, 188
anxiety, 17, 27–8, 187–8
    anger, difference from, 42, 44
    attentiveness, relationship to, 54–5
    and emotional primes, 52
    information processing, 27, 34
    measures of, 55–6
    primary emotion, as, 188
    surveillance system, 35
Arceneaux, Kevin, 8, 110–11
Armstrong, Terry R., 48
Asian tsunami crisis, 3, 7
Atkeson, Lonna Rae, 8, 26, 67, 70, 110, 113, 138, 142, 184
attentiveness
    and emotion, 56–8
    and media frames, 187, 190
attributions of blame, 20, 84, 92, 97–8, 185
    accuracy motivated reasoning, 84, 91

attributions of blame (*cont.*)
  affective attributions, theory of,
      16–18, 34–8, 82, 86, 94, 103,
      187
  anger, effect of, 100–3, 188.
      See also anger
  anxiety, effect of, 82–7, 92–3, 98
  black respondents, differences in,
      93–7
  directionally motivated reasoning,
      82, 89–91, 104
  explanations of, 35
  extraordinary events, during, 36–8
  hypotheses about, 80, 83–6, 95–6,
      185
  measures of, 122–34
    level of agreement with blame
      frames, 77, 82–3, 87–91
  models of, 85–7, 94–6
    control variables, 85
    results, 61, 85–93, 96, 98,
      103–4, 185, 189–90, 199
    survey measures, 77–80, 84–7,
      92–3, 96
  party identification/partisanship,
      effects of, 80–2, 92, 94
  race, effect of, 18–19, 93–7
Averill, James R., 43, 98

Baetz, Uergen, 197
Ball-Rokeach, S. J., 49
Bamberger, Robert L., 53
Banducci, Susan A., 138–9
Banks, Antoine J., 17, 29, 36–8,
      42–3
Barabas, Jason, 33
Barber, Bernard, 136
Barnes, Michael D., 51
Bartels, Larry M., 18, 26, 58, 93, 198
Bartels, Mathias, 33, 52
Bartlett, Dan, 11
Baumgartner, Frank R., 1–2, 27, 39,
      160, 190
Beach, L. R., 25, 34
Bean, Clive S., 142
Beaudoin, Christopher, 49

Beer, Samuel H., 111
Begin, Guy, 35
Bellantoni, Christina, 12
Benjamin, Scott, 68
Bennett, W. Lance, 25, 27
Berelson B. R., 26
Betancourt, Hector, 43
Bevc, Christine, 31, 52, 65
Beverlin, Matthew, 2, 17–18, 23, 27,
      36, 39, 77, 93–4, 99, 128,
      160, 183–4, 190–1
Bird, Carol, 43
Birkland, Thomas A., 1–2, 4, 22, 27,
      39, 77, 160, 183, 190–1
Black Friday, 193
Blair, Irene, 43
Blanco, Kathleen, 11, 19, 40, 62–3,
      69–70, 72, 77, 81, 83, 107–8,
      111–30, 133–4, 188
Blum, Scott, 2
Blumenthal, Ralph, 65
Bobo, Lawrence D., 18, 58, 93
Bodenhausen, Galen, 43
Bohannon, John Neil, III, 8
Bolsen, Toby, 33
Borgstedt, Kirsten, 28, 43
Borelli, Stephen A., 110
Bowen, Shelly Ann, 63
Bowler, Shaun, 138
BP Gulf Oil spill, 12–13
Brader, Ted, 17, 26, 29, 36, 53
Brambor, Thomas, 132
Brennan, Kathleen, 138, 161
Brown, Aaron, 47, 65
Brown, Michael, 11, 31, 67–8,
      163–4, 174
Bryant, Lisa, 67, 70, 113, 184
Buckner, Randy L., 8
Bucy, Erik P., 7, 32, 184, 192
Budson, Andrew E., 8
Burke, Peter J., 18, 128
Burton, Paul W., 138, 159
Bush, George W., 7, 11, 13, 31, 40,
      63, 70, 74, 77, 83, 107–8,
      111–34, 141, 163, 183, 188,
      198

administration, 11, 68, 80, 82,
    170, 174, 178
Bush, George H. W., 40, 198

California firestorms, 9, 11
Campbell, Angus, 26
Capelos, Theresa, 55–6, 193
Carlo, G., 33, 52
Carrillo, Nancy, 138, 142
Carver, Charles S., 42
Cassese, Erin, 2, 42–4, 56, 99, 129,
    177
catastrophe. *See* extraordinary
    events
CBS, 14, 47–8, 50, 71, 77
CBS News/New York Times poll,
    77
Centerbar, D., 43
Challenger explosion, 2, 5, 8, 27
Chandler, Carla, 17, 43
Chanley, Virginia A., 2
Chernobyl, 2
Chertoff, Michael, 62, 67–9
Chong, Dennis, 18, 30, 32, 35, 38,
    128
Christenson, James A., 142
Chubb, John E., 110
Citrin, Jack, 136–8
Civettini, Andrew J. W., 42
Clark, William, 132
Clinton, Bill, 7
Clore, Gerald, 43
CNN, 14, 47–54, 62–3, 65–6, 68,
    70, 72, 106, 164
CNN/USA Today poll, 49
Cohen, Cathy, 96
Cohen, Jeffrey E. L., 108
Cohen, Roxane Silver, 2
Collins, Allan, 43
Columbine High School shootings,
    2, 5
confidence in government, 20,
    136–41. *See also* external
    efficacy
anger, effects of, 141, 151–3, 189
anxiety, effects of, 150–1, 153

attributions, effects of, 139–41,
    150–1, 153
catastrophic moments and,
    139–41
democracy, role in, 20, 135–7, 199
experiment about, 155
control variables, 153, 156
measures and treatments, 155
research design, 155
results, 96, 153, 155–6, 185,
    189–90, 199
hypotheses about, 141, 156, 185
long-term effects on, 138,
    155–6. *See also* confidence
    in government, experiment
    about
measures of confidence for types
    of crises, 147–9, 151
control variables, 148–9
generalized confidence index,
    152
model of, 147–53
results, 147, 149, 185, 189–90,
    199
party identification, effects of,
    154
Conover, Pamela Johnston, 26, 42
Converse, Philip E., 24, 26, 156
Cook, Timothy E., 138
Cooper, Anderson, 68
Cooper, Christopher A., 138, 161
Craig, Stephen C., 138
Crittenden, Kathleen S., 35
Croom, Thomas, 67, 70, 113, 184
Cropanzano, Russell, 43
Cross, Victoria Symons, 8
Cuc, Alexandru, 8

Dahl, Robert A., 135
Dateline, 49
Davidson, Joe, 182
Davidson, Richard J., 13, 42
Davis, Anne K., 17, 29, 36–8, 42–3
Davis, Darren W., 192–3
Davis, Geoff, 137
Defleur, M. I., 49

Delehanty, William, 2, 17–18, 23, 36, 93–4, 99, 128, 184
Delli Carpini, Michael X., 24, 108, 139
Dennis, Jack L., 138
Department of Homeland Security, 11, 19, 67, 69, 83
  National Response Plan, 69
Detenber, Benjamin H., 33, 52
Devroy, Ann, 7
DiMaggio, Paul, 25–6, 34
disaster. *See* extraordinary events
Doan, Alesha, 2, 39, 190
Domke, D., 30
Donovan, Todd, 138
Downs, Anthony, 24, 26
Drew, Christopher, 65
Druckman, James N., 30, 32, 35, 38, 42
Dryzek, J. K., 199
Dukakis, Michael, 97

Easton, David B., 136, 138
Edelman, Murray, 7
Eisenberg, Nancy, 33, 52
Elder, Keith, 63
Elliot, Michael, 31
Ellis, Christopher, 42
Ellsworth, Phoebe C., 43
emotion. *See* anger, anxiety, surprise
emotional primes. *See* media
Enticott, P. G., 33, 52
Entman, Robert M., 25, 30, 198
Erber, Ralph, 136
Erbring, Lutz, 138
Erbs, Michael, 33, 52
Erickson, Brittany C., 51
evaluations of leaders, 19–20, 115–34
  anger, effects of, 119, 129–34
  anxiety, effects of, 119, 129–30, 134
  attributions, effects of, 108–11, 116, 119, 121–2
  dominant attribution frame, 116–18

economics, effect of, 109–10
federalism, effect of.
  See federalism
hypotheses about, 115–18, 120–1, 129, 185
model of, 118–20, 123–6, 129
  research design/framework, 115
  control variables, 115, 118–20, 128–9, 131
  results, 87, 114, 117–18, 120–1, 126–8, 130–3, 185, 189–90, 199
  survey measures, 107, 112, 116, 119–20, 123, 127, 130–3
party identification/partisanship, effects of, 108–9, 119–20, 122, 132, 192–5
and political responsibility, 109–11
race, effect of, 120, 128
experiment, survey. *See* confidence in government, experiment about
external efficacy, 20
  anger, effects of, 143, 146, 189
  anxiety, effects of, 141, 144–5
  attribution, effects of, 139–41, 144
  catastrophic moments and, 139
  definition of, 136
  hypotheses about, 141–3, 149, 153, 185
  measure of, 142–6
  model of, 142
    control variables, 142–3, 146
    results, 92, 143–7, 185, 189–90, 199
  party identification, effects of, 142–3, 146–7
  short- and long-term influences, 138. *See also* confidence in government
extraordinary events
  attributions during.
    See attributions of blame
  collective dimension, 4, 7, 195
  definition of, 4

political context of, 27–9
"extraordinary politics" versus
    "normal politics," 24–8

Fabes, Rickard A., 33, 52
Failure of Initiative, A, 13
Fan, D. P., 30
Federal Emergency Management
    Agency (FEMA), 11–13,
    19, 67–9, 77, 83, 112, 121,
    163–4, 174, 191
federalism, 20, 110–11, 121, 133.
    See also evaluations of
    leaders
  and assigning responsibility,
    111–13, 133–4
  and attributions of blame, 67,
    114–16
  party identification/partisanship,
    effects of, 113
  problems of, 69, 112
  theory of, 111
Federico, Christopher M., 18, 128
Feldman, Stanley, 2, 18, 23, 26,
    28–9, 42–4, 55–6, 58, 93–4,
    96, 99, 128–9, 177, 184, 193
Ferree, Karen E., 110
Fiddick, Laurence, 43
Finkel, Steven E., 142
Finn, Kathy, 12
Fiorina, Morris P., 109–10
Fischer, Henry W., III, 63
Fischhoff, Baruch, 43
Fischle, Mark, 142
Fischoff, Stuart, 32, 49–50
Fisher, Marc, 51, 63, 66, 73
Fishkin, J., 199
Fiske, Susan T., 28
Fitzgerald, P. B., 33, 52
Foley, Kerry, 8
Folkes, Valerie S., 43
Forsterling, Friedrich, 17
Fox News Channel (FNC), 14,
    47–54, 65–6, 68, 71–2
Frank, Thomas, 3
Freitas, Kate, 35

Friedman, Barbara, 63–5
Fujoka, Yuki, 28, 33

Gabrieli, John D. E., 8
Gaines, Brian J., 25
Gainous, Jason, 138
Gallup, 49, 195
Gallup/CNN/ USA Today poll, 49
Gamson, William A., 2, 30
Gay, Claudine, 18, 128
Gelman, Andrew, 26
Genovese, Michael A., 7
Gibson, Charles, 52
Gilens, Martin, 97
Gilliam, Franklin D., Jr., 97
Ginsberg, Benjamin, 136
Giuliani, Rudolph, 7, 40
Glover, Saundra, 63
Goldberg, Julie H., 43, 165
Goldenberg, Edie N., 138
Golder, Matt, 132
Gomez, Brad T., 8, 35, 67, 106, 110
Gonzalez, Roxana M., 235
Grabe, Maria Elizabeth, 32–3
Graber, Doris, 30–3, 48, 66, 75
Graham, Sandra, 17, 43
Grant, J. Tobin, 110
Gratz, Sami, 8
Great Depression, 26, 193–4
Green, Donald P., 136, 138
Greitemeyer, Tobias, 43, 98–9
Griffin, Stephen M., 69
Gronke, Paul, 138
Guarino, Mark, 12
Gugliotta, Guy, 65
Guimond, Serge, 35
Gulf of Tonkin, 34
Gulf oil spill, 191
Gulf War, 198

Haider-Markel, Donald P., 2, 17–18,
    22–3, 35–6, 93–4, 99, 128,
    184
Haidt, Jonathan, 43
Haiti, earthquake in 13–14
Hall, Mimi, 13

Hall, Thad, 184
Hanson, Carl L., 51
Hastie, R., 27
Hayes, Bernadette C., 142
Heath, Brad, 12
Hero, Rodney, 138
Herring, S.E., 33, 52
Hetherington, Marc J., 137
Hewstone, Miles, 17, 28, 35, 95
Hirst, William, 8
Hoenig, John M., 197
Hoffner, Cynthia A., 28, 33
Horton, Willie, 97
Hougland, James G., Jr., 142
Howard, Judith A., 35
Howell, Susan E., 108
Hoy, K. E., 33, 52
Hsu, Spencer, 70
Huddy, Leonie, 2, 18, 23, 28–9,
       42–4, 55–6, 58, 93–4, 96, 99,
       128–9, 177, 184, 193
Hurricane Andrew, 5, 198
Hurricane Katrina, 143
    aftermath of, 2, 13–14, 65, 139,
       183
    attention to. *See* attentiveness
    collective crisis, as, 10–11
    emotional response of public, 10,
       56–60
       news source, by, 58
       and race, 58–9
    evaluations of leaders, 107–8
    media coverage of, 10, 113, 136–7
       attributions of blame, 60–1,
       government blame frames,
       18, 60, 65–70, nature of
       the storm frame, 18, 60–3,
       societal breakdown frame,
       18, 60, 63–5, television
       source, by, 70–2, timing, 72–4
    emotional primes, 50–4
       episodic framing, 51
    policy proposals, effect on, 161–3,
       182
    political symbol, as, 12–13
    public attentiveness to, 48–50

Hurricane Rita, 11, 56, 74, 120, 128,
       138, 147–9, 165
Hutchings, Vincent L., 17, 29, 36–8,
       42–3

Ibrahim, Amal G. S., 28, 33
Ignatieff, Michael, 136–7
Iraq War, 42, 99
Iyengar, Shanto, 8, 35, 51, 97, 111,
       138–9, 160

Jackson, Darren C., 42
Jacoby, William G., 26
Japan, earthquakes in 14, 196–7
Jenkins-Smith, Hank C., 6
Jennings, M. Kent, 2, 9, 182
Jerit, Jennifer, 33
Jervis, Rick, 13
Johnson, Devon, 165
Johnson, Marcia K., 8
Johnston, P. J., 33, 52
Jones, Bryan D, 1–2, 27, 39, 160,
       190
Joslyn, Mark R., 2, 22, 35

Kahn, Kim Fridkin, 26
Kalin, Ned H., 42
Kane, James G., 138
Karp, Jeffrey A., 137–9
Keele, Luke, 17, 27–9, 36–8, 42–4,
       177, 236
Keeter, Scott, 24, 108, 139
Keltner, Dacher, 42
Kennedy, John F., assassination, 1, 8
Kenney, Patrick J., 26
Kernell, Samuel, 7
Key, V. O., 105, 109, 198
Khatib, Nadia, 55–6, 193
Kleinfield, N. R., 65
Kiewiet, D. Roderick, 110
Kim, Young Mie, 2
Kinder, Donald R., 110, 139
King, Gary, 26, 87
King, James D., 108
Kingdon, John W., 1, 27, 39, 160,
       190

Kirson, D., 43
Knight, Kathleen, 26
Knotts, H. Gibbs, 138, 161
Kornbrot, Diana E., 8
Kramer, Geoffrey P., 43
Kramer, Gerald H. 43, 109
Kuklinski, James H., 25
Kuligowski, Erica, 31, 52, 65
Kumins, Lawrence, 53
Kunda, Ziva, 25, 28, 34
Kuo, Alexander G., 36, 184
Kurtz, Howard, 51, 66, 68
Kvavilashvili, Lia, 8

Ladner, Matthew, 26
Lahav, Gallya, 28–9, 55, 193
Lang, Annie, 28, 32–3, 50, 53
Langer, Gary, 107
Lanoue, David J, 110
Lau, Richard R., 25–6, 42, 110, 136
Lavine, Howard, 35
Lawrence, Regina G., 25, 27
Lawrence, Robert, 136
Lazarsfeld, P. F., 26
Lengell, Sean, 13
Lerner, Jennifer S., 42–3, 165
Levi, Margaret, 136
Levin, Alan, 13
Levin, Gary, 49
Lewis, C. W., 2, 22
Lewis, Kelly, 33
Lewis-Beck, Michael S., 26
Lexis-Nexis, 11–12
Leyden, Kevin M., 110
Linton, Susan, 43
Lipton, Eric, 31, 65, 137
Livingston, Steven, 25, 27
Lodge, Milton, 25, 35–6, 82
Los Angeles Times, 66
Lowery, David, 137
Lowi, Theodore J., 7
Lowry, Robert C., 110
Lubell, Mark, 136
Luks, Samantha, 18, 128, 140
Lustig, Cindy, 8
Lyle, Keith B., 8

MacCash, Doug, 65
Macgregor-Morris, Rosanne, 43
MacKuen, Michael, 17, 27–9, 36–8,
     42–4, 82, 177
MacLeod, Colin, 43
Madison, James, 112
Maestas, Cherie, 67, 70, 113, 184
magnetic resonance imaging (MRI),
     33
Malhotra, Neil, 36, 184
Marcus, George E., 17, 27–9, 36–8,
     42–4, 82, 177, 236
Marsh, Michael, 111
Martinez, Michael D., 138
Mather, Mara, 8
Mathews, Andrew, 43
Matthew, Richard, 2
McAllister, D. W., 25, 34
McClosky, Herbert, 137
McDermott, Jim, 12
McDermott, Rose, 42
McDonald, Bryan, 2
McFadden, Robert, 65
McGowen, Ernest, 97
McGraw, Kathleen, 63, 66, 113
McIntyre, Emily, 51
McPhee, W. N., 26
Meacham, Aaron T., 51
Mebane, Walter R., 110
media. *See also* Hurricane Katrina,
     media coverage of
  coverage of extraordinary events,
       8–9, 17, 29, 32–4, 191, 195
    active phase, 30–1
    blaming government, 9, 18, 31
    emotional primes, 32–3, 191,
      definition of, 50
    norms during, 30–2
    second phase, 30–1
    third phase, 30–1
  coverage of Hurricane Katrina.
       See Hurricane Katrina
  framing, 9, 19, 30, 32, 34
  norms, 25
Meksin, Robert, 8
Mendelberg, Tali, 97, 199

Merolla, Jennifer L., 7, 29, 32, 34, 38, 42, 184, 192–3
methodology, 14
  advantages and limits, 14–15
  control variables, 14–15
  experimental data, 20, 137
  Hurricane Katrina as a test case, 9–10
  hypothesis, 14
  media data, 14
    transcript coding, 47–8, 60–1
    video coding, 46–8, 53
  survey data, 14, 48
Meyer, W. U., 28, 53
Mill, John Stuart, 199
Miller, Arthur H., 138
Miller, Jon, 2, 22
Miller, Nancy, 63
Miller, P., 33, 52
Miller, Warren E., 26
Mirani, Jennifer, 8
mirror neuron system (MNS), 33, 52
Mitchell, Karen J., 8
Mitchell, T. R., 25, 34
Modigliani, Andre, 2, 30
Mogg, Karin, 43
Molnar-Szakacs, Istavn, 33, 52
Mondak, Jeffery J., 118
Morrell, Michael E., 142
motivated reasoning. *See* public opinion
MSNBC, 50
Murphy, Cullen, 11, 183
Mutz, Diana C., 8, 194

Nagin, Ray, 11, 19, 40, 63–4, 69, 72, 74, 77, 107–8, 113–30, 133–4
National Guard, 112, 119, 121
NBC, 14, 47–8, 50, 71
Nelson, Thomas E., 8
Neuman, W. Russell, 17, 28–9, 36–8, 42–3, 82
New Orleans Convention Center, 52
New Orleans Times Picayune, 66

New York Times, 12, 51, 195
New York Times Magazine, 136
Newhagen, John E., 28, 53
Newsweek, 70
Nickerson, R. S., 26
Nielson ratings, 48
Niemi, Richard G., 110
Niepel, M., 28
Norpoth, Helmut, 26
Norrander, Barbara, 26
Novilla, Len M., 51
NPR, 108
Nuijten, Koos, 32–3, 50–1
Nugent, John D., 137

Obama, Barack, 13, 183
O'Brien, Soledad, 68
O'Byrne, James, 65
O'Connor, C., 43
Ochsner, Kevin N., 8
O 'Harrow, Robert, Jr., 12
Oklahoma City bombing, 1–2, 4, 7, 27, 34, 191
Orth, Deborah A., 108
Ortony, Andrew, 43
Osborne, Danny, 17, 43, 98–9

Page, Benjamin I., 28
Pakistan, earthquake in 2005, 3
Palmer, Douglas L., 35
Pataki, George, 40
Park, Byungho, 33, 50
Partin, Randall, 8, 110
Pearl Harbor, attack on, 1, 8
Peeters, Allerd, 32–3, 50–1
Peffley, Mark, 106, 110
Pennington, N., 27
Penrod, S. D., 27
Persian Gulf crisis, 2
Petersen, Michael Bang, 42–4, 130, 134, 177
Pew Research Center, 48, 50, 66, 70, 93
Peyton, Buddy, 25
Phelps, Elizabeth, 8
Philpot, Tasha S., 97

Pike, Kenneth C., 35
Pinney, Neal, 136
Piotrowski, Chris, 48
Piper, Crystal, 63
Princeton Survey Research
     Associates International, 48
Pollock, Philip H., III, 136
Popkin, Samuel L., 25
Potter, Hillary, 18
Poulin, Michael, 2
Poulin, R., 33, 52
Powell, G. Bingham, 110
Prior, Markus, 28
Proposition 2, 137
public opinion, 20, 23
  affective attributions, result of,
     39–42
  extraordinary events, 1–3, 23
  motivated reasoning, 25, 35,
     37–8
     accuracy motivations, 34, 37–8
     directional motivations, 25–6,
        34, 36–8
  and partisanship, 25–6
  and predispositions, 35, 37–9
public policy opinion
  anger, effects of, 165–9, 172,
     175–6, 182, 189
  anxiety, effects of, 165, 167–9,
     172, 175–6, 178, 180–2, 188
  attributions, effects of, 164,
     166–8, 171–5, 177–82
  black respondents, differences in,
     170, 176
  catastrophic moments and, 181–2
  hypotheses about, 164–6, 170,
     172, 178–9, 185
  measures of
     confidence for types of crises,
        165, 167, 169, 171–2, 175,
        181–2
     support for appointing an
        independent commission,
        166, 170–2, 175–7
     support for limiting the
        president, 164–6, 170–81

     support for victim penalties,
        168–72, 175, 177
  models of, 169–73, 176, 181
     control variables, 163, 168–9,
        178
     results, 98, 170, 175–6, 178–82,
        185, 189–90, 199
     survey measures, 165, 167, 170,
        172–3, 176–9
  party identification/partisanship,
     effects of, 176, 178, 180–1
Purdum, Todd S., 11, 183

Quirk, Paul J., 25

race and attributions of blame.
     See attributions of blame
Ramesh, Subha, 110
Rapoport, Ronald, 26
Reagan, Ronald, 42
Redlawsk, David P., 25–6, 42
Reese, Stephen, 31
Reeves, Byron, 28, 53
Reisenzein, Rainer, 28
Reiss, Jason E., 33, 52
Responsible Electorate, The, 105
Revkin, Andrew C., 31
Ricchiardi, Sherry, 71
Risen, James, 31
Robertson, Campbell, 12
Robinson, Eugene, 12, 48
Roedema, Thomas M., 52
Roesch, Scott C., 43, 98–9
Rogers, Reuel, 18, 128
Rohde, David, 65
Roig-Franzia, Manuel, 70
Roper Center for Public Opinion
     Research, iPOLL Databank,
     48–9, 195
Ruddy, Christopher, 108
Rudolph, Thomas J., 35, 77–106,
     110
Rudolph, Udo, 17, 28, 43, 98–9
Russell, Gordon, 64
Russert, Tim, 68
Rutenberg, Jim, 11

Sack, Kevin, 12
Sanders-Jackson, Ashley, 33, 50
Savage, Charlie, 163
Scarborough, Joe, 68
Schacter, Daniel L., 8
Schaller, M., 33, 52
Schiffer, Adam, 25, 27
Schlagman, Simone, 8
Schloz, John T., 136
Schneider, Saundra K., 69, 184
Schützwohl, Achim, 28, 43
Schwartz, J., 43
Sears, David O., 110, 137
Seattle Times, 64
Sebelius, Kathleen, 11
September 11 attacks, 1–5, 7–8, 11,
    19–20, 27–8, 31, 34, 40, 55,
    69, 99, 155–6, 182–3, 191–3,
    195, 198
Shah, D. V., 30
Shambaugh, George, 2
Shane, Scott, 31, 65
Shanks, John M., 137
Shapiro, Robert Y., 28
Sharp, Elaine B., 35
Shaver, P., 43
Shea, C., 33, 52
Shell, R., 33, 52
Sheppard, Lori A., 43
shock. *See* surprise
Shoemaker, Pamela J., 28, 31–3
Shults, Christopher W., 33
Sigelman, Lee, 18, 128, 137
Silva, Carol L., 6
Silver, Brian D., 138, 159, 192–3
Simons, Jon S., 8
Simons, Robert F., 33, 52
Sinclair, Besty, 184
Small, Deborah A., 235
Smith, Craig A., 43
Smith, Shepard, 47, 71
Sniderman, Paul, 137
Sornette, Didier, 2–3
Soss, Joe, 142
Spezio, Michael L., 42
Stanley, Harold W., 110

Steenbergen, Marco, 42
Steger, Wayne, 26
Stegmaier, Mary, 26
Stein, Robert M., 8, 110–11
Stenner-Day, Karen, 142
Stets, Jan E., 18, 128
Stock, Paul V., 63–5
Stokes, Donald E., 26
Stolberg, Sheryl Gay, 11
Stone, Deborah A., 39, 190
Stone, Walter J., 26
Suckow, Kathleen, 43
Sundquist, James, 110
surprise, 28
    and attentiveness, 32, 54
    attributions, role in, 36
    information processing, 34
    measures of, 55
    surveillance system and, 28
Sweeney, Kathryn A., 18, 58
Sylvester, Judith, 49, 51, 63

Tabor, Charles S., 25, 28–9, 36, 55,
    82, 193
Tate, Katherine, 128
Taylor, Kay, 33
Tetlock, Philip E., 25, 34, 43, 166
Thomas, Evan, 64, 68
Three Mile Island, 2
Tiedens, Larissa Z., 43
Tierney, Kathleen, 31, 52, 65
Tilley, James, 111
Time Magazine, 7
Tolbert, Caroline, 138
Tomz, Michael, 87
Treaster, Joseph, 65
Triangle Shirtwaist Factory fire in
    1911, 197
Tuchman, Gary, 52
Tuchman, Gaye, 30
Tyler, Tom R., 106, 110, 136, 138,
    161

U.S. Census, 57
U.S. Congress, 137
U.S. Constitution, 135

U.S. House, 13, 69
USA Today, 12, 49, 164, 195

Vaidya, Chandan J., 8
Valentino, Nicholas A., 17, 29, 36–8, 42–3
Van Belle, Douglas A., 48
Van der Brug, Wouter, 2, 23
Vanderleeuw, James M., 108
Varette, Julie A., 43
Vedlitz, Arnold, 160, 190
Verkuilen, Jay, 25
Vettehen, Paul Hendriks, 32–3, 50–1
Virginia Tech massacre, 5
Vogel, Ronald J., 110
Von Drehle, David, 197

Wang, Zeng, 33, 50
War on Terror, 28
Washington Post, 12, 51, 70, 182
Wason, P. C., 26
Waterman, Richard W., 6
Waterman, Sarah, 77, 184
Watts, Fraser N., 43
Watts, M. D., 30
Wayne, Stephen J., 242
Weatherford, M. Stephen, 110
Weiner, Bernard, 17, 28, 35, 43, 98–9

Weiss, Howard M., 43
Weissberg, Robert, 138
Welch, Susan, 18, 128
Wenger, Dennis, 63–5
White, Ismail K., 96–7, 170
Whitten, Guy D., 110
Whoriskey, Peter, 65
Wild, Barbara, 33, 52
Williams, John T., 106, 110
Williams, Timothy, 12
Williams, J. Mark G., 43
Wilson, Brian D., 33, 50
Wilson, J. Matthew, 8, 35, 67, 106, 110
Wittenberg, Jason, 87
Wlezien, Christopher, 26
Wolak, Jennifer, 17, 27–9, 36–8, 42–4, 177, 236
Wood, B. Dan, 2, 39, 160, 190
Wylie, Kristin, 97

Xirasagar, Sudha, 63

Ye, Jiali, 28, 33

Zaller, John, 25, 34–5, 198
Zechmeister, Elizabeth J., 7, 29, 32, 34, 38, 42, 184, 192–3
Zhao, Xiaoquan, 32–3
Zillmann, Dolf, 33